LAB MANUAL

TO ACCOMPANY THE ALTERNATE VERSION OF

STARTING OUT WITH C++

FOURTH EDITION

by Tony Gaddis, Judy Walters, and Godfrey Muganda

Dean DeFino
Salisbury University

Michael Bardzell
Salisbury University

Judy Walters
North Central College

Scott/Jones, Inc.
P.O. Box 696
El Granada, CA 94018
Voice: **650-726-2436**
Facsimile: **650-726-4693**
E-mail: **marketing@scottjonespub.com**
Web site: **www.scottjonespub.com**
ISBN 1-57676-128-2

Lab Manual to Accompany the Alternate Version of Starting Out with C++, Fourth Edition,
by Tony Gaddis, Judy Walters, and Godfrey Muganda
Dean DeFino, Michael Bardzell, and Judy Walters

Printed in Canada.

ZYX 543

ISBN: 1-57676-128-2

The publisher wishes to acknowledge the memory and influence of James F. Leisy. Thanks, Jim. We miss you.

Text Design: Cecelia G. Morales
Composition: Cecelia G. Morales and Joshua Faigen, Folio Publishing Services
Production: Leslie Austin, Heather Bennet, and Audrey Anderson
Proofreading: Kristin Furino, Holbrook Communications
Book Manufacturing: WebCom

Scott/Jones Publishing Company
Editorial Group: Richard Jones, Denise Simon, and Patricia Miyaki
Production Management: Audrey Anderson
Marketing and Sales: Victoria Chamberlin, Richard Jones, and Leata Holloway
Business Operations: Michelle Robelet, Cathy Glenn, and Bill Overfelt

---

Contents

Lab Manual Introduction

To the Student

Formal computer laboratories are an essential part of your course. They provide an environment where you can gain valuable programming skills. They allow you, under the guidance of your instructor, to experiment with the concepts introduced in the course. You can try things and see firsthand what certain statements and programming constructs do. You can use the techniques presented in class in programs that solve actual, practical problems. To facilitate your learning, and allow you to try out a number of different things in each lab session, this Lab Manual provides pre-developed code for you to complete or edit. It then guides you through the steps needed to turn the code into successfully working programs, preparing you to later create your own programs.

The Lab Manual consists of fifteen "Lesson Sets" which cover the first thirteen chapters of the textbook. There is one lesson set for each chapter of the text, except for Chapters 6 and 7 which have two lesson sets each. Since the length of scheduled lab sessions varies from one institution to another, each lesson set has been broken into two lessons. These are designated in the manual as Lesson A and Lesson B. If you have a 1½- to 2-hour weekly lab it is likely your instructor will have you complete both lessons during your lab period. If you have two 50-minute to 1-hour weekly labs, you will likely be asked to complete Lesson A (half a lesson set) during the first lab session and Lesson B during the second session. If you have only a single 50-minute to 1-hour weekly lab, your instructor will let you know which parts of the lesson set to do each week. You may be asked to do some of the work during lab time and some for homework.

Each lesson set contains the following learning activities.

Pre-lab Reading Assignment. This material provides a good review of the key concepts introduced in the corresponding text chapter and prepares you for the activities you will be carrying out in the lab assignments. It also presents additional examplcs, many of which are later used in the lab assignments themselves. It is very important that you read this material carefully before coming to lab.

Pre-lab Writing Assignment. This section consists of short and easy questions on the pre-lab reading material so you can make sure you understood it. Some instructors collect and grade these assignments.

Lesson A and Lesson B Lab Assignments. Each lesson consists of one to three separate labs and is designed so that all the labs in the lesson can be completed in approximately one hour. Of course, since everyone works at their own pace, you may need more or less time than this. If you need more time, your instructor may ask you to complete the lesson for homework. Some instructors assign all the labs, and some assign just part of them. Your instructor will tell you which labs to do and what exactly they want handed in.

To the Instructor

Closed laboratories in computer programming are a vital component of the learning experience, creating an environment where students can develop valuable programming skills under the guidance of an instructor. Many different opinions concerning the content of such labs have been generated over the past few years, ranging from programming assignments to scheduled exercises using prepared materials. This manual emphasizes the latter approach, with pre-developed code for the students to complete or edit. The lab assignments do not involve sophisticated problems since the point of the labs is to allow students to master basic concepts and techniques by applying them in a practical forum. Most chapters also include "Student-Generated Programming Assignments" that ask students to independently create small programs. These assignments, which can be assigned as lab activities for students who finish early or as post-lab homework, are not intended as a substitute for larger programming assignments. They are small programs in which students can apply the material covered in the labs.

The Lab Manual consists of fifteen "Lesson Sets" which cover the first thirteen chapters of the textbook. There is one lesson set for each chapter of the text, except for Chapters 6 and 7 which have two lesson sets each. Since the length of scheduled lab sessions varies from one institution to another, each lesson set has been broken into two lessons. These are designated in the manual as Lesson A and Lesson B. Students who have a 1½- to 2-hour weekly lab should be able to complete both lessons during a single lab period. Students with two 50-minute to 1-hour weekly labs should be able to complete Lesson A (half a lesson set) during their first lab session and Lesson B during their second session. If students have only a single 50-minute to 1-hour weekly lab, the instructor can assign just some of the labs from each lesson set or can assign some work to be done in lab and the rest to be done for homework. A suggested assignment schedule for various scenarios is provided below. Of course it is impossible to set a time frame for each student in a given lab. It is natural that some students will finish early, while others will need more than the suggested time allotment. Since all of the labs are self-contained with solutions to each problem, any of them can be assigned to students for independent self-study as well as used in a formalized lab setting. Solutions to all the problems of each lesson set are provided to instructors adopting the text.

Each lesson set begins with a pre-lab reading and writing assignment to be done by students before they come to lab. Following this are the Lesson A and Lesson B lab assignments. Since student-written programs should be attempted only after exposure to a complete concept, the "Student-Generated Code Assignments" are always the last lab activity in Lesson B. Most of these provide several different assignment "options" so the instructor can select the one most appropriate for a given class, or can vary the assignments given to different sections or in different semesters (quarters). Additional options for programming assignments can be found at the end of each chapter in the text. More detailed information on each of the lesson set components follows.

Pre-lab Reading Assignment. This prepares students for the activities found in the lab assignments. While most of the material presented is also covered in the text, this section gives a good review of the key concepts and provides additional examples, some of which are then used in the labs themselves. Students should thus be required to read this section before coming to lab.

Pre-lab Writing Assignment. This consists of short and easy questions on the pre-lab reading material so that the students can check to make sure they understood it. Some instructors like to collect these assignments to ensure that students did the pre-lab reading before coming to lab. Answers to these questions are provided on-line to instructors adopting the text.

Lesson A and Lesson B Lab Assignments. These are done during the lab time, one lesson per hour. Possible solutions to all lab assignments are provided on the instructor's disk.

Use of the ISO/ANSI Standard. This lab manual conforms to the ISO/ANSI standard and introduces some of those features, such as the use of `string` objects, in early lessons. The directives

```
#include <iostream>
using namespace std;
```

are used in all programs, conforming to the standard. Other standards followed throughout the manual include the use of library header files without the `.h` extension, the Boolean data type, and the `fixed` and `showpoint` floating-point directives.

Other Standards. Throughout the labs, `main` is treated as a value returning function since this is increasingly used in professional settings. The lessons sometimes refer to non-returning functions as procedures. Although this is not in keeping with C++ terminology, we make this distinction both for exposure to the general terminology found in the field and to describe the unique purpose of a value returning function.

The Instructor's Notes. The Instructor's Notes found on-line contain the following sections for each lesson set:

- *Objectives for Students.* The Objectives for Students in the Instructor's Notes are similar to the Purpose sections that appear in the student manual. The objectives listed are geared more for the lab work while the student Purpose section covers the reading material as well. In some lesson sets they are the same. The objectives are listed for the convenience of the instructor.
- *Assumptions.* This section gives a brief list of what students should already know before attempting each lesson. It is generally assumed that the students have completed and understood the previous lessons and that they have read and understood the pre-lab reading material for the current lesson set.
- *Pre-lab Writing Assignment Solutions.* This section contains the answers to the Pre-lab Writing Assignment.
- *Lab Assignments.* This section first lists the labs for Lesson A and Lesson B and then gives a more detailed description of each lab. Solutions have been provided on-line for all labs. These of course are just suggested solutions, as there are often many ways to accomplish the same thing.

Suggested Lab Assignment Schedules

One-semester course with 1½ to two hours of lab a week:

Week 1	Lesson Set 1
Week 2	Lesson Set 2
Week 3	Lesson Set 3
Week 4	Lesson Set 4
Week 5	Lesson Set 5
Week 6	Lesson Set 6.1
Week 7	Lesson Set 6.2
Week 8	Lesson Set 7.1
Week 9	Lesson Set 7.2
Week 10	Lesson Set 8
Week 11	Lesson Set 9
Week 12	Lesson Set 10
Week 13	Lesson Set 11
Week 14	Lesson Set 12
Week 15	Lesson Set 13

One-semester course with 50 minutes to 1 hour of lab a week:

Instructors are encouraged to pick and choose labs based on the needs of individual classes. One possibility is to have students do one lesson set per week, but only complete Lesson A in lab each week. The instructor can then select which, if any, activities from Lesson B are to be done for homework.

		In Lab	Optional Homework
Week 1	Lesson Set 1	Lab 1.1–1.3	Lab 1.4–1.5
Week 2	Lesson Set 2	Lab 2.1–2.2	Lab 2.3–2.4
Week 3	Lesson Set 3	Lab 3.1–3.3	Lab 3.4–3.6
Week 4	Lesson Set 4	Lab 4.1–4.3	Lab 4.4–4.5
Week 5	Lesson Set 5	Lab 5.1–5.2	Lab 5.3–5.5
Week 6	Lesson Set 6.1	Lab 6.1–6.2	Lab 6.3–6.4
Week 7	Lesson Set 6.2	Lab 6.5–6.6	Lab 6.7–6.8
Week 8	Lesson Set 7.1	Lab 7.1–7.3	Lab 7.4
Week 9	Lesson Set 7.2	Lab 7.5–7.6	Lab 7.7–7.8
Week 10	Lesson Set 8	Lab 8.1–8.2	Lab 8.3–8.5
Week 11	Lesson Set 9	Lab 9.1–9.3	Lab 9.4
Week 12	Lesson Set 10	Lab 10.1–10.3	Lab 10.4–10.6
Week 13	Lesson Set 11	Lab 11.1–11.2	Lab 11.3–11.5
Week 14	Lesson Set 12	Lab 12.1–12.3	Lab 12.4–12.6
Week 15	Lesson Set 13	Lab 13.3–13.4	Lab 13.2–13.3

LESSON SET

1 Introduction to Programming and the Translation Process

PURPOSE

1. To become familiar with the login process and the C++ environment used in the lab
2. To understand the basics of program design and algorithm development
3. To learn, recognize and correct the three types of computer errors:

   syntax errors
   run-time errors
   logic errors

4. To learn the basics of an editor and compiler and be able to compile and run existing programs
5. To enter code and run a simple program from scratch

PROCEDURE

1. Students should read the Pre-lab Reading Assignment before coming to lab.
2. Students should complete the Pre-lab Writing Assignment before coming to lab.
3. In the lab, students should complete Labs 1.1 through 1.4 in sequence. Your instructor will give further instructions as to grading and completion of the lab.

Contents	Prerequisites	Approximate completion time	Page number	Check when done
Pre-lab Reading Assignment		20 min.	2	
Pre-lab Writing Assignment	Pre-lab reading	10 min.	6	
Lesson 1A				
Lab 1.1 Opening, Compiling and Running Your First Program	Pre-lab reading	20 min. (Including overview of local system)	7	
Lab 1.2 Compiling a Program with a Syntax Error	Familiarity with the environment Finished Lab 1.1	15 min.	7	

continues

Lab 1.3 Running a Program with a Run-Time Error	Understanding of run-time errors	15 min.	8
Lesson 1B			
Lab 1.4 Working with Logic Errors	Understanding of logic errors	15 min.	9
Lab 1.5 Writing Your First Program	Finished Labs 1.1 through 1.4	35 min.	10

PRE-LAB READING ASSIGNMENT

Computer Systems

A **computer system** consists of all the components (hardware and software) used to execute the desires of the computer user. **Hardware** is the electronic physical components that can retrieve, process, and store data. It is generally broken down into five basic components:

Central Processing Unit (CPU)	This is the unit where programs are executed. It consists of the **control unit**, which oversees the overall operation of program execution, and the **arithmetic/logic unit** (ALU), which performs the mathematical and comparison operations.
Main Memory	area where programs and data are stored for use by the CPU while a program is running
Secondary Storage	where programs and data are stored for use at a later time
Input Devices	devices used to get programs and data into the computer (e.g., a keyboard)
Output Devices	devices used to get programs and data from the computer (e.g., a printer)

Software consists of a sequence of instructions to perform some pre-defined task. These labs concentrate on the software portion of a computer system.

Introduction to Programming

A **computer program** is a series of instructions written in some computer language that performs a particular task. Many times beginning students concentrate solely on the language code; however, quality software is accomplished only after careful design that identifies the user's needs, data, processes, and anticipated outcomes. For this reason it is critical that students learn good design techniques before attempting to produce a quality program. Design is guided by an **algorithm**, which is a plan of attacking some problem. Algorithms are used for many tasks, whether a recipe for a cake, a guide to study for an exam, or the specifications of a rocket engine.

Problem example: Develop an algorithm to find the average of five test grades.

An algorithm usually begins with a general broad statement of the problem.

Find the average of five test grades

From here we can further refine the statement by listing commands that will accomplish our goal.

Read in the grades	Find the average	Write out the average

Each box (sometimes called a node) may or may not be refined further depending on its clarity to the user. This refinement process continues until we have a listing of steps understandable to the user to accomplish the task. For example, **Find the average** may be refined into the following two nodes.

Total = sum of 5 grades	Average = total/5

Starting from left to right, a node that has no refinement becomes part of the algorithm. The actual algorithm (set of steps to solve a problem) is listed in bold.

Find the average of five test grades

Read in the grades

Find the average

Total = sum of 5 grades
Average = total/5

Write out the average

From this algorithm, a program can be written in C++.

The Translation Process

Computers are strange in that they understand only a sequence of 1s and 0s. The following looks like nonsense to us but, in fact, is how the computer reads and executes everything that it does:

10010001111010101110010001110001000

Because computers only use two numbers (1 and 0), this is called **binary** code. One can imagine how complicated programming would be if we had to learn this very complex language. That, in fact, was how programming was done many years ago; however, today we are fortunate to have what are called **high level languages** such as C++. These languages are geared more for human understanding and thus make the task of programming much easier. However, since the computer only understands low level binary code (often called machine code), there must be a translation process to convert these high level languages to machine code. This is often done by a **compiler**, which is a software package that translates high level languages into machine code. Without it we could not run our programs. The figure below illustrates the role of the compiler.

The compiler translates source code into object code. The type of code is often reflected in the extension name of the file where it is located.

Example: We will write source (high level language) code in C++ and all our file names will end with `.cpp`, such as:

```
firstprogram.cpp    secondprogram.cpp
```

When those programs are compiled, a new file (object file) will be created that ends with `.obj`, such as:

```
firstprogram.obj    secondprogram.obj
```

The compiler also catches grammatical errors (called **syntax errors**) in the source code. Just like English, all computer languages have their own set of grammar rules that have to be obeyed. If we turned in a paper with a proper name (like John) not capitalized, we would be called to task by our teacher, and probably made to correct the mistake. The compiler does the same thing. If we have something that violates the grammatical rules of the language, the compiler will give us error messages. These have to be corrected and a grammar-error-free program must be submitted to the compiler before it translates the source code into machine language. In C++, for example, instructions end with a semicolon. The following would indicate a syntax error:

```
cout <<"Hi there" <<endl
```

Since there is no semicolon at the end, the compiler would indicate an error, which must be corrected as follows:

```
cout <<"Hi there" <<endl;
```

After the compile process is completed, the computer must do one more thing before we have a copy of the machine code that is ready to be executed. Most programs are not entirely complete in and of themselves. They need other program modules previously written that perform certain routine operations such as data input and output. Our programs need these attachments in order to run. This is the function of the **linking process**. Suppose you are writing a term paper on whales and would like a few library articles attached to your report. You would go to the library, get a copy of the articles (assuming it would be legal to do so), and attach them to your paper before turning it in. The **linker** does this to your program. It goes to a "software library" of program routines and attaches the appropriate code to your program. This produces what is called the executable code, generated in a file that often ends with `.exe`.

Example: `firstprogram.exe    secondprogram.exe`

The following figure summarizes the translation process:

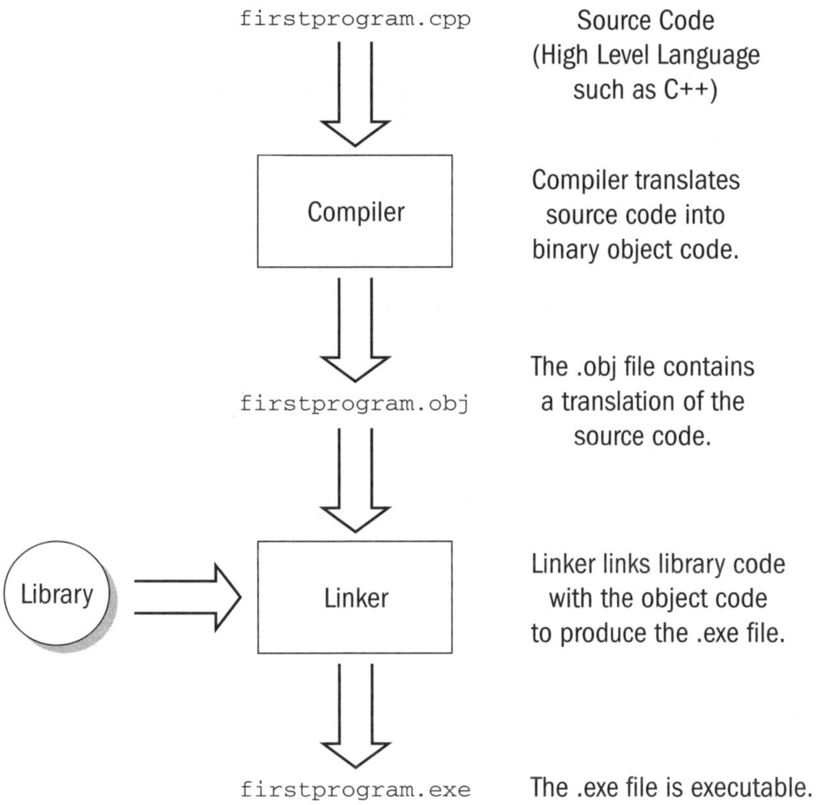

Once we have the executable code, the program is ready to be run. Hopefully it will run correctly and everything will be fine; however, that is not always the case. During "run time" we may encounter a second kind of error called a **run-time error**. This error occurs when we ask the computer to do something it cannot do. Look at the following sentence:

You are required to swim from Naples, Italy to New York in five minutes.

Although this statement is grammatically correct, it is asking someone to do the impossible. Just as we cannot break the laws of nature, the computer cannot violate the laws of mathematics and other binding restrictions. Asking the computer to divide by 0 would be an example of a run-time error. We would get executable code; however, when the program tries to execute the command to divide by 0, the program will stop with a run-time error. Run-time errors, particularly in C++, are usually more challenging to find than syntax errors.

Once we run our program and get neither syntax nor run-time errors, are we free to rejoice? Not exactly. Unfortunately, it is now that we may encounter the worst type of error: the dreaded **logic error**. Whenever we ask the computer to do something, but mean for it to do something else, we have a logic error. Just as there needs to be a "meeting of the minds" between two people for meaningful communication to take place, there must be precise and clear instructions that generate our intentions to the computer. The computer only does what we ask it to do. It does not read our minds or our intentions! If we ask a group of people to cut down the tree when we really meant for them to trim the bush, we have a communication problem. They will do what we ask, but what we asked and what we wanted are two different things. The same is true for the computer. Asking it to multiply by 3 when we want something doubled is an example of a logic error. Logic errors are the most difficult to find and correct because there are no error messages to help us locate the problem. A great deal of programming time is spent on solving logic errors.

Integrated Development Environments

An integrated development environment (IDE) is a software package that bundles an editor (used to write programs), a compiler (that translates programs) and a run-time component into one system. For example, the figure below shows a screen from the Microsoft Visual C++ integrated development environment.

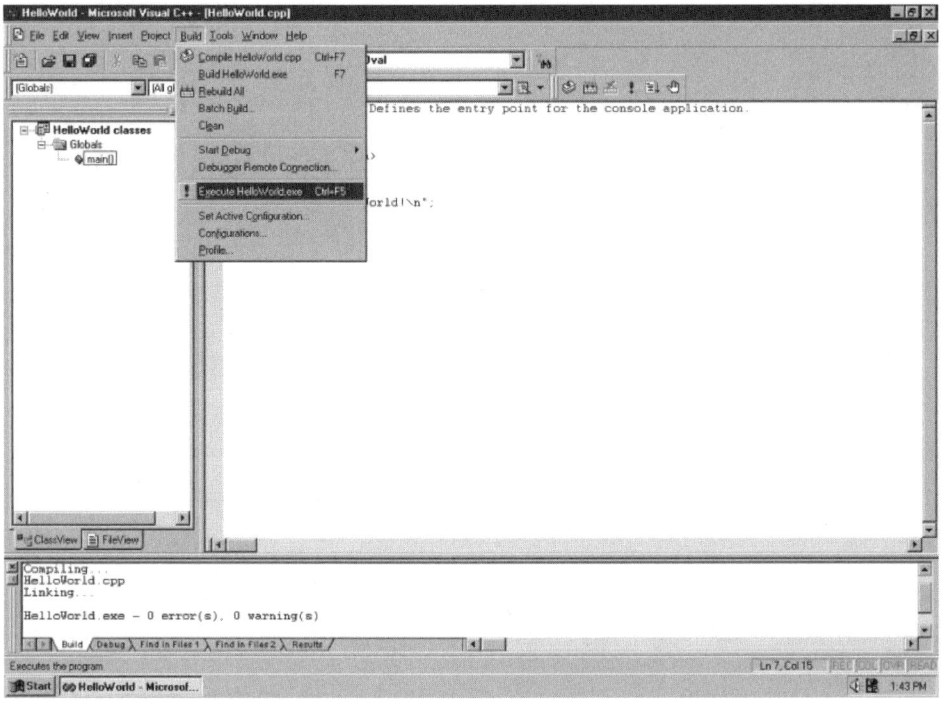

Other systems may have these components separate, which makes the process of running a program a little more difficult. You should also be aware of which operating system you are using. An **operating system** is the most important software on your computer. It is the "grand master" of programs that interfaces the computer with your requests. Your instructor will explain your particular system and C++ environment so that you will be able to develop, compile, and run C++ programs on it.

PRE-LAB WRITING ASSIGNMENT

Fill-in-the-Blank Questions

1. Compilers detect _______________ errors.
2. Usually the most difficult errors to correct are the _______________ errors, since they are not detected in the compilation process.
3. Attaching other pre-written routines to your program is done by the _______________ process.

4. ______________ code is the machine code consisting of ones and zeroes that is read by the computer.
5. Dividing by zero is an example of a ______________ error.

Learn the Environment That You Are Working In

The following information may be obtained from your instructor.

1. What operating system are you using?
2. What C++ environment are you working in?
3. If you are not working in an integrated environment, what are the compile, run, and edit commands that you will need?

LESSON 1A

Your instructor may assign either Appendix A, Appendix B, or Appendix C depending on your environment. Appendix A is for labs using Microsoft Visual C++ .NET, Appendix B is for labs using Visual C++, and Appendix C is for labs using UNIX. If you are using an environment other than these, your instructor will give you instructions for this first lesson and ask you to complete Lab 1.1 below. If you are using a pre-standard C++ compiler you will need to make the following changes to all the programs in this lab manual.

1. Add `.h` to all included files. So, for example, `#include <iostream>` will be changed to `#include <iostream.h>`
2. Eliminate the `using namespace` statement.

LAB 1.1 Opening, Compiling, and Running Your First Program

Exercise 1: Log on to your system based on your professor's instructions.

Exercise 2: Bring in the `firstprog.cpp` program from the Set 1 folder. The code follows.

```
// This is the first program that just writes out a simple message.

#include <iostream>              // needed to do C++ I/O
using namespace std;

int main ()
{
   cout << "Now is the time for all good men" << endl;
   cout << "to come to the aid of their party." << endl;

   return 0;
}
```

Exercise 3: Compile the program.

Exercise 4: Run the program and write what is printed on the screen.

LAB 1.2 Compiling a Program with a Syntax Error

Exercise 1: Bring in program `semiprob.cpp` from the Set 1 folder. The code follows.

```
// This program demonstrates a compile error.

#include <iostream>
using namespace std;

int main()
{
   int number;
   float total;

   cout << "Today is a great day for lab."
   cout << endl << "Let's start off by typing a number of your choice." << endl;
   cin  >> number;

   total = number * 2;
   cout << total << " is twice the number you typed." << endl;

   return 0;
}
```

Exercise 2: Compile the program. Here we have our first example of the many syntax errors that you no doubt will encounter in this course. The error message you receive may be different depending on the system you are using, but the compiler insists that a semicolon is missing somewhere. Unfortunately, where the message indicates that the problem exists, and where the problem actually occurs may be two different places. To correct the problem, place a semicolon after the following line.

```
cout << "Today is a great day for lab."
```

Most syntax errors are not as easy to spot and correct as this one.

Exercise 3: Re-compile the program and when you have no syntax errors run the program and input 9 when asked. Record the output.

Exercise 4: Try running it with different numbers. Record your output.

Do you feel you are getting valid output?

LAB 1.3 Running a Program with a Run-Time Error

Exercise 1: Bring in program `runprob.cpp` from the Set 1 folder. The code follows.

```
// This program will take a number and divide it by 2.

#include <iostream>
using namespace std;

int main()
{
   float number;
   int divider;
```

continues

```
   divider = 0;

   cout << "Hi there!" << endl;
   cout << "Please input a number and then hit return." << endl;
   cin  >> number;

   number = number / divider;

   cout << "Half of your number is " << number << endl;

   return 0;
}
```

Exercise 2: Compile the program. You should get no syntax errors.

Exercise 3: Run the program. You should now see the first of several run-time errors. There was no syntax or grammatical error in the program; however, the program is asking the computer to break a law of math by dividing by zero. It cannot be done. On some installations, you may see this as output that looks very strange. Correct this program by having the code divide by 2 instead of 0.

Exercise 4: Re-compile and run the program. Type 9 when asked for input. Record what is printed.

Exercise 5: Run the program using different values. Record the output.

Do you feel that you are getting valid output?

LESSON 1B

LAB 1.4 Working with Logic Errors

Exercise 1: Bring in program `logicprob.cpp` from the Set 1 folder. The code follows.

```
// This program takes two values from the user and then swaps them
// before printing the values. The user will be prompted to enter
// both numbers.

#include <iostream>
using namespace std;

int main()
{
   float firstNumber;
   float secondNumber;

   // Prompt user to enter the first number.
   cout << "Enter the first number" << endl;
   cout << "Then hit enter" << endl;
   cin  >> firstNumber;
```

continues

```
    // Prompt user to enter the second number.
    cout << "Enter the second number" << endl;
    cout << "Then hit enter" << endl;
    cin  >> secondNumber;

    // Echo print the input.
    cout << endl << "You input the numbers as "
         << firstNumber << " and " << secondNumber << endl;

    // Now we will swap the two values.
    firstNumber = secondNumber;
    secondNumber = firstNumber;

    // Output the values.
    cout << "After swapping, the values of the two numbers are "
         << firstNumber << " and " << secondNumber << endl;

    return 0;
}
```

Exercise 2: Compile the program. You should get no syntax errors.

Exercise 3: Run the program. It has no syntax or run-time errors, but it certainly has a logic error. This logic error may not be easy to find. Most logic errors create a challenge for the programmer. Your instructor may ask you not to worry about finding and correcting the problem at this time.

LAB 1.5 Writing Your First Program (Optional)

Exercise 1: Develop a design that leads to an algorithm and a program to convert kilometers to miles. Your program should read in a number representing the number of kilometers traveled and output it in miles. 1 kilometer = 0.621 miles. Call this program `kilotomiles.cpp`

Exercise 2: Compile the program. If you get compile errors, try to fix them and re-compile until your program is free of syntax errors.

Exercise 3: Run the program. Is your output what you expect from the input you gave? If not, try to find and correct the logic error and run the program again. Continue this process until you have a program that produces the correct result.

LESSON SET

2 Introduction to the C++ Programming Language

PURPOSE

1. To briefly introduce the C++ programming language
2. To show the use of memory in programming
3. To introduce variables and named constants
4. To introduce the assignment operator
5. To introduce various data types:
   - Integer
   - Character
   - Floating-point
   - Boolean
   - String
6. To introduce the `cout` statement
7. To demonstrate the use of arithmetic operators

PROCEDURE

1. Students should read the Pre-lab Reading Assignment before coming to lab.
2. Students should complete the Pre-lab Writing Assignment before coming to lab.
3. In the lab, students should complete Labs 2.1 through 2.4 in sequence. Your instructor will give further instructions as to grading and completion of the lab.

Contents	Prerequisites	Approximate completion time	Page number	Check when done
Pre-lab Reading Assignment		20 min.	12	
Pre-lab Writing Assignment	Pre-lab reading	10 min.	17	
Lesson 2A				
Lab 2.1 Working with the `cout` Statement	Pre-lab reading	20 min.	17	
Lab 2.2 Working with Constants, Variables, and Arithmetic Operators	Understanding of variables and operators	30 min.	18	

continues

Lesson 2B			
Lab 2.3 Rectangle Area and Perimeter	Understanding of basic components of a program	30 min.	19
Lab 2.4 Working with Characters and Strings	Completion of Labs 2.1–2.3	30 min.	19

PRE-LAB READING ASSIGNMENT

The C++ Programming Language

Computer programming courses generally concentrate on program design that can be applied to any number of programming languages on the market. It is imperative, however, to apply that design to some particular language. This course uses C++, a popular object-oriented language.

For now, we can think of a C++ program as consisting of two general divisions: header and main. The **header**, or **global section**, gives preliminary instructions to the compiler. It consists of comments that describe the purpose of the program, as well as information on which library routines will be used by the program (see Lesson Set 1).

```
// This program prints to the screen the words:
//   PI = 3.14
//   Radius = 4
//   Circumference = 25.12

#include <iostream>
using namespace std;

const double PI = 3.14;

int main()
{
     float radius;
     radius = 4.0;

     cout << "PI = " << PI << endl;
     cout << "Radius = " << radius << endl;
     cout << "Circumference = " << 2 * PI * radius << endl;

     return 0;
}
```

Everything in bold, i.e., everything above the `int main()` statement, is considered the header or global section. Everything in italics, i.e., everything below and including the `int main()` statement, is the main section.

Comments are included in every program to document what a program does and how it operates. These statements are ignored by the computer but are valuable to the programmers who must update or fix the program. In C++, comments begin with //, which is an indication to the compiler to ignore everything from the // to the end of the line. Comments can also cross line boundaries by beginning with /* and ending with */. Notice that the first four lines of the previous program all begin with // and thus are comments. Those same lines could also have been written as the following:

```
/* This program prints to the screen the words:
     PI = 3.14
     Radius = 4
     Circumference = 25.12
*/
```

The next statement, the #include statement, indicates which libraries will be needed by the program.

```
#include <iostream>
```

Recall from Lesson Set 1 that every program needs other program modules attached to it so that it may execute properly. Your instructor will generally tell you which libraries are needed for each particular programming assignment; however, in time you will learn this task for yourself.

Every C++ program has a **main** function, which indicates the start of the executable instructions. Every main must begin with a left brace { and end with a right brace }. The statements inside those braces will be explained as we progress through this lesson.

Memory

Memory storage is the collection of locations where instructions, and data used by the instructions, are temporarily stored. Recall from Lesson Set 1 that a computer only understands sequences of 1s and 0s. These are binary digits or **bits** (binary digits). Eight of these brought together are called a **byte**, which is the most common unit of storage. These chunks of memory can be thought of as hotel mailboxes at the registration desk. The size of each of those boxes indicates the type of mail that can be stored there. A very small mailbox may only hold notes or postcards. Larger mailboxes can hold letters, while even larger ones can hold packages. Each mailbox is identified by a number or name of an occupant. We have identified two very important attributes of these mailboxes: the name or number, which indicates the mailbox that is being referenced, and the size, which indicates what type of "data" can be placed there.

Example: **postcards Jim** could be an indication that the mailbox called Jim can only hold postcards, while the statement **packages Mary** would indicate that the mailbox called Mary could hold large packages. Memory locations in a computer are identified by the same two attributes: data type and name.

Much of programming is getting data to and from memory locations, so it is imperative that the programmer tell the computer the data type and name of each memory location that he or she intends to use. In the sample program the statement **float radius** does just that. float is a data type that indicates what kind of data can be stored and radius is the name for that particular memory location.

Variables and Constants

The ability to change or not change the data stored could be a third attribute of these memory locations. Components of memory in which data values stored can change during the execution of the program are called **variables**. In the sample program, radius is a variable. Notice that it is defined inside the main function. In general variables, like radius, should not be defined in the header or global section of the program. Components of memory in which data values stored are initialized once and may never be changed during the execution of the program are called **named constants** or **constant variables**. They are often defined in the global section and are preceded (in C++) by the word `const`. PI, in the sample program, is an example of a named constant. Its value, 3.14, will not change during the execution of the program.

Identifiers in C++

Identifiers are used to name variables, constants and many other components of a program. They consist exclusively of letters, digits, and the underscore _ character. They cannot begin with a digit and cannot duplicate reserved words used in C++ such as `int` or `if`. All characters in C++ are case sensitive; thus memory locations called simple, Simple, and SIMPLE are three distinct locations. Many programmers make constants all uppercase and variables predominantly lowercase characters. We have followed this convention with the identifiers radius and PI.

The statements

```
const double PI = 3.14;
float radius;
```

are called **definitions**. They reserve by name enough memory to hold the data type specified.

Variables, like constants, can be given an initial value when they are defined, but that value is not permanent and can be altered. For example:

```
int count = 7;       // defines a variable memory location called
                     // count that initially has the value of 7
count = count + 1;   // count is now altered
```

The Assignment Operator

The = symbol in C++ is called the **assignment operator** and is read "is assigned the value of." It assigns the variable on its left-hand side the value on its right-hand side. Notice how it is used in the above two statements. In the first case count "is assigned the value of" 7. In the second case count "is assigned the value of" one greater than its previous value. Do not be misled that the C++ assignment operator looks like an equal sign. It is very different. We can say, for example, count = 7; but we cannot say 7 = count; since 7 is not the name of a variable or named constant that can be assigned a value.

Data Types

As noted earlier, computer memory is composed of units identified by a data type and a name (like the room number of a hotel mailbox). The data type indicates what kind of data can be stored in this location, thus setting its size.

Integer Data Type

Integers are real numbers that do not contain any fractional component. They take up less memory than numbers with fractional components. C++ has three data types that are integers: `short`, `int`, and `long`. The difference is strictly in the amount of memory (number of bytes) they reserve, short reserving the least and long reserving the most. Larger integers may need the long data type. The following three statements define integer variables in C++.

```
short count;
int sum;
long total;
```

Floating-Point Data Type

In computer science, 3 = 3.0 is not a true statement. The number on the left is an integer while the number on the right is a real, or floating-point, number (a number that has a fractional component). Although mathematically the two are equal, the computer stores them as different data types. C++ uses both **`float`** and **`double`** to indicate floating-point numbers, with `double` using more memory than `float`. The following two statements define floating-point variables in C++.

```
float average;
double nationalDebt;
```

Character Data Type

Character data includes the letters of the alphabet (upper and lower cases), the characters representing digits 0–9, and special characters such as ! ? . , *. Each character data item is enclosed in single quotes to distinguish it from other data types. Thus `'8'` is different than `8`. The first is a character while the second is an integer. The following statement defines a C++ character variable initialized to `'b'`.

```
char letter = 'b';
```

Boolean Data Type

The Boolean data type, named after the mathematician George Boole, allows only two values: true and false, which are internally represented as non-zero and zero, respectively. The following statement defines a Boolean variable initialized to false.

```
bool found = false;
```

String Type

A variable defined to be character data can store only one character in its memory location, which is not very useful for storing names. A **string class** has become part of standard C++ and, although not a primitive data type defined by the language, it can be used as a type for storing a whole set of characters in a memory location. In order for this to be accomplished we must "include" the string library (`#include <string>`) in the program header. The following statement defines a string initialized to `"John"`. Note that, unlike a character, a string must be enclosed in double quotes.

```
string name = "John";
```

Fundamental Instructions

Most programming languages, including C++, consist of five fundamental instructions from which all code can be generated.

1. **Assignment Statements**: These statements use the assignment operator (described earlier) to place values in memory locations. The left side of an assignment statement (before the = sign) consists of a single variable name. The right side (after the = sign) consists of an **expression**. An expression is something that can be "evaluated" to arrive at a single value. It can be something as simple as a literal number (like 7) or a single variable, which of course has a single value, or can involve a complicated

set of operations that must be carried out to arrive at a single value. That value is placed in the memory location of the variable on the left.

Example:

```
int count;
int total;

count = 5;       // 5 is stored in the memory location called count.

total = count;   // Since count is holding a 5, the right-hand side
                 // evaluates to 5. Thus 5 is stored in total.
                 // count's value remains unchanged.

count = 3 + 4;   // The right-hand side is evaluated to produce a 7.
                 // count is assigned the value of 7, which replaces
                 // its earlier value of 5.

total = total + count;   // The right-hand side is evaluated (5+7)
                         // and 12 is stored in total, replacing its
                         // previous value of 5.
```

2. **Output Statements**: These instructions send information from the computer to the outside world. This information may be sent to the screen or to some file. In C++ the **cout <<** statement sends information to the screen. **#include <iostream>** must be in the header for cout to be used. The following statement sends whatever value is stored in the variable total to the screen.

   ```
   cout << total;
   ```

   We can output literal strings (such as "The total is ") by enclosing them in double quotes as shown below. The << operator acts as a separator for multiple outputs. The endl causes subsequent output to begin on a new line. The semicolon is the C++ statement terminator.

   ```
   cout << "The total is " << total << endl;
   ```

   The remaining three fundamental instructions will be explained in future labs.

3. **Input Statements**: These statements bring in data to the computer. (Lesson Set 3)
4. **Conditional Statements**: These instructions test conditions to determine which path of instructions to execute. (Lesson Set 4)
5. **Loops**: These instructions indicate the repetition of a set of instructions. (Lesson Set 5)

Arithmetic Operators

Programming has the traditional arithmetic operators:

Operation	C++ Symbol
addition	+
subtraction	-
multiplication	*
division	/
modulus	%

Integer division occurs when both the numerator and denominator of the divide operation are integers (or numbers stored in variables defined to be integers). The result in this case is always an integer. As an example, 14/3 will give the answer 4, not 4.667. Notice that the decimal part of the result is truncated, or "chopped off," rather than the result being rounded to the nearest integer. The modulus operator, which can be used only with integers, gives the remainder of a division operation between two integers. 14 % 3 produces a 2.

Example:

```
int count = 9;
int div = 2;
int remainder;
int quotient;

quotient = count / div;     // quotient will be assigned a 4
remainder = count % div;    // remainder will be assigned a 1
```

Go back and review the sample program on the first page of the Pre-lab Reading Assignment. By now you should understand most of the statements.

PRE-LAB WRITING ASSIGNMENT

Fill-in-the-Blank Questions

1. A ______________________ is a memory location whose value cannot change during the execution of the program.
2. ______________ is a data type that holds only numbers with no fractional component.
3. ______________ is a data type that holds numbers with fractional components.
4. ______________ is an arithmetic operator that gives the remainder of a division problem between two integers.
5. `cout <<` is an example of the ______________ fundamental instruction.
6. ______________ data types only have two values: true and false.
7. One byte consists of ______________ bits.
8. // or /* in C++ indicates the start of a ______________.
9. A ______________ is a memory location whose value can change during the execution of the program.

LESSON 2A

LAB 2.1 Working with the `cout` Statement

Bring in program `name.cpp` from the Set 2 folder. The code is as follows.

```
// This program will write the name, address, and telephone
// number of the programmer.

#include <iostream>
using namespace std;
```

continues

```
int main()
{
   // Fill in this space to write your first and last name.
   // Fill in this space to write your address.
   // Fill in this space to write your city, state, and zip.
   // Fill in this space to write your telephone number.

   return 0;
}
```

Exercise 1: Fill in the code where indicated so that the program will do the following:

Write your first and last name on one line. Remember that to output a string value, such as "John Smith", you must use double quotes. Write your address on the next line. Outputting an `endl` will cause subsequent output to appear on the next line. Write your city, state, and zip on the next line. Write your telephone number on the next line. Compile and run the program.

Example: Deano Beano
123 Markadella Lane
Fruitland, Md. 55503
489-555-5555

Exercise 2: Change the program so that a blank line separates the telephone number from the address. Compile and run the program.

Exercise 3: Change the program so that the following (but with your name and address) is printed. Try to get the spacing exactly like that shown below. Compile and run the program.

```
************
   Programmer: Deano Beano
               123 Markadella Lane
               Fruitland, Md. 55503

   Telephone:  489-555-5555

************
```

LAB 2.2 Working with Constants, Variables, and Arithmetic Operators

Bring in the file `circlearea.cpp` from the Set 2 folder. The code follows.

```
// This program will output the circumference and area
// of the circle with a given radius.

// PLACE YOUR NAME HERE.

#include <iostream>
using namespace std;

const float PI = 3.14;
const float RADIUS = 5.4;
```

continues

```
int main()
{  _____ area;                        // definition of area
   float circumference;               // definition of circumference

   circumference = 2 * PI * RADIUS; // computes circumference

   area = ____________;               // computes area

   // Write a cout statement that will output (with description)
   // the circumference of the circle.

   // Write a cout statement that will output (with description)
   // the area of the circle.

   return 0;
}
```

Exercise 1: Fill in the blanks and the `cout` statements so that the output will produce the following:

```
The circumference of the circle is 33.912
The area of the circle is 91.5624
```

Exercise 2: Change the data type of `circumference` from `float` to `int`. Run the program and record the results.

The circumference of the circle is ______________.

The area of the circle is ______________.

Explain what happened to get the above results.

LESSON 2B

LAB 2.3 Rectangle Area and Perimeter

Exercise 1: Using Lab 2.2 as an example, develop a program that will calculate the area and perimeter of a rectangle. The length and width can be given as constants. (`LENGTH = 8 WIDTH = 3`)

Exercise 2: Compile and run your program. Continue to work on it until you get the following output.

```
The area of the rectangle is 24
The perimeter of the rectangle is 22
```

LAB 2.4 Working with Characters and Strings

The following program illustrates the use of characters and strings. The `char` data type allows only one character to be stored in its memory location. The `string` data type (actually a C++ string object, rather than a data type built into the C++ language) allows a sequence of characters to be stored in one memory location.

Bring in the file `stringchar.cpp` from the Set 2 folder. The code follows.

```
// This program demonstrates the use of characters and strings.
// PLACE YOUR NAME HERE.

#include <iostream>
#include <string>
using namespace std;

// definition of constants
const string FAVORITESODA = "Brand X"; // strings get double quotes
const char   BESTRATING = 'A';          // characters get single quotes

int main()
{
   char   rating;          // 2nd highest product rating
   string favoriteSnack;   // most preferred snack
   int    numberOfPeople;  // number of people in the survey
   int    topChoiceTotal;  // number of people who prefer the top choice

   // Write lines of code to do the following:
   // Assign the value of "crackers" to favoriteSnack.
   // Assign a grade of 'B' to rating.
   // Assign the number 250 to numberOfPeople.
   // Assign the number 148 to topChoiceTotal.

   // Fill in the blanks of the following:
   cout << "The number one soda is  " << ____________ << endl;
   cout << "The number one snack is " << ____________ << endl;
   cout << "Out of " << _____________ << " people "
        << _________ << " chose these items!" << endl;
   cout << "Each of these products received a rating of " << ______;
   cout << " from our expert tasters." << endl;
   cout << "The other products were rated no higher than a "
        << _________ << endl;
}
```

Exercise 1: Fill in the indicated code, then compile and run the program. Continue to work on the program until you have no compile, run-time, or logic errors. NOTE: There is a very important statement missing from this code. Check the other programs in previous labs to find what it is. When you compile, you will get a warning that will help you determine what it might be.

Exercise 2: Is it possible to change the choice of `FAVORITESODA` by adding code within the main module of the program? Why or why not?

Exercise 3: Is it possible to change the choice of `favoriteSnack` by adding code within the program? Why or why not?

LESSON SET

3 Expressions, Input, Output, and Data Type Conversions

PURPOSE

1. To learn input and formatted output statements
2. To learn data type conversions (coercion and casting)
3. To work with constants and mathematical functions
4. To introduce the concept of files

PROCEDURE

1. Students should read the Pre-lab Reading Assignment before coming to lab.
2. Students should complete the Pre-lab Writing Assignment before coming to lab.
3. In the lab, students should complete labs assigned to them by the instructor.

Contents	Prerequisites	Approximate completion time	Page number	Check when done
Pre-lab Reading Assignment		20 min.	22	
Pre-lab Writing Assignment	Pre-lab reading	10 min.	28	
LESSON 3A				
Lab 3.1 Working with the `cin` Statement	Confidence in use of data types	15 min.	29	
Lab 3.2 Formatting Output	Basic understanding of `cout` and formatted output	15 min.	30	
Lab 3.3 Arithmetic Operations and Math Functions	Understanding of pre-defined functions `pow` and `sqrt`	20 min.	31	
LESSON 3B				
Lab 3.4 Working with Type Casting	Understanding of type casting (implicit and explicit data conversion)	15 min.	32	

continues

Lab 3.5 Reading and Writing to a File	Basic understanding of reading and writing files	15 min.	33
Lab 3.6 Student-Generated Code Assignments	Understanding of all concepts (except files) covered in this section.	30 min.	34

PRE-LAB READING ASSIGNMENT

Review of the `cout` Statement

The `cout` statement invokes an output stream, which is a sequence of characters to be displayed to the screen.

Example: `cout << "Hi there";`

The **insertion operator** `<<` inserts the string of characters `Hi there` into the output stream that goes to the screen. The `cout` statement can be thought of as an **`ostream`** (output stream) data type.

Input Instructions

Just as the `cout` statement transfers data from the computer to the "outside" world, the **`cin`** statement transfers data into the computer from the keyboard.

Example: `cin >> grade;`

The **extraction operator** `>>` extracts an item from the input stream. In this case, since `grade` is an integer, this instruction will wait for an integer to be entered at the keyboard and then will place that number in the memory location called `grade`.

Just as `cout` is of type `ostream`, `cin` is considered to be an **`istream`** (input stream) data type. In order to use `cin` and `cout` in a C++ program, the `#include <iostream>` directive should be included in the header. The `>>` extraction operator also serves as a separator between input variables, allowing more than one memory location to be loaded with a single `cin` instruction.

Example:

```
float rate;
float hours;

cin >> rate >> hours;
```

The `cin` statement will wait for two floating-point numbers (separated by at least one blank space) to be input from the keyboard. The first will be stored in `rate` and the second in `hours`.

There is one problem with the example above; it does not indicate to the user for what data the `cin` statement is waiting. Remember that the `cin` statement is expecting data from the user at the keyboard. For this reason, every `cin` statement should be preceded by a `cout` statement that indicates to the user the data to be input. A `cout` statement when used in this manner is called a prompt.

Example:

```
cout << "Please input the hourly pay rate"
     << " and then the number of hours worked." << endl;
cin  >> rate >> hours;
```

Storing and Inputting Strings

Often we want to read in and store a string, such as a person's name, in a variable. Since the `char` data type can only hold a single character, we must define a variable that is able to hold a whole set of characters. We can do this in one of two ways.

```
string name;
char name[12];
```

The first statement defines `name` as a string object using the C++ `string` class. This is the type of string most commonly used in your text and throughout this manual. Notice that when we define a variable to be a string object, we do not have to specify its size. The second method defines `name` as an **array** of characters. Arrays will be dealt with in more detail in a later lesson, but for now just think of an array as a set of contiguous memory spaces where we can store something, like a set of characters, together. In C++ programming, this type of string is commonly called a C-string. When using this method to define a string, the programmer must indicate how many characters it can hold. The above statement allows `name` to hold 12 characters, 11 for the name plus one that must be reserved to hold `'\0'`, the special end-of-string character.

Example 1 (using a string object):

```
string name;
cout << "What is your name? ";
cin  >> name;
cout << "Hi " << name << endl;
```

Example 2 (using a C-string):

```
char name[12];
cout << "What is your name? ";
cin  >> name;
cout << "Hi " << name << endl;
```

Even though the above examples will work, we normally do not use `cin >>` to read in strings. This is because of the way it handles **whitespace** (blank spaces, tabs, and line breaks). When `cin >>` is reading numeric data, leading whitespace is ignored and the read continues until a non-numeric character is encountered. When `cin >>` is reading into a variable defined as a string or character array, however, the reading stops if a blank space is encountered within the string. Thus, in the above examples, a name like "John" could be entered, but "John Smith" could not be. We can get around this restriction by using special functions for reading whole lines of input. When using string objects, we can do this with the `getline` function. The simplest format for this function is `getline(cin, stringname)`. Thus, in Example 1 above, we could read a name like John Smith into the `name` variable with the statement

```
getline(cin, name);
```

When using C-strings, we can read whole lines of input using `cin.getline(stringname, length)`, where `length` specifies the maximum number of characters the C-string can hold. Thus, in Example 2 above, we could read a name like John Smith into the `name` variable with the statement

```
cin.getline(name, 12);
```

This will allow a maximum of 11 characters to be read in and stored in `name`, reserving a character to hold the `'\0'`, which is automatically placed in the C-string following the final character in the string.

Here is another example that uses strings.

Example:

```
string name;                  // Define a string object.
float rate, hours, pay;       // More than one variable can be defined in a
                              // single statement providing they are of the
                              // same data type and are separated by commas.

cout << "Please enter employee name." << endl;
getline(cin, name);

cout << "Enter hourly pay rate and then the number of hours worked." << endl;
cin  >> rate >> hours;

pay = rate * hours;
cout << "Employee name: " << name << "   Gross pay: " << pay  << endl;
```

To convert the above example to use a C-string allowing a name of up to 19 characters, you would make the following two changes.

1) Replace the string definition with `char name[20];`
2) Replace the `getline` statement with `cin.getline(name, 20);`

Remember that `getline` and `cin.getline` are only used for inputting strings. When reading in numeric data, you should just use `cin`.

Formatted Output

C++ has special instructions that allow the user to control output attributes such as spacing, data format, and decimal point precision as well as other features. For these special instructions to work, the `#include <iomanip>` directive must be included in the header (global section).

Example:

```
cout << fixed;              // This forces the output to be in decimal
                            // format, instead of scientific notation.

cout << showpoint;          // This makes all floating-point output
                            // show a decimal point, even if the
                            // values are whole numbers.

cout << setprecision(n);    // This forces all floating-point numbers
                            // to be rounded to n decimal places.
```

The above could all be combined into one statement as shown below.

```
cout << fixed << showpoint << setprecision(2);
```

The order in which these items, called stream manipulators, appear does not matter. The above statement could just as correctly have been written

```
cout << setprecision(2) << fixed << showpoint;
```

Spacing is handled by an indication of the width of the field that the number, character, or string is to be placed in. It can be done with `cout.width(n);` where `n` is the width size. However, it is more commonly done by `setw(n)` within a `cout` statement.

Example:
```
float price = 9.5;
float rate = 8.76;
cout << setw(10) << price << setw(7) << rate;
```

The above statements will print the following:

```
       9.5   8.76
```

There are seven blank spaces before 9.5 and three blank spaces between the numbers. The numbers are right justified. The computer memory stores this as follows:

							9	.	5				8	.	7	6

Note: So far we have used `endl` for a new line of output. The `'\n'` is an escape sequence which can be used as a character in a string to accomplish the same thing.

Example: Both of the following will do the same thing.

```
cout << "Hi there\n";          cout << "Hi there" << endl;
```

Expressions

Recall from Lesson Set 2 that the assignment statement consists of two parts: a variable on the left and an expression on the right. The expression is converted to one value that is placed in the memory location corresponding to the variable on the left. These expressions can consist of variables, constants, and literals combined with various operators. It is important to remember the mathematical precedence rules that are applied when evaluating these expressions.

Precedence Rules of Arithmetic Operators

1. Anything grouped in parentheses is top priority
2. Unary negation: for example: `-8`
3. Multiplication, Division and Modulus `* / %`
4. Addition and Subtraction `+ -`

Example:
```
( 8 * 4/2 + 9 - 4/2 + 6 * (4+3) )
( 8 * 4/2 + 9 - 4/2 + 6 * 7 )
( 32 /2   + 9 - 4/2 + 6 * 7 )
(   16    + 9 - 4/2 + 6 * 7 )
(   16    + 9 -  2  + 6 * 7 )
(   16    + 9 -  2  + 42 )
(      25     -  2  + 42 )
(           23      + 42 )  =    65
```

Converting Algebraic Expressions to C++

One of the challenges of learning a new computer language is the task of changing algebraic expressions to their equivalent computer instructions.

Example: `4y(3-2)y+7`

How would this algebraic expression be implemented in C++?

```
4 * y * (3-2) * y + 7
```

Other expressions are a bit more challenging. Consider the quadratic formula:

$$\frac{-b \pm \sqrt{b^2 - 4ac}}{2a}$$

To write this formula we need to know how to indicate the square root and squaring functions in C++.

Several predefined math library routines are contained in the `cmath` library. In order to use these we must have the `#include <cmath>` directive in the header.

Exponents in C++ are handled by the `pow(number,exp)` function, where `number` indicates the base and `exp` is the exponent. For example,

2^3 would be written as `pow(2,3)`

5^9 would be written as `pow(5,9)`

Square roots are handled by `sqrt(n)`. For example,

$\sqrt{9}$ would be written as `sqrt(9)`

Look at the following C++ statements and try to determine what they are doing.

```
formula1 = ( -b + sqrt(pow(b,2) -(4 * a * c))) / (2 * a);
formula2 = ( -b - sqrt(pow(b,2) -(4 * a * c))) / (2 * a);
```

(These are the roots from the quadratic formula in C++ format.)

Data Type Conversions

Recall the discussion of data types from Lesson Set 2. Whenever an integer and a floating-point variable or constant are mixed in an operation, the integer is changed temporarily to its equivalent floating-point. This automatic conversion is called **implicit type coercion**.

Consider the following:

```
int count;
count = 7.8;
```

We are trying to put a floating-point number into an integer memory location. This is like trying to stuff a package into a mailbox that is only large enough to contain letters. Something has to give. In C++ the floating-point is **truncated** (the entire fractional component is cut off) and, thus, we have loss of information.

Type conversions can be made explicit (by the programmer) by using the following general format:

```
static-cast <DataType>(value)
```

This is called **type casting** or **type conversion**.

Example:

```
int count;
float sum = 10.89;

count = sum;                          // Float to integer. This is type coercion.
count = static-cast <int>(sum); // Also float to integer. This is
                                      // type casting.
```

In both cases `count` receives a 10, but `sum` remains 10.89.

If two integers are divided, the result is an integer that is truncated. This can create unexpected results.

Example:

```
int num_As = 10;
int totalGrade = 50;
float percent_As;

percent_As = num_As / totalGrade;
```

In this problem we would expect `percent_As` to be .20 since 10/50 is .20. However, since both `num_As` and `totalGrade` are integers, integer division is performed, which results in a truncated number. In this case it is 0. Whenever a smaller integer value is divided by a larger integer value the result will always be 0. We can correct this problem by type casting.

```
percent_As = static-cast <float>(num_As)/totalGrade;
```

Although the variable `num_As` itself remains an integer, the type cast causes the divide operation to use a copy of the `num_As` value which has been converted to a float. Thus a float is being divided by the integer `totalGrade` and the result will be a floating-point number. The result is now placed in `percent_As`, giving the .20 value we expect.

Files

So far in our examples, program input has always come from the keyboard and output has always gone to the monitor. However, input can come from files instead of from the keyboard and output can go to files instead of to the screen. To do either of these things, `#include <fstream>` should be included in the header so that files can be created and accessed. A file containing data to be input to the computer should be defined as an **`ifstream`** data type while an output file should be defined as **`ofstream`**.

Sample Program 3.1

Suppose we have a data file called `grades.dat` that contains three grades, and we want to take those grades and output them to an output file that we will call `finalgrade.out`. The following code shows how this can be done in C++.

```
#include <fstream>                   // needed to use files
using namespace std;

int main()
{
   float grade1, grade2, grade3;      // This defines 3 float variables.

   ifstream dataFile;                 // This defines an input file stream.
                                      // dataFile is the "internal" name that we
                                      // will use for the file grades.dat

   ofstream outFile;                  // This defines an output file stream.
                                      // outFile is the "internal" name that we
                                      // will use for the file finalgrade.out

   outFile << fixed << showpoint;     // These can be used with output files
                                      // as well as with cout.

   dataFile.open("grades.dat");       // This ties the internal name, dataFile,
                                      // to the actual file, grades.dat

   outFile.open("finalgrade.out");    // This ties the internal name, outFile, to
                                      // the actual file, finalgrade.out.

   dataFile >> grade1 >> grade2 >> grade3; // This reads the values from the
                                           // input file into the 3 variables.

   outFile << grade1 << endl;              // These 3 lines write the values
   outFile << grade2 << endl;              // stored in the 3 variables out to
   outFile << grade3 << endl;              // the output file.

   return 0;
}
```

PRE-LAB WRITING ASSIGNMENT

Fill-in-the-Blank Questions

1. What is the final value (in C++) of the following expression?

   `(5 - 16 / 2 * 3 + (3 + 2 / 2) - 5)` ________________.

2. How would the following expression be written in C++?

   $2x + 3^4$

   ____

3. Implicit conversion is also known as data type ________________.
4. Explicit type conversion is also known as type ________________.
5. List the preprocessor directive that must be included for `cin` and `cout` to be used in a C++ program. ________________
6. List the preprocessor directive that is used to allow data and output files to be used in a program. ________________

7. Blank spaces, tabs, and line breaks in an input line or data file are referred to as ___________________.
8. The << in a cout statement is called the _______________ operator.
9. The #include <_______________> directive is needed for formatted output.
10. The '\n' is a special character that ___________________.

LESSON 3A

LAB 3.1 Working with the cin Statement

Bring in the program bill.cpp from the Set 3 folder. The code follows.

```
// This program will read in the quantity of a particular item and its price.
// It will then print out the total price.
// The input will come from the keyboard and the output will go to
// the screen.

// PLACE YOUR NAME HERE.

#include <iostream>
#include <iomanip>
using namespace std;

int main()
{
   int   quantity;           // number of items purchased
   float itemPrice;          // price of each item
   float totalBill;          // total price of all items

   cout << setprecision(2) << fixed << showpoint; // formatted output

   cout << "Input the number of items bought" << endl;
   // Write an input statement that brings in the quantity.

   // Write a prompt to ask for the price.
   // Write an input statement that brings in the price of each item.

   // Write an assignment statement that determines the totalbill.

   // Write an output statement that prints total bill,
   // with a label to the screen.

   return 0;
}
```

Exercise 1: Complete the program as directed above. Then compile and run it, inputting 22 for the number of items bought and 10.98 for the price of each item. The output should match the results shown below.

Sample run of the program

```
Please input the number of items bought
22

Please input the price of each item
10.98

The total bill is $241.56
```

Exercise 2: Once you have the program working, change the instruction

```
cout << setprecision(2) << fixed << showpoint;
```

to

```
cout << setprecision(2) << showpoint;
```

Rerun the program with the same data given in Exercise 1 above and record your results. What do you think the `fixed` attribute in the `cout` statement does?

Exercise 3: Now put the `fixed` attribute back in and change the instruction to make the precision 4. Rerun the program with the same data given in Exercise 1 and record your results. What do you think the `setprecision( )` attribute in the `cout` statement does?

The attribute `showpoint` forces all floating-point output to show a decimal point even if the values are whole numbers. In some environments this is done automatically.

LAB 3.2 Formatting Output

Look at the following table:

```
  PRICE    QUANTITY

   1.95       8
  10.89       9
```

Assume that from the left margin, PRICE takes up 15 spaces. We could say that the numbers are right justified in a 15-width space. Starting where the PRICE ends, the next field (QUANTITY) takes up 12 spaces. We can use the output formatting instructions from Lab 3.1 and the statement `setw(n)`, where `n` is some integer, to indicate the width to produce such tables.

Bring in the program `tabledata.cpp` from the Set 3 folder. The code follows.

```
// This program will bring in two prices and two quantities of items
// from the keyboard and print those numbers in a formatted chart.

// PLACE YOUR NAME HERE.
```

continues

```
#include <iostream>
#include ___________ // Include the library needed for formatted output.
using namespace std;

int main()
{
   float price1, price2;     //the price of 2 items
   int   quantity1, quantity2;    //the quantity of 2 items

   cout << setprecision(2) << fixed << showpoint;
   cout << "Input the price and quantity of the first item" << endl;
   // Write an input statement that reads in price1 and
   // quantity1 from the keyboard.

   // Provide a prompt for the second price and quantity.
   // Write an input statement that reads in price2 and
   // quantity2 from the keyboard.

   cout << setw(15) << "PRICE" << setw(12) << "QUANTITY\n\n";

   // Write an output statement that prints the first price
   // and quantity. Be sure to use setw() statements.

   // Write an output statement that prints the second price
   // and quantity.

   return 0;
}
```

Exercise 1: Finish the code above as directed. Note that two or more data items can be input at one time by having at least one blank space between them before hitting the enter key. Compile the program and run it using the input shown below to obtain the following results.

```
Input the price and quantity of the first item
1.95 8

Input the price and quantity of the second item
10.89 9

          PRICE    QUANTITY

           1.95          8
          10.89          9
```

LAB 3.3 Arithmetic Operations and Math Functions

Bring in the program `righttrig.cpp` from the Set 3 folder. The code follows.

```
// This program will input the value of two sides of a triangle and then
// determine the length of the third side in order to make it a right triangle.

// PUT YOUR NAME HERE.
```

continues

```
#include <iostream>
#include <cmath>        // needed for math functions like sqrt()
using namespace std;

int main()
{
   float a, b;         // the smaller two sides of the triangle
   float hyp;          // the hypotenuse (side 3) calculated by the program

   cout << "Please input the value of the two sides." << endl;
   cin  >> a >> b;

   // Write a statement to calculate the hypotenuse and assign it to hyp.

   cout << "The sides of the right triangle are "
        << a << " and " << b << endl;
   cout << "The hypotenuse is " << hyp << endl;

   return 0;
}
```

The formula for finding the hypotenuse is $hyp = \sqrt{a^2 + b^2}$.

How can this be implemented in C++? Hint: One way to do this is by using two pre-defined math functions (one of them twice) learned in this lesson. One of them will be "inside" the other.

Exercise 1: Complete the code as instructed. Then compile and run the program using inputs of 9 and 3 for the two sides. Your output should look similar to the sample that follows.

```
Please input the value of the two sides.
9 3
The sides of the right triangle are 9 and 3
The hypotenuse is 9.48683
```

Exercise 2: Alter the program so that the sample run now looks like the following:

```
Please input the value of the two sides: 9 3
The sides of the right triangle are 9 and 3
The hypotenuse is 9.49
```

Note: To print the hypotenuse rounded to two decimal places you must `#include` another library as well as use the formatting features discussed in the earlier labs of this lesson. Notice that the formatting change is made only to the value of the hypotenuse and not to the values of 9 and 3.

LESSON 3B

Lab 3.4 Working with Type Casting

Bring in the program `batavg.cpp` from the Set 3 folder. The code follows.

```
// This program will determine a batting average.
// The number of hits and at bat are given internally in the program.

// PUT YOUR NAME HERE.

#include <iostream>
using namespace std;

const int ATBATS = 421;
const int HITS = 123;

int main()
{
   int batavg;

   batavg = HITS / ATBATS;

   cout << "The batting average is " << batavg << endl;

   return 0;
}
```

Exercise 1: Run this program and record the results. The batting average is ___________.

Exercise 2: There is a logical error in this program centering around data types. Try changing the data type of `batavg` from `int` to `float` and then compile and run the program again. Did that solve the problem?

Exercise 3: Continue to work with this program until you get the correct result. Do not change the data type of the two named constants. Instead, use a typecast to solve the problem.

The correct result should be 0.292162.

LAB 3.5 Reading and Writing to a File

Bring in `billfile.cpp` from the Set 3 folder. The code follows.

```
// This program will read in the quantity of a particular item and its price.
// It will then print out the total price. The input will come from a
// data file and the output will go to an output file.

// PUT YOUR NAME HERE.

#include <fstream>       // needed to use files
#include <iomanip>
using namespace std;
```

continues

```
int main()
{
   ifstream dataIn;       // defines an input stream for a data file
   ofstream dataOut;      // defines an output stream for an output file
   int   quantity;        // number of items purchased
   float itemPrice;       // price of each item
   float totalBill;       // total price of all items

   dataIn.open("transaction.dat"); // These 2 statements open the files.
   dataOut.open("bill.out");

   __________ << setprecision(2) << fixed << showpoint;
                                 // format output in the output file

   // Write an input statement that brings the quantity and price
   // of the item in from the data file.

   // Write an assignment statement that determines the totalbill.

   // Write an output statement that prints total bill, with a label,
   // to the output file.

   return 0;
}
```

Exercise 1: Notice that this is an altered version of Lab 3.1. This program gets the information from a data file and places the output in an output file. You must create the data file. Your instructor will tell you how to do this and where to put it. Create a data file called `transaction.dat` that contains the following information:

```
22
10.98
```

Exercise 2: Complete the program code as directed by filling in the blank and by writing the statements needed to read the data from the file and print the result to the `bill.out` file using the formatting illustrated below. Compile and run the program. Then verify that the result, which will be in the `bill.out` file rather than on the screen, is correct as shown below.

```
The total bill is $241.56
```

LAB 3.6 Student-Generated Code Assignments

Option 1: Write a program that will read in 3 grades from the keyboard and will print the average (to 2 decimal places) of those grades to the screen. It should include good prompts and labeled output. Use the examples from the earlier labs to help you. You will want to begin with a design. The Lesson Set 1 Pre-lab Reading Assignment gave an introduction for a design similar to this problem. Notice in the sample run that the answer is stored in fixed-point notation with two decimal points of precision.

Sample run

```
Please input the first grade
97

Please input the second grade
98.3

Please input the third grade
95

The average of the three grades is 96.77
```

Option 2: The Woody furniture company sells the following three styles of chairs:

Style	**Price Per Chair**
American Colonial	$ 85.00
Modern	$ 57.50
French Classical	$127.75

Write a program that will input the number of chairs sold for each style. It will print the total dollar sales of each style as well as the total sales of all chairs in fixed-point notation with two decimal places.

Sample run

```
Please input the number of American Colonial chairs sold
20
Please input the number of Modern chairs sold
15
Please input the number of French Classical chairs sold
5
The total sales of American Colonial chairs $1700.00
The total sales of Modern chairs $862.50
The total sales of French Classical chairs $638.75
The total sales of all chairs $3201.25
```

Option 3: Write a program that will input total sales (sales plus tax) that a business generates for a particular month. The program will also input the state and local sales tax percentage. It will output the total sales plus the state tax and local tax to be paid. The output should be in fixed notation with 2 decimal places.

Sample run

```
Please input the total sales for the month
1080
Please input the state tax percentage in decimal form (.02 for 2%)
.06
Please input the local tax percentage in decimal form (.02 for 2%)
.02

The total sales for the month is $1080.00
The state tax for the month is $64.80
The local tax for the month is $21.60
```

LESSON SET

4 Conditional Statements

PURPOSE

1. To work with relational operators
2. To work with conditional statements
3. To learn and use nested `if` statements
4. To learn and use logical operators
5. To learn and use the `switch` statement

PROCEDURE

1. Students should read the Pre-lab Reading Assignment before coming to lab.
2. Students should complete the Pre-lab Writing Assignment before coming to lab.
3. In the labs, students should complete the labs assigned to them by the instructor.

Contents	Prerequisites	Approximate completion time	Page number	Check when done
Pre-lab Reading Assignment		20 min.	38	
Pre-lab Writing Assignment	Pre-lab reading	10 min.	44	
LESSON 4A				
Lab 4.1 Relational Operators and the `if` and `if/else` Statements	Basic understanding of `if` and `if/else` statements	15 min.	45	
Lab 4.2 `if/else if` Statements	Basic understanding of nested `if/else if` statements	20 min.	46	
Lab 4.3 Logical Operators and Nested `if` Statements	Basic understanding of logical operators and nested `if` statements	15 min.	47	
LESSON 4B				
Lab 4.4 The `switch` Statement	Understanding of the `switch` statement	15 min.	48	
Lab 4.5 Branch Errors	Understanding of Files and Branching Statements	20 min.	49	
Lab 4.6 Student-Generated Code Assignments	Basic understanding of conditional statements	30 min.	51	

PRE-LAB READING ASSIGNMENT

Relational Operators

You have already seen that the statement `total = 5` is an assignment statement; that is, the integer 5 is placed in the variable called `total`. Nothing relevant to our everyday understanding of equality is present here. So how do we deal with equality in a program? How about greater than or less than? C++ allows the programmer to compare numeric values using **relational operators**. They are the following:

>	Greater than
<	Less than
>=	Greater than or equal to
<=	Less than or equal to
==	Equal to
!=	Not equal to

An expression of the form `num1 > num2` is called a **relational expression**. Note that it does *not* assert that `num1` is greater than `num2`. It actually tests to see if this is true. So relational expressions are Boolean. Their value must be either *true* or *false*. The statement `cost!=9` is false if `cost` has value 9 and true otherwise. Consider the following code:

```
int years;
years = 6;        // assignment statement (years is assigned the value 6.)
years == 5;       // relational expression (Does years equal 5?)
years = years - 1;
years == 5;
```

In this sequence the first occurrence of `years == 5` is a false statement whereas the second occurrence is true. Can you see why?

The `if` Statement

Sometimes we may want a segment of code executed only under certain conditions. To do so, we use **conditional statements**. For example, if you are writing a payroll program to compute wages, then the program should only compute overtime pay *if* the employee worked more than 40 hours in a given week. Otherwise, when the program is executed the overtime portion of the code should be bypassed. An **`if` statement** is one kind of conditional statement.

Consider the following program:

Sample Program 4.1

```
// This program prints "You Pass" if a student's average is
// 60 or higher and prints "You Fail" otherwise.

#include <iostream>
using namespace std;

int main()
{
   float average;
```

continues

```
    cout << "Input your average: ";
    cin  >> average;

    if (average >= 60)       // note the use of a relational operator
       cout << "You Pass" << endl;

    if (average < 60)
       cout << "You Fail" << endl;

    return 0;
}
```

Note that it is not possible for this program to print out both "You Pass" and "You Fail". Only one of the `if` statements will be executed. Later we will see a way to write this program without using two `if` statements.

If you want to conditionally execute several statements using `if`, the following syntax is required:

```
if (expression)
{  statement_1;
   statement_2;
         :
   statement_n;
}
```

Note the curly braces surrounding the set of statements to be conditionally executed.

In the examples shown so far, relational operators have been used to compare numeric constants and variables. Characters and string objects can also be compared with these operators. For example:

```
char letter = 'C';
string word = "bat";

if (letter == 'A')                   // This is false
   cout << "The letter is A.";       // so this will not print.

if (word < "cat")                    // This is true
   cout << "The word bat comes "     // so this will print.
        << "before the word cat.";
```

The `if/else` Statement

In Sample Program 4.1 we used two `if` statements. A more elegant approach would be to use the **`if/else` statement** as follows:

```
if (average >= 60)
    cout << "You Pass" << endl;
else
    cout << "You Fail" << endl;
```

In every `if/else` statement, the program can take only one of two possible paths. Multiple statements can be handled using curly braces in the same way as the `if` statement.

The `if/else if` Statement

The `if/else` statement works well if there are only two possible paths to follow. However, what if there are more than two possibilities? For example, suppose we need to decide what kind of vacation to take based on a yearly work bonus:

- if the bonus is less than $1,000, we set up a tent and camp out in the back yard
- if the bonus is less than $10,000 and greater than or equal to $1,000, we go to Disney World
- if the bonus is $10,000, we go to Hawaii

We could code this using the **`if/else if`** statement as follows:

```
float bonus;

cout << "Input yearly bonus amount: ";
cin >> bonus;

if (bonus < 1000)
   cout << "Another vacation at home." << endl;

else if (bonus < 10000)
   cout << "Off to Disney World!" << endl;

else if (bonus == 10000)
   cout << "Let's go to Hawaii!" << endl;
```

Can you explain why the first `else if` conditional statement does not require a greater than or equal to 1000 condition?

In general we can use as many `else if` expressions as needed to solve a given problem.

The Trailing `else`

What happens in the code above if the bonus entered is greater than $10,000? Actually, nothing will happen since none of the conditional expressions are true in this case. Sometimes it is advantageous to add a final or **trailing `else`** at the end of a chain of `if/else if` statements to handle all other cases. For example, we could modify the code to read:

```
if (bonus < 1000)
   cout << "Another vacation at home" << endl;
else if (bonus < 10000)
   cout << "Off to Disney World!" << endl;
else if (bonus == 10000)
   cout << "Let's go to Hawaii!" << endl;
else
{  cout << bonus << " is not a valid bonus." << endl;
   cout << "Please rerun the program with valid data" << endl;
}  // Note the necessary use of the curly brackets here.
```

Of course, few would complain about a bonus greater than $10,000 and the Hawaii trip could still be done on this budget. However, if the maximum possible bonus is $10,000, then the trailing `else` will let the user know that an illegal value has been entered.

Nested `if` Statements

Often programmers use an `if` statement within another `if` statement. For example, suppose a software engineering company wants to screen applicants first for experienced programmers and second for C++ programmers specifically. One possible program is the following:

Sample Program 4.2

```
// This program illustrates the use of nested if statements.

#include <iostream>
using namespace std;

int main()
{
   char programmer, cPlusPlus;

   cout << "Before we consider your application, answer the following"
        << endl;
   cout << " yes (enter Y) or no (enter N)." << endl << endl;

   cout << "Are you a computer programmer? ";
   cin  >> programmer;

   if (programmer == 'Y')
   {  cout << "Do you program in C++? ";
      cin  >> cPlusPlus;

      if (cPlusPlus == 'Y')
         cout << " You look like a promising candidate for employment."
              << endl;
      else if (cPlusPlus == 'N')
          cout << " You need to learn C++ before further consideration."
               << endl;
      else
          cout << " You must enter a capital Y or N." << endl;
    }

    else if (programmer == 'N')
       cout << " You are not currently qualified for employment."
            << endl;
    else
       cout << " You must enter a capital Y or N." << endl;

    return 0;
}
```

Note how C++ programmers are identified using a nested `if` statement. Also note how the trailing `else` is used to detect invalid input.

Logical Operators

By using relational operators, C++ programmers can create relational expressions which evaluate to *true* or *false*. Programmers can also combine truth values into a single expression by using **logical operators**. For example, instead of a statement such as "if it is sunny, then we will go outside," one may use a statement such as "if it is sunny and it is warm, then we will go outside." Note that this statement has two smaller statements "it is sunny" and "it is warm" joined by the **AND** logical operator. To evaluate to *true*, both the sunny and warm requirements must be met.

The **OR** operator is similar to the AND operator in that it connects two statements. In this case the expression evaluates to *true* if either (or both) of the two expressions is *true*. In English there is an ambiguity about the meaning of the word *or*. In the statement "tonight at 8:00 I will go to the concert in the park or I will go to the stadium to see the ball game," the word **or** is *exclusive*. That is, I can go to the concert or to the game but not both. However, in the statement "I need to draw an ace or a king to have a good poker hand," the word **or** is *inclusive*. In other words, I can draw a king, an ace, or even both and I will have a good hand. In computer science there is no such ambiguity. We always use the second meaning of the word *or*. So, in the statement "if it is sunny or it is warm, then we will go outside," there are three scenarios where we will go outside: if it is sunny but not warm, if it is warm but not sunny, or if it is sunny and warm.

A third logical operator, the **NOT** operator, negates a single statement. For example, "it is sunny" can be negated by "it is not sunny."

The symbols used by C++ for logical operators are the following:

Operator	Symbol	Example
AND	&&	`if height > 72 && weight > 200`
OR	||	`if height > 72 || weight > 200`
NOT	!	`if (!(height > 72))`

Two or more logical operators can be combined in a single C++ statement as shown here.

```
if (dollars <= 0 || !(accountActive) )
    cout << " You may not withdraw money from the bank";
```

It is good programming practice to enclose the operand after the (!) operator in parentheses. Unexpected things can happen in complicated expressions if you do not. When will this code execute the `cout` statement? What type of variable do you think `accountActive` is?

The `switch` Statement

We have already seen how `if` statements can affect the branching of a program during execution. Another way to do this is using the **`switch` statement**. It is also a conditional statement. The `switch` statement uses the value of an integer expression to determine which group of statements to branch through. Sample Program 4.3 illustrates the syntax.

Sample Program 4.3

```
// This program uses a switch statement to create an
// appropriate output based on the grade a student earned.

#include <iostream>
using namespace std;

int main()
{
   char grade;

   cout << "What grade did you earn in Programming I?" << endl;
   cin  >> grade;

   switch(grade)    // The switch statement begins here.
   {
      case 'A':cout << "You got an A. Excellent work!" << endl;
               break;
      case 'B':cout << "You got a B. Good job." << endl;
               break;
      case 'C':cout << "Earning a C is satisfactory." << endl;
               break;
      case 'D':cout << "D is passing, but there is a problem." << endl;
               break;
      case 'F':cout << "You failed. Better luck next time." << endl;
               break;
      default: cout << "You did not enter A, B, C, D, or F." << endl;

   }
   return 0;
}
```

Note the use of the curly braces that enclose the cases. Observe also the use of the `break;` after each `case`. You will investigate what this does in one of the lab exercises. Consider the variable `grade`. It is defined as a character data type and the `case` statements have character arguments such as `'B'`. This seems to contradict what we said above, namely that the `switch` statement uses the value of integer expressions to determine branching. However, this apparent contradiction is resolved by the compiler automatically converting character data into the integer data type. Finally, notice the role of the `default` statement. The `default` branch is followed if none of the case expressions match the given `switch` expression.

Testing for File Open Errors

In Lesson Set 3 you were introduced to input and output files. Sample Program 3.1 used the following code to open the input file `grades.dat`:

```
ifstream dataFile;
dataFile.open("grades.dat");
```

Obviously there will be a problem if the file `grades.dat` does not exist or is not in the correct location. To determine if the file is opened successfully we could use the following code:

Example:

```
ifstream dataFile;
dataFile.open("grades.dat");
if (!dataFile)
{
      cout << "Error opening file.\n";
      cout << "Perhaps the file is not where indicated.\n";

}
```

In Lesson Set 13 you will see the advantage of adding a `return 1;` statement after the second `cout` statement in this code. However, until value-returning functions have been introduced (Lesson Set 6.2), it is best to postpone this discussion. When using file I/O, you should always test to make sure the file is opened successfully. If the file cannot be opened, an error message should be displayed to the user, like the message in the example code, to indicate the problem.

PRE-LAB WRITING ASSIGNMENT

Fill-in-the-Blank Questions

1. The two possible values for a relational expression are _______________ and _______________.
2. C++ uses the _______________ symbol to represent the AND operator.
3. The `switch` statement and `if` statements are examples of _______________ statements.
4. In C++ the meaning of the OR logical operator is _______________ (inclusive / exclusive).
5. C++ uses the _______________ symbol to represent the OR operator.
6. It is good programming practice to include the operand after the NOT operator in _______________.
7. The `switch` statement uses the value of a(n) _______________ expression to determine which group of statements to branch through.
8. In a `switch` statement the _______________ branch is followed if none of the `case` expressions match the given `switch` expression.
9. C++ _______________ (does / does not) allow string objects to be compared with relational operators.
10. The C++ symbol for equality is _______________.

LESSON 4A

LAB 4.1 Relational Operators and the `if` and `if/else` Statements

Bring in the file `compare.cpp` from the Set 4 folder. The code follows.

```
// This program tests whether or not an initialized value
// (num2 = 5) is equal to a value input by the user.

// PLACE YOUR NAME HERE.

#include <iostream>
using namespace std;

int main( )
{
   int num1,                  // num1 is not initialized
   num2 = 5;                  // num2 is initialized to 5

   cout << "Please enter an integer" << endl;
   cin  >> num1;

   cout << "num1 = " << num1 << " and num2 = " << num2 << endl;

   if (num1 = num2)
      cout << "Hey, that's a coincidence!" << endl;

   if (num1 != num2)
      cout << "The values are not the same." << endl;

   return 0;
}
```

Exercise 1: Run the program several times using a different input each time. If you input a 5, what is output? If you input a 7, what is output? Does the program do what you expect? If so, explain what it is doing. If not, locate the error and fix it.

Exercise 2: Modify the program so that the user inputs both values to be tested for equality. Update the starting comment to reflect this change. Make sure you have a prompt for each input. You will no longer need to initialize `num2`. Test the revised program with pairs of values that are the same and that are different.

Exercise 3: Modify the revised Exercise 2 program by adding an additional `cout` statement so that when the numbers are the same it prints the following lines.

```
The values are the same.
Hey, that's a coincidence!
```

Again, test the program with pairs of values that are the same and that are different. What happens if you forget the curly braces in the `if` statement? Take them out and see. Then put them back in.

Exercise 4: Modify (and then test) the revised Exercise 3 program by replacing the two `if` statements with a single `if/else` statement.

LAB 4.2 `if/else if` Statements

Bring in the file `grades.cpp` from the Set 4 folder. The code follows.

```
//  This program prints "You Pass" if a student's average
//  is 60 or higher and prints "You Fail" otherwise.

// PLACE YOUR NAME HERE.

#include <iostream>
using namespace std;

int main()
{
   float average;                    // holds the grade average

   cout << "Input your average: ";
   cin  >> average;

   if (average > 60)
      cout << "You Pass" << endl;

   if (average < 60)
      cout << "You Fail" << endl;

   return 0;
}
```

Exercise 1: Run the program three times, first inputting 80 for average, then 55, and then 60. Record the results in each case. Were they what you expected? What happened when you input 60 as the average? Modify the first `if` statement so that the program will also print "`You Pass`" if the average equals 60.

Exercise 2: Modify the program so that it uses an `if/else` statement rather than two `if` statements.

Exercise 3: Now modify your program from Exercise 2 to allow four grade categories. Do this by replacing the `if/else` statement you used in Exercise 2 with an `if/else if` statement. If the average is 90 or higher, the program should print "Excellent". If it is 80 or higher, but less than 90, it should print "Good". For an average of 65 or higher, but less than 80, it should print "Fair". Finally, for anything else (i.e., below 65), it should print "Poor". Test your program with averages that are at the extreme top and bottom of each range as well as within each range. That is, test the "Excellent" range with 100, with 90, and with something in between. Do the same for the other three ranges.

Exercise 4: What will happen to your program from Exercise 3 if you enter a negative value such as –12? Try it. Add a final `else` clause to your `if/else if` statement to print an error message if a negative number is entered.

LAB 4.3 Logical Operators and Nested `if` Statements

Bring in the file `insurance.cpp` from the Set 4 folder. The code follows.

```
// This determines a client's automobile insurance category based
// on gender and age. It illustrates the use of logical operators
// and nested if statements.

// PLACE YOUR NAME HERE.

#include <iostream>
using namespace std;

int main()
{
   char gender;
   int  age,
        category = 0;

   cout << "Enter your gender (M for male or F for female): ";
   cin  >> gender;
   cout << "Enter your age: ";
   cin  >> age;

   if (gender == 'M')
   {  if (age < 21)
         category = 1;
      else
         category = 3;
   }
   else if (gender == 'F')
   {  if (age < 21)
         category = 2;
      else
         category = 4;
   }

   if (category != 0)
      cout << "Gender: " << gender << "    Age: " << age
           << "    Insurance category: " << category << endl;
   else
      cout << "Illegal gender entered" << endl;

   return 0;
}
```

Exercise 1: What output would you expect for each of the following? Trace the code and complete the **Expected** results column before running the program.

	Expected	**Observed**
Female age 19	__________	__________
Female age 23	__________	__________
Male age 20	__________	__________
Male age 21	__________	__________

Now run the program four times, using the above data, and complete the **Observed** results column. Be sure to enter the gender with an upper case letter. Were your expectations correct?

Exercise 2: Now try running the program for a 23-year-old female, but enter the gender in lower case. What happened? We can fix this problem by using the logical OR operator. Replace the line that reads

```
if (gender == 'M')
```

with the line

```
if (gender == 'M' || gender == 'm')
```

Make a similar change on the statement that tests if `gender` equals 'F'. Retest the program for a 23 year old female where the gender is entered in lower case. Does it work correctly now?

Exercise 3: Modify the program from Exercise 2 to utilize an `if/else if` statement (instead of nested `if` statements) by using the logical AND operator to test `gender` and `age` in the same statement. The first test you will need is shown below. Use inner parentheses to ensure that the OR gets done before the AND.

```
if ( (gender == 'M' || gender == 'm') && age < 21)
```

LESSON 4B

LAB 4.4 The `switch` Statement

Bring in the file `switch.cpp` from the Set 4 folder. This is Sample Program 4.3 from the Pre-lab Reading Assignment. The code follows.

```
// PLACE YOUR NAME HERE.

#include <iostream>
using namespace std;

int main()
{
   char grade;

   cout << "What grade did you earn in Programming I?" << endl;
   cin  >> grade;

   switch(grade)    // The switch statement begins here.
   {
      case 'A':cout << "You got an A. Excellent work!" << endl;
               break;
      case 'B':cout << "You got a B. Good job." << endl;
               break;
```

continues

```
      case 'C':cout << "Earning a C is satisfactory." << endl;
               break;
      case 'D':cout << "D is passing, but there is a problem." << endl;
               break;
      case 'F':cout << "You failed. Better luck next time." << endl;
               break;
      default: cout << "You did not enter A, B, C, D, or F." << endl;

   }
   return 0;
}
```

Exercise 1: What do you think will happen if you run the code and enter a lower case 'a'? Try it and see if you were correct. You can solve this problem by having two cases (one for the upper case letter and one for its lower case equivalent) execute the same output statement. Do this by adding an 'a' case just before the 'A' case, as shown below.

```
case 'a':
case 'A':cout << "You got an A. Excellent work!" << endl;
         break;
```

Do the same thing for the 'B', 'C', 'D', and 'F' cases. Recompile and rerun the program. Test it to make sure it works correctly for all grades, both upper and lower case.

Exercise 2: Remove the `break` statements from each of the cases. Then rerun the program and see what happens when a grade of 'B' is entered. What is the effect on the execution of the program?

Exercise 3: Put the `break` statements back in. Then add an additional `switch` statement right after the grade is input (i.e., before the `switch` statement shown above) that prints "YOU PASSED!" for a grade of D or better. Use the sample run given below to model your output.

Sample Run

```
What grade did you earn in Programming I?
A
YOU PASSED!
You got an A. Excellent work!
```

Exercise 4: Rewrite the program from Exercise 3 without any `switch` statements. Replace the top `switch` statement with an `if` statement and the bottom one with an `if/else if` statement. Did you use a trailing `else` in your new version? If so, what did it correspond to in the original program with the `switch` statement?

Lab 4.5 Branch Errors

Bring in the file `payprog.cpp` & `overtime.dat` from Set 4 folder. The code follows:

```
#include <fstream>
#include <iostream>
using namespace std;

// This program reads from a file the maximum hours (before overtime is
// calculated) as well as the overtime rate. It then has hours worked
```

continues

```
// and the pay rate entered from the keyboard. The program determines
// the gross pay based on the overtime rate and hours worked. It also
// prints out a message if the gross pay is over $5,000.

// PLACE YOUR NAME HERE.

int main()
{
   float maxHours;  // maximum hours worked before overtime is calculated
   float overRate;  // rate of overtime pay (ex. 1.5 is time and a half)
   float hoursWorked;
   float ratePerHour;
   float grossPay;
   ifstream getData;

   // Fill in the code to open getData. The actual data file is called
   // overtime.dat.

   // Fill in the code to check if getData can be found.  This should include
   // an if statement and a cout statement that indicates the file could not
   // be found.


   // Fill in the code to read maxHours and overRate from the file.

   cout << "Please input the number of hours worked this week" << endl;
   cin >> hoursWorked;
   cout << "Please input rate per hour" << endl;

   cin >> ratePerHour;

   if (hoursWorked > maxHours)
   {
       cout << "This individual worked overtime " << endl;
       grossPay = (ratePerHour * maxHours) + (ratePerHour *overRate *
                                            (hoursWorked - maxHours));
       cout << "The gross pay is $" << grossPay << endl;
   }
   else
       cout << "This individual did not work overtime" << endl;
       grossPay = (ratePerHour * hoursWorked);
       cout << "The gross pay is $" << grossPay << endl;

   if (grossPay > 5000);
       cout << "You earned more than $5,000 this week!!!" << endl;

   return 0;
}
```

Exercise 1: Fill in the code as indicated in the program. Then run the program with the following data: 30 (for hours worked) 10 (for rate per hour). NOTE: the data file has 40 hours as the maximum number of hours and 1.5 at the overtime rate.

What is printed?

Rerun the program with the following data: 50 (for hours worked) and 20 (for rate per hour).

What is printed?

Exercise 2: There are obviously a few things wrong with this program (logic errors). Correct the program so that it produces the correct output.

Sample Run 1:

```
Please input the number of hours worked this week: 30
Please input rate per hour: 10
This individual did not work overtime
The gross pay is $300
```

Sample Run 2:

```
Please input the number of hours worked this week: 50
Please input rate per hour: 20
This individual worked overtime
The gross pay is $1100
```

LAB 4.6 Student-Generated Code Assignments

Option 1: Write a program that prompts users for their quarterly water bill for the last four *quarters*. The program should find and output their average *monthly* water bill. If the average bill exceeds $75, the output should include a message indicating that too much water is being used. If the average bill is at least $25 but no more than $75, the output should indicate that a typical amount of water is being used. Finally, if the average bill is less than $25, the output should contain a message praising the user for conserving water. Use the sample run below as a model for your output.

Sample Run 1

```
Please input your water bill for quarter 1: 300
Please input your water bill for quarter 2: 200
Please input your water bill for quarter 3: 225
Please input your water bill for quarter 4: 275

Your average monthly bill is $83.33. You are using excessive amounts of water.
```

Sample Run 2

```
Please input your water bill for quarter 1: 100
Please input your water bill for quarter 2: 150
```

continues

```
Please input your water bill for quarter 3: 75
Please input your water bill for quarter 4: 125

Your average monthly bill is $37.50. You are using a typical amount of water.
```

Option 2: Modify Option 1 to read the quarterly water bill amounts in from a file. In this case the prompts for the data should be omitted. The file `water.dat`, provided on the student disk, contains the data values shown in Sample Run 1.

Option 3: The local T-shirt shop sells shirts that retail for $12. Quantity discounts are given as follows:

Number of Shirts	Discount
5–10	10%
11–20	15%
21–30	20%
31 or more	25%

Write a program that prompts the user for the number of shirts required and then computes the total price. Make sure the program accepts only non-negative input. Use the following sample runs to guide you:

Sample Run 1

```
How many shirts would you like? 4
The cost per shirt is $12 and the total cost is $48.
```

Sample Run 2

```
How many shirts would you like? 0
The cost per shirt is $12 and the total cost is $0.
```

Sample Run 3

```
How many shirts would you like? 8
The cost per shirt is $10.80 and the total cost is $86.40.
```

Sample Run 4

```
How many shirts would you like? -2
Invalid Input: Please enter a non-negative integer.
```

Option 4: The University of Guiness charges $3000 per semester for in-state tuition and $4500 per semester for out-of-state tuition. In addition, room and board is $2500 per semester for in-state students and $3500 per semester for out-of-state students. Write a program that prompts the user for their residential status (i.e., in-state or out-of-state) and whether they require room and board (Y or N). The program should then compute and output their bill for that semester.

Use the sample output below:

Sample Run 1

```
Please input "I" if you are in-state or "O" if you are out-of-state: I
Please input "Y" if you require room and board and "N" if you do not: N

Your total bill for this semester is $3000.
```

Sample Run 2

```
Please input "I" if you are in-state or "O" if you are out-of-state: O
Please input "Y" if you require room and board and "N" if you do not: Y

Your total bill for this semester is $8000.
```

LESSON SET

5 Looping Statements

PURPOSE

1. To introduce counter- and event-controlled loops
2. To work with the `while` loop
3. To work with the `do-while` loop
4. To work with the `for` loop
5. To work with nested loops

PROCEDURE

1. Students should read the Pre-lab Reading Assignment before coming to lab.
2. Students should complete the Pre-lab Writing Assignment before coming to lab.
3. In the lab, students should complete labs assigned to them by the instructor.

Contents	Prerequisites	Approximate completion time	Page number	Check when done
Pre-lab Reading Assignment		20 min.	56	
Pre-lab Writing Assignment	Pre-lab reading	10 min.	63	
LESSON 5A				
Lab 5.1 Working with the `while` Loop	Basic understanding of the `while` loop	25 min.	64	
Lab 5.2 Working with the `do-while` Loop	Basic understanding of `do-while` loop	25 min.	66	
LESSON 5B				
Lab 5.3 Working with the `for` Loop	Understanding of `for` loops	25 min.	67	
Lab 5.4 Nested Loops	Understanding of nested `for` loops	25 min.	69	
Lab 5.5 Student-Generated Code Assignments	Understanding of loop control structures	homework	70	

PRE-LAB READING ASSIGNMENT

Increment and Decrement Operators

To execute many algorithms we need to be able to add or subtract 1 from a given integer quantity. For example, both of the statements below **increment** the value of `count` by one.

```
count = count + 1;
count += 1;
```

Similarly, the following two statements **decrement** the value of `count` by one.

```
count = count - 1;
count -= 1;
```

C++ also provides an **increment operator** ++ and a **decrement operator** -- to perform these tasks. There are two modes that can be used:

```
count++;      // increment operator in the postfix mode
count--;      // decrement operator in the postfix mode

++count;      // increment operator in the prefix mode
--count;      // decrement operator in the prefix mode
```

The two increment statements both execute exactly the same. So do the two decrement operators. The difference lies in when the increment or decrement is performed if the operator appears in a statement that contains other operations as well. Consider the following code:

```
int age = 49;
if (age++ > 49)
    cout << "Congratulations - You have made it to the"
         << " half-century mark !" << endl;
```

In this code, the `cout` statement will not execute. The reason is that in the postfix mode the comparison between `age` and 49 is made *first.* Then the value of `age` is incremented by one. Since 49 is not greater than 49, the `if` conditional is false. Things are much different if we replace the postfix operator with the prefix operator:

```
int age = 49;
if (++age > 49)
    cout << " Congratulations - You have made it to the"
         << " half-century mark !" << endl;
```

In this code `age` is incremented first. So its value is 50 when the comparison is made. The conditional statement is true and the `cout` statement is executed.

The `while` Loop

Often in programming one needs a statement or block of statements to repeat during execution. This can be accomplished using a **loop**. A loop is a control structure that causes repetition of a block of code within a program. C++ has three types of loops. The first we will consider is the **`while` loop**. The syntax is the following:

```
while (expression)
{
      statement_1;
      statement_2;
           :
      statement_n;
}
```

If there is only one statement, then the curly braces can be omitted. When a `while` loop is encountered during execution, the expression is tested to see if it is true or false. The block of statements is repeated as long as the expression is true. Notice that the `while` loop is a **pre-test loop**. This means the expression to be tested is at the top of the loop. If it is initially false, the statements in the loop are never executed at all. Sample Program 5.1 illustrates the use of the `while` loop.

Sample Program 5.1

```
#include <iostream>
using namespace std;

int main()
{
   int num = 5;
   int factorial = 1;

   while (num > 0)
   {  factorial = factorial * num;
      num--;
   }
   cout << " 5! =" << factorial << endl;

   return 0;
}
```

This program computes 5! = 5*4*3*2*1 and then prints the result to the screen. Note how the `while` loop works. Since `num = 5` when the `while` loop is first encountered, the expression (`num > 0`) is true and so the block of statements in the body of the loop is executed at least once. In fact, the block is executed five times. The decrement operator decreases the value of `num` by one every time the block is executed. During the fifth **iteration** of the loop (i.e., the fifth time its code is executed) `num` becomes 0, so the next time the expression is tested `num > 0` is false and the loop is exited. Then the `cout` statement is executed.

What do you think would happen if we eliminated the `num--` statement from the above code? Without it, `num` would always have a value of 5, so the expression `num > 0` would always be true! If we tried to execute the modified program, the result would be an **infinite loop**, i.e., a block of code that will repeat forever. Thus the decrementing of `num` is essential to properly control the loop in the above example. Note that the two statements

```
factorial = factorial * num;
num--;
```

could have been combined into a single statement:

```
factorial = factorial * num--;
```

However, many instructors advise against doing this since it decreases readability.

One must be very cautious when using loops to ensure that the loop will terminate. Sample Program 5.2 below illustrates another example where the user may have trouble with termination.

Sample Program 5.2

```
#include <iostream>
using namespace std;

int main()
{
   char letter = 'a';

   while (letter != 'x')
   {
      cout << "Please enter a letter" << endl;
      cin  >> letter;
      cout << "The letter you entered is " << letter << endl;
   }

   return 0;
}
```

Note that this program requires input from the user during execution. Infinite loops can be avoided, but it would help if the user knew that the `'x'` character terminates the execution. Without this knowledge the user could continually enter characters other than `'x'` and never realize how to terminate the program. An improved prompt to the user would solve this problem and make the program more user friendly.

Counters

One common way to control how many times to repeat a loop is by using a **counter**. For example, suppose we want to find the average of five test scores. First we must input and add the five scores. We could do this with a counter-controlled loop as shown in Sample Program 5.3. Notice how the variable named `test` works as a counter.

Sample Program 5.3

```
#include <iostream>
using namespace std;

int main()
{
   int score = 0;         // the individual score read in
   float total = 0.0;     // the total of the scores
   float average = 0.0;   // the average of the scores
   int test = 1;          // counter that tells which score we are
                          // currently dealing with and that
                          // controls the loop

   while (test <= 5)      // Note that test will be 1 the first time
   {                      // the expression is tested.
      cout << "Enter your score on test " << test << ": ";
      cin  >> score;

      total = total + score;
      test++;
   }
```

continues

```
   average = total / 5;

   cout << "Your average based on " << 5
        << " test scores is " << average << endl;

   return 0;
}
```

Note how the above program could be made more flexible by adding an integer variable called `numScores` that could be used in place of the hard-coded value 5. In the lab assignments you will be asked to do this.

Sentinel Values

Another way to control the execution of a loop is by using a **sentinel value**, a special value that signals that it is time to leave the loop. Suppose in the above example we do not know exactly how many test scores there will be. We could just input them and add them to `total` until the sentinel value is input, signaling that there are no more scores to be read. Sample Program 5.4 revises the previous program to control the loop with a sentinel value. The sentinel value used in this case is –1 since it is an invalid test score. It would not make sense to use a sentinel value between 0 and 100 since this is the range of valid test scores. Notice that the first read is done before the `while` loop. If the first value the user enters is a –1, the loop will never be executed and no scores will be added to the total. Notice also that a counter is still used to keep track of the number of test scores entered, but it does not control the loop.

Sample Program 5.4

```
#include <iostream>
using namespace std;

int main()
{
   int score = 0;          // the individual score read in
   float total = 0.0;      // the total of the scores
   float average = 0.0;    // the average of the scores
   int test = 1;           // counter that tells which score we are
                           // currently dealing with and that
                           // counts the total number of scores read in

   cout << "Enter your score on test " << test  // Read the 1st score
        << " (or -1 to exit): ";
   cin  >> score;

   while (score != - 1)   // While we have not yet input the sentinel
   {                       // value, do the loop.
      total += score;      // Add the score to the total
      test++;              // Increment test number
      cout << "Enter your score on test " << test // Read the next score
           << " (or -1 to exit): ";
      cin  >> score;
   }
```

continues

```
    if (test > 1)          // If test = 1, no scores were entered.
    {  average = total / (test-1);

       cout << "\nYour average based on " << (test-1)
            << " test scores is " << average << endl;
    }
    return 0;
}
```

Why was `test-1` used to compute the average rather than `test`? What would happen if we tried to find the average when `test = 1`?

Data Validation

One important use of the `while` loop is for doing data validation. A value can be input by the user and then a `while` loop test can check to see if the value is valid. If it is, the loop body will be skipped. However, if the value is not valid, the loop body will be entered and the user can be prompted to enter a new value. Since that new value will then be checked again by the loop test, the user will not be allowed to exit the loop until a valid value is entered. The following example illustrates this use of a `while` loop.

```
cout << "Enter your department number (1-5): ";
cin  >> dept;
while (dept < 1 || dept > 5)
{   cout << "Valid departments are 1-5. Please re-enter: ";
    cin  >> dept;
}
```

The `do-while` Loop

As mentioned earlier, the `while` loop is a pre-test, or top test, loop. If the test expression in the `while` loop is initially false, then no iterations of the loop will be executed. Sometimes the programmer wants to ensure that a loop is executed at least once. In this case a **post-test loop** should be used. With a post-test loop, the expression to be tested appears at the bottom of the loop, so it is never tested until the body of the loop has been executed a first time. C++ provides the **`do-while` loop** for this purpose. The syntax is the following:

```
do
{
      statement_1;
      statement_2;
            :
      statement_n;
} while (expression);
```

If there is only one statement, then the curly braces can be omitted.

To emphasize the difference between the `while` loop (top test) and the `do-while` loop (bottom test) consider the following example.

`while` loop

```
int num1 = 5;
int num2 = 7;

while (num1 > num2)
{
   num1++;
   num2--;
}
cout << num1 << "  " << num2;
```

`do-while` loop

```
int num1 = 5;
int num2 = 7;

do
{  num1++;
   num2--;
} while (num1 > num2);

cout << num1 << "  " << num2;
```

In the case of the `while` loop (left-hand code), the statements `num1++` and `num2--` will never be executed since the test expression `(num1 > num2)` is initially false. The `cout` statement will print `5  7`. In the case of the `do-while` loop (right hand code), the body of the loop will be executed once before the expression is tested and found to be false. The `do-while` loop will then be exited and the `cout` statement will print `6  6`.

The `for` Loop

The **`for` loop** is often used for applications that require a counter. The syntax for the `for` loop is the following:

```
for (initialization; test; update)
{
   statement_1;
   statement_2;
      :
   statement_n;
}
```

Notice that there are three expressions inside the parentheses of the `for` statement.

1. The *initialization* expression is normally used to set the initial value of a variable called the **loop control variable**.
2. The *test* expression, as with a `while` loop, is used to determine whether or not to remain in the loop. If it evaluates to true, the statements in the body of the loop are executed again. If it evaluates to false, the loop is exited. Also, like a `while` loop, the `for` loop is a top test loop. It is tested before the loop is ever entered. If the test expression is initially false, the statements in the loop body will never be executed.
3. The *update* expression is normally used to increment, or otherwise alter, the value of the loop control variable so that the loop will eventually be exited. It is not executed before the first loop iteration. Rather, it executes at the end of each iteration before the next test expression is evaluated.

Sample Program 5.5 illustrates the use of the `for` loop. In this example it is being used to find the average (mean) of the first n positive integers. We do this by adding $1 + 2 + 3 + \ldots + n$ and then dividing by n. Note this should just give us the value in the "middle" of the list $1, 2, \ldots, n$.

Sample Program 5.5

```
// This program has the user input a number n and then finds the
// mean of the first n positive integers.

#include <iostream>
using namespace std;

int main()
{
   int n;
   int total = 0;
   int number;                              // the loop control variable
   float mean;

   cout << "Please enter a positive integer: ";
   cin  >> n;

   for (number = 1; number <= n; number++)
   {
      total = total + number;
   }                                        // Curly braces are optional
                                            // since there is only one statement.

   mean = static-cast <float>(total) / n;   // Note the use of the typecast operator.

   cout << "The mean average of the first " << n
        << " positive integers is " << mean << endl;

   return 0;
}
```

Note that the counter in the `for` loop of Sample Program 5.5 is `number`. It increments from 1 to *n* during execution. Several other features of this code also need to be addressed. First of all, why is the typecast operator needed to compute the mean? What do you think would happen if it were removed? Second, what would happen if we entered zero or a negative number for *n,* instead of a positive number as instructed? Finally, what would happen if the value input for *n* were a float such as 2.99 instead of an integer? Lab 5.3 will demonstrate what happens in these cases.

Nested Loops

Often programmers need to use a loop within a loop, or **nested loops**. Sample Program 5.6 provides a simple example of a nested loop. This program finds the average number of hours per day spent programming by each student over a three-day weekend. The outer loop controls the number of students and the inner loop allows the user to enter the number of hours a given student worked each of the three days. Note that the inner loop is executed three times for each iteration of the outer loop.

Sample Program 5.6

```
// This program finds the average time spent programming by a
// student each day over a three-day period.

#include <iostream>
using namespace std;

int main()
{
   int numStudents;
   float numHours, total, average;
   int student, day;            // These are the counters for the loops.

   cout << "This program will find the average number of hours a day that" << endl
        << "each given student spent programming over a long weekend."
        << endl << endl;

   cout << "How many students are there?: " ;
   cin  >> numStudents;

   for (student = 1; student <= numStudents; student++)
   {
      total = 0;
      for (day = 1; day <= 3; day++)
      {
         cout << "Enter the number of hours worked by student "
              << student << " on day " << day << ": ";
         cin  >> numHours;

         total = total + numHours;
      }

      average = total / 3;

      cout << endl;
      cout << "The average number of hours per day spent programming by"
           << " student " << student << " is " << average << endl << endl;
   }
   return 0;
}
```

In Lab 5.4 you will be asked to modify this program to make it more flexible.

PRE-LAB WRITING ASSIGNMENT

Fill-in-the-Blank Questions

1. A block of code that repeats forever is called a(n) ____________________.
2. To keep track of the number of times a particular loop is repeated, one can use a(n) ________________.
3. A `do-while` loop is a(n) ________________ test loop that is always executed at least once.

4. A `while` loop is a(n) ______________ loop that will never be executed if the test expression is initially false.
5. In the conditional `if (++number < 9)`, `number` is incremented ___________ (before / after) it is compared to 9.
6. In the conditional `if (number++ < 9)`, `number` is incremented ___________ (before / after) it is compared to 9.
7. A loop within a loop is called a(n) ______________________________.
8. To write out the first 12 positive integers and their cubes, a natural choice would be to use a(n) ______________ loop.
9. A(n) ______________ value is used to indicate the end of a list of values. It can be used to control a loop.
10. In a nested loop, the _____________ (inner / outer) loop goes through all of its iterations for each iteration of the _____________ (inner / outer) loop.

LESSON 5A

LAB 5.1 Working with the `while` Loop

Bring in program `testavg.cpp` from the Set 5 folder. (This is Sample Program 5.3 from the Pre-lab Reading Assignment). The code follows.

```
// PLACE YOUR NAME HERE.

#include <iostream>
using namespace std;

int main()
{
   int score = 0;          // the individual score read in
   float total = 0.0;      // the total of the scores
   float average = 0.0;    // the average of the scores
   int test = 1;           // counter that tells which score we are
                           // currently dealing with and that
                           // controls the loop

   while (test <= 5)       // Note that test will be 1 the first
   {                       // time the expression is tested.
      cout << "Enter your score on test " << test << ": ";
      cin  >> score;

      total = total + score;
      test++;
   }

   average = total / 5;

   cout << "Your average based on " << 5
        << " test scores is " << average << endl;

   return 0;
}
```

Exercise 1: Run the program once to see how it works.

Exercise 2: Make the program more flexible by adding an integer variable called `numScores`. Prompt the user to input this value. This variable should then be used in place of the hard-coded value 5 throughout the program. Rerun your modified program using several different values for `numScores`.

Bring in program `sentinel.cpp` from the Set 5 Folder. The code follows.

```
// This program illustrates the use of a sentinel in a while loop.
// The user is asked for monthly rainfall totals until a sentinel
// value of -1 is entered. Then the total rainfall is displayed.

// PLACE YOUR NAME HERE.

#include <iostream>
using namespace std;

int main()
{
   // Fill in the code to define the variable month and initialize it to 1.
   float total = 0, rain;

   cout << "Enter the total rainfall for month " << month
        << " (or -1 to quit): ";
   // Fill in the code to read in the value for rain.

   // Fill in the code to start a while loop that iterates
   // while rain does not equal -1.
   {
      // Fill in the code to update total by adding rain to it.
      // Fill in the code to increment month by one.

      cout << "Enter the total rainfall for month " << month
           << " (or -1 to quit): ";
      // Fill in the code to read in the value for rain.
   }

   if (month == 1)
      cout << "No data has been entered." << endl;
   else
      cout << "The total rainfall for the " << month-1
           << " months is " << total << " inches." << endl;

   return 0;
}
```

Exercise 3: Fill in the indicated code to complete the above program. Then compile and run the program several times with various inputs. Record your results. Are they correct?

Exercise 4: What happens if you enter –1 first? Try it and see. What happens if you enter only values of 0 for each month? Try it and see. Is there any numerical data that you should not enter?

Exercise 5: What is the purpose of the following code in the program above?

```
if (month == 1)
      cout << "No data has been entered" << endl;
```

Why does the last `cout` statement output `month -1` instead of `month`?

LAB 5.2 Working with the `do-while` Loop

Bring in the program `dowhile.cpp` from the Set 5 folder. The code follows.

```
// This program displays a hot beverage menu and prompts the user
// to make a selection. A switch statement determines which item
// the user has chosen. A do-while loop repeats until the user
// selects item E from the menu.

// PLACE YOUR NAME HERE.

#include <iostream>
#include <iomanip>
using namespace std;

int main()
{
   // Fill in the code to define an integer variable called numCups,
   // a floating-point variable called cost,
   // a character variable called beverage,
   // and a Boolean variable called validBeverage.

   cout << fixed << showpoint << setprecision(2);

   do
   {
      cout << endl << endl;
      cout << "***Hot Beverage Menu***" << endl << endl;
      cout << "A: Coffee          $1.00" << endl;
      cout << "B: Tea             $ .75" << endl;
      cout << "C: Hot Chocolate   $1.25" << endl;
      cout << "D: Cappuccino      $2.50" << endl;
      cout << "E: Exit the program     " << endl << endl;

      cout << "Enter the beverage A,B,C, or D you desire" <<endl
           << "(or E to exit the program): ";
      // Fill in the code to read in beverage.

      cout << "How many cups would you like ? ";
      // Fill in the code to read in numCups.

      validBeverage = false;

      // Fill in the code to begin a switch statement
      // that is controlled by beverage.
      {
         case 'a':
         case 'A': cost = 1.00;
                   validBeverage = true;
                   break;
         // Using the 'a' and 'A' cases as a model,
         // fill in the code to give the cases for tea (.75),
         // hot chocolate (1.25), and cappuccino (2.50).
```

continues

```
            case 'e':
            case 'E': cout << " Please come again" << endl;
                      break;
            default : cout << // Fill in the code to write a message
                                // indicating an invalid selection.
         }

         if (validBeverage == true)
         { // Write an output statement that calculates
           // and prints the total cost. You do not need a totalCost
           // variable to do this.
         }
      } while (beverage != 'E' && beverage != 'e');

      // Fill in the appropriate return statement.
}
```

Exercise 1: Fill in the indicated code to complete the above program. Then compile and run the program several times with various inputs. Try all the possible relevant cases and record your results.

Exercise 2: When you enter an E, the program quits, but only after asking the user a question it should not ask in this case. What is the question? Modify the program so that it only asks this question when it should.

Exercise 3: What do you think will happen if you do not enter A, B, C, D, or E? Try running the program and inputting another letter. If you have made the correct modification in Exercise 2, the program should also now run correctly when a bad input is entered.

Exercise 4: Replace the line

```
if (validBeverage == true)
```

with the line

```
if (validBeverage)
```

and run the program again. Does it behave the same as it did before?

LAB 5.3 Working with the `for` Loop

Bring in program `for.cpp` from the Set 5 folder (This is Sample Program 5.5 from the Pre-lab Reading Assignment.) The code follows.

```
// This program has the user input a number n and then finds the
// mean of the first n positive integers.  It uses a while loop
// for data validation and a for loop to accumulate the total of
// the integers from 1 to n.

// PLACE YOUR NAME HERE.

#include <iostream>
using namespace std;
```

continues

```
int main()
{
   int n;
   int total = 0;
   int number;                    // the loop control variable
   float mean;

   cout << "This program finds the average of the first n integers.\n";
   cout << "Please enter a positive integer: ";
   cin  >> n;

   while (n <= 0)
   {  cout << "Only positive integers are valid. Please re-enter: ";
      cin  >> n;
   }

   for (number = 1; number <= n; number++)
   {
      total = total + number;
   }                                       // Curly braces are optional
                                           // since there is only one statement.

   mean = static-cast <float>(total) / n; // Note the use of the typecast operator.

   cout << "The mean average of the first " << n
        << " positive integers is " << mean << endl;

  return 0;
}
```

Exercise 1: Why is the typecast operator needed to compute the mean in the statement `mean = static-cast <float>(total)/n;`? What do you think would happen if it were removed? Replace this line of code with `mean = total / n;` and try running the program. Make sure that you try both even and odd values for *n*. Record the result in each case. Are they correct? Now put `static-cast <float>(total)` back in the program.

Exercise 2: What happens if you enter zero or a negative number instead of a positive number as instructed? Try both of these and record the results.

Exercise 3: What happens if you enter a float such as 2.99 instead of an integer for *n?* Try it and record the result.

Exercise 4: Modify the code so that it computes the mean of the consecutive positive integers $n, n + 1, n + 2, \ldots, m$, where the user chooses n and m. For example, if the user picks 3 and 8, then the program should find the mean of 3, 4, 5, 6, 7, and 8, which is 5.5. This is somewhat tricky and requires several modifications to the program. Validate that the first number the user enters, `n`, is greater than zero and that the second number entered, `m`, is greater than `n`. Be sure to update the user prompts and the comments to document what the revised program does.

LAB 5.4 Nested Loops

Bring in program `nested.cpp` from the Set 5 folder (this is Sample Program 5.6 from the Pre-lab Reading Assignment). The code follows.

```
// This program finds the average time spent programming by a
// student each day over a three-day period.

// PLACE YOUR NAME HERE.

#include <iostream>
using namespace std;

int main()
{
   int numStudents;
   float numHours, total, average;
   int student, day;             // These are the counters for the loops.

   cout << "This program will find the average number of hours a day" << endl
        << "each given student spent programming over a long weekend."
        << endl << endl;

   cout << "How many students are there?: " ;
   cin  >> numStudents;

   for (student = 1; student <= numStudents; student++)
   {
      total = 0;                 // total must be reset to 0 for each student
      for (day = 1; day <= 3; day++)
      {
         cout << "Enter the number of hours worked by student "
              << student << " on day " << day << ": ";
         cin  >> numHours;

         total = total + numHours;
      }

      average = total / 3;

      cout << endl;
      cout << "The average number of hours per day spent programming by"
           << " student " << student << " is " << average << endl << endl;
   }
   return 0;
}
```

Exercise 1: Note that the inner loop of this program is always executed exactly three times, once for each day of the long weekend. Modify the code so that the inner loop iterates `numDays` times, where `numDays` is a positive integer input by the user. In other words, let the user decide how many days to consider just as they choose how many students to consider.

Sample Run

```
This program will find the average number of hours a day
each given student spent programming over a long weekend.

How many students are there?: 2
Enter the number of days in the long weekend: 2

Enter the number of hours worked by student 1 on day 1: 4.5
Enter the number of hours worked by student 1 on day 2: 6

The average number of hours per day spent programming by student 1 is 5.25

Enter the number of hours worked by student 2 on day 1: 9
Enter the number of hours worked by student 2 on day 2: 3.25

The average number of hours per day spent programming by student 2 is 6.125
```

Exercise 2 (Optional): Modify the program from Exercise 1 so that it also finds the average number of hours per day that each student studied biology as well as spent programming. For each student you will need a prompt and an input for each subject as well as additional variables in which to store the additional information. For each student have the program print out the two averages and tell which subject the student, on average, spent more time on.

Lab 5.5 Student-Generated Code Assignments (Homework)

Option 1: Write a program that surveys a set of people and tallies their beverage choices from the following options:

1. Coffee 2. Tea 3. Coke 4. Orange Juice

The program should input and count each person's choice until a sentinel value of 5 is entered. Once this occurs, the program should display the total number of respondants and the totals for each beverage. The program should validate the user inputs to ensure that only valid numbers (1-5) are entered.

Sample Run

```
Program to Tally beverage choices


Enter choice for person #1
 (1. Coffee   2. Tea   3. Coke   4. Orange Juice   5. Quit Program): 2

Enter choice for person #2
 (1. Coffee   2. Tea   3. Coke   4. Orange Juice   5. Quit Program): 3

Enter choice for person #3
 (1. Coffee   2. Tea   3. Coke   4. Orange Juice   5. Quit Program): 4

Enter choice for person #4
 (1. Coffee   2. Tea   3. Coke   4. Orange Juice   5. Quit Program): 4

Enter choice for person #5
 (1. Coffee   2. Tea   3. Coke   4. Orange Juice   5. Quit Program): 1
```

```
Enter choice for person #6
 (1. Coffee   2. Tea   3. Coke   4. Orange Juice   5. Quit Program): 2

Enter choice for person #7
 (1. Coffee   2. Tea   3. Coke   4. Orange Juice   5. Quit Program): 0
choice must be between 1 and 5.  Please re-enter: 4

Enter choice for person #8
 (1. Coffee   2. Tea   3. Coke   4. Orange Juice   5. Quit Program): 5

The total number of people surveyed is 7. The results are as follows:

Beverage     Number of Votes
****************************
Coffee          1
Tea             2
Coke            1
Orange Juice    3
```

Option 2: Suppose Dave drops a watermelon off a high bridge and lets it fall until it hits the water. If we neglect air resistance, then the distance d in meters fallen by the watermelon after t seconds is $d = 0.5 * g * t^2$, where the acceleration of gravity $g = 9.8$ meters/second^2. Write a program that asks the user to input the number of seconds that the watermelon falls and the height of the bridge, in meters, above the water. The program should validate that the value the user enters for the number of seconds is greater than or equal to 1 and that the value entered for the height of the bridge is greater than or equal to 10. The program should then calculate the distance fallen for each second from $t = 0$ until the value of t input by the user. If the total distance fallen is greater than the height of the bridge, then the program should tell the user that the distance fallen is not valid.

Sample Run 1

```
Please input the time of fall in seconds:  2
Please input the height of the bridge in meters: 100

Time Falling (seconds) Distance Fallen (meters)
*******************************************
0                      0
1                       4.9
2                      19.6
```

Sample Run 2:

```
Please input the time of fall in seconds: 4
Please input the height of the bridge in meters: 50
```

```
Time Falling (seconds) Distance Fallen (meters)
*******************************************
0                       0
1                       4.9
2                       19.6
3                       44.1
4                       78.4

Warning-Bad Data: The distance fallen exceeds the height of the bridge.
```

Option 3: Write a program that prompts the user for the number of tellers at Nation's Bank in Hyatesville that worked each of the last three years. For each worker the program should ask for the number of days out sick for each of the last three years. Data validation should be done to ensure that the number of tellers is greater than or equal to 2 and that the number of sick days for each teller is not negative (i.e., is zero or greater). The output should display the number of tellers, the average number of days per year each teller was out sick, and the total number of days missed by all the tellers over the last three years. Format the output so it displays with one decimal point. See the sample output below.

Sample Run

```
How many tellers worked at Nation's Bank during the last three years? 2

How many days was teller 1 out sick during year 1? 5
How many days was teller 1 out sick during year 2? 8
How many days was teller 1 out sick during year 3? 2
Teller 1 missed an average of 5.0 days per year.

How many days was teller 2 out sick during year 1? 1
How many days was teller 2 out sick during year 2? 0
How many days was teller 2 out sick during year 3? 3
Teller 2 missed an average of 1.3 days per year.

The 2 tellers were out sick for a total of 19.0 days during the last three
years.
```

LESSON SET

6.1 Introduction to Void Functions (Procedures)

PURPOSE

1. To introduce the concept of void functions (procedures)
2. To work with void functions (procedures) that have no parameters
3. To introduce and work with void functions (procedures) that have pass by value and pass by reference parameters

PROCEDURE

1. Students should read the Pre-lab Reading Assignment before coming to lab.
2. Students should complete the Pre-lab Writing Assignment before coming to lab.
3. In the lab, students should complete labs assigned to them by their instructor.

Contents	Prerequisites	Approximate completion time	Page number	Check when done
Pre-lab Reading Assignment		20 min.	74	
Pre-lab Writing Assignment	Pre-lab reading	10 min.	80	
LESSON 6.1A				
Lab 6.1 Functions with No Parameters	Confident in use of control structures	15 min.	81	
Lab 6.2 Pass by Value	Basic understanding of pass by value. Use of string class for Ex. 3	35 min.	81	
LESSON 6.1B				
Lab 6.3 Pass by Reference	Basic understanding of pass by reference	25 min.	83	
Lab 6.4 Student-Generated Code Assignments	Basic understanding of pass by reference and value	30 min.	85	

PRE-LAB READING ASSIGNMENT

Modules

You have already learned that structured programs are well organized and documented. Another key element of structured programs is their modularity: the breaking of code into small units, each of which carries out a well defined task. When these units, or **modules**, do not return a value they are called **procedures** in most languages and are called **void functions** in C++. Although *procedures* is the authors' preferred term, this manual uses the word **function** to describe both void functions (discussed in this lesson set) and **value-returning functions** (studied in the next lesson set), as this is the terminology used in C++.

The `int main()` section of our program is a function and, up until now, has been the only coded module used in our programs. We also have used predefined functions such as `pow` and `sqrt` which are defined in library routines that we "imported" to our program with the `#include <cmath>` directive. We now explore the means of breaking our own code into modules. In fact, the `main` function should contain little more than "calls" to other functions. We can think of the `main` function as a contractor who hires sub-contractors to perform certain duties: plumbers to do the plumbing, electricians to do the electrical work, etc. The contractor is in charge of the order in which these sub-contract jobs are issued.

The `int main()` function consists mostly of calls to functions just like the contractor issuing commands to sub-contractors to come and do their jobs. A computer basically does many simple tasks that, when combined, carry out a set of complex operations. Determining how to modularize a program into separate tasks is one of the skills learned in software engineering, the science of developing quality software.

In simple programs most functions are called, or invoked, by the `main` function. Calling a function basically means starting the execution of the instructions contained in that module. In the following example, the task of printing a program description for the user has been placed in its own module, the `description` function.

Example

```
#include <iostream>
using namespace std;

void description();   // Function prototype

int main()
{
   cout << "Welcome to the Payroll Program." << endl;
   description();      // Call to the function
   cout << "We hope you enjoyed this program." << endl;

   return 0;
}

void description()    // The function heading
{
   cout << "*****************************************************" << endl << endl;
   cout << "This program takes two numbers (pay rate & hours)" << endl;
   cout << "and outputs gross pay. "<< endl;
   cout << "*****************************************************" << endl << endl;
}
```

In this example, three areas have been highlighted. Starting from the bottom we have the function itself, which is often called the function definition.

The function **heading** `void description()` consists of the name of the function preceded by the word `void`. The word `void` means that this function will not return a value to the module that called it. The function name is followed by a set of parentheses. Just like the `main` function, all functions begin with a left brace and end with a right brace. In between these braces are the instructions of the function. In this case they consist solely of `cout` statements that tell what the program does.

Notice that this function comes after the `main` function. How is this function activated? It must be called by either the `main` function or another function in the program. In this case, the function is called by `main` with the simple instruction `description();`

A **call** to a function could be classified as the sixth fundamental instruction (see Lesson Set 2). Notice that it consists only of the name of the function (not the word `void` preceding it) followed by the set of parentheses and a semicolon. By invoking its name in this way, the function is called at that moment. The program executes the body of instructions found in that function and then returns to the calling function (`main` in this case) where it executes the remaining instructions following the call. Let us examine the order in which the instructions are executed.

The `main` function begins by executing the following instruction.

```
cout << "Welcome to the Payroll Program." << endl;
```

Then the call to the `description` function is encountered, which causes the following instructions to be executed.

```
cout << "************************************************" << endl << endl;
cout << "This program takes two numbers (pay rate & hours)" << endl;
cout << "and outputs gross pay. " << endl;
cout << "************************************************" << endl << endl;
```

After all the instructions in `description` are executed, control returns to `main` and the next instruction in `main` after the function call is executed:

```
cout << "We hope you enjoyed this program." << endl;
```

Looking again at the example program, notice that the first highlighted section is found before `main()` in what we call the global section of the program. It is called a **prototype** and looks just like the function heading except it has a semicolon at the end. Since our example has the definition of the function after the call to the function, the program would give us an error when we tried to call it if we did not have some kind of signal to the computer that the definition will be forthcoming. That is the purpose of the prototype. It tells the compiler that a `void` function called `description` will be defined somewhere after the `main` function. If the `description` function had been placed in the file before the `main` function which calls it, then the prototype would not have been necessary. However, most C++ programs are written with prototypes so that `main()` can be the first function.

Pass by Value

Sometimes a function needs data "passed" to it to perform its designated tasks. For example, if a function is to find the square root of a number, then it needs that number passed to it by the calling function. Data is passed to a function through

parameters. Not all functions need parameters, as seen in the previous example. We call these parameter-less functions. However, it is common for functions to need data passed to them through parameters in order to carry out their task. Sample Program 6.1a, which is an extension of the previous example program, illustrates the use of parameters. This program uses a function called `paycheck` to take a pay rate and hours worked and produce gross pay based on those numbers.

Sample Program 6.1a

```
#include <iostream>
using namespace std;

// Function prototypes
void description();
void paycheck(float, int);

int main()
{
   float payRate;
   int hours;

   cout << "Welcome to the Payroll Program." << endl;

   description();                   // call to the description function

   cout << endl << "Please input the pay per hour." << endl;
   cin >> payRate;

   cout << endl << "Please input the number of hours worked." << endl;
   cin >> hours;
   cout << endl << endl;

   paycheck(payRate, hours);        // call to the paycheck function

   cout <<"We hope you enjoyed this program." << endl;

   return 0;
}

/********************************************************
 *                      description                     *
 * This function prints a program description.          *
 ********************************************************/

void description()
{
   cout << "************************************************" << endl << endl;
   cout << "This program takes two numbers (pay rate & hours)" << endl;
   cout << "and outputs gross pay. "<< endl;
   cout << "************************************************" << endl << endl;
}

/********************************************************
 *                      paycheck                        *
 * This function computes and outputs gross pay, using *
 * values passed into its rate and time parameters.    *
 ********************************************************/
```

continues

```
void paycheck(float rate, int time)
{
   float gross;

   gross = rate * time;
   cout << "The pay is " << gross << endl;
}
```

The bold sections of this program show the development of the paycheck function. Observe that the parameters (and/or their data types) used by this function appear, in one form or another, inside the parentheses of the call, the heading and the prototype. Parameters are the components of communication to and from a function and the call to that function. In order to find the gross pay the paycheck function needs the rate per hour and the number of hours worked to be passed to it. The call provides this information by having these two parameters inside the parentheses of the call `paycheck(payRate,hours);` The paycheck function heading must also have two corresponding parameters.

```
void paycheck(float rate, int time)
```

Note that the names used in the function heading (rate and time) need not match the names used for these items in the call to the function (payRate and hours), but they still match up in a one-to-one correspondence. That is, payRate (the first parameter in the call) gets passed into rate (the first parameter in the function heading) and hours (the second parameter in the call) gets passed into time (the second parameter in the function heading). So, although the names do not have to match, it is important that the order in which the parameters are listed in a function call and in a function heading agree. The parameters in a function call are called **actual parameters** (or **arguments**) and the parameters in a function heading are called **formal parameters**.

Compare the call to the paycheck function with the function heading.

Call	Function heading
`paycheck(payRate, hours);`	`void paycheck(float rate, int time)`

1. The call does not have any word preceding the name whereas the function heading has the word void preceding its name.
2. The call must *not* give the data type of its actual parameters whereas the function heading *must* give the data type of its formal parameters.
3. Although the formal parameters may have the same name as their corresponding actual parameters, they do not have to be the same. The first actual parameter, payRate, is paired with rate, the first formal parameter. This means that the value of payRate is given to rate. The second actual parameter, hours, is paired with time, the second formal parameter, and gives time its value. Corresponding (paired) parameters must have the same data type. Notice that payRate is defined as float in the main function and thus it can legally match rate, which is also defined as float in the function heading. hours is defined as int so it can be legally matched (paired) with time, which is defined as int in the function heading.
4. The actual parameters (payRate and hours) pass their values to their corresponding formal parameters. Whatever value is read into payRate in the main function will be given to rate in the paycheck function. This is called **pass by value**. It means that payRate and rate are two distinct

memory locations. Whatever value is in `payRate` at the time of the call will be placed in `rate`' s memory location as its initial value. It should be noted that if function `paycheck` were to alter the value of `rate`, it would not affect the value of `payRate` back in the `main` function. In essence, pass by value is like making a copy of the value in `payRate` and placing it in `rate`. Whatever is done to that copy in `rate` has no effect on the value in `payRate`. Recall that a formal parameter could have the same name as its corresponding actual parameter; however, they would still be two different locations in memory.

How does the computer know which location to go to if there are two with the same name? The answer is found in a concept called **scope**. Scope refers to the location where a variable or memory location is active in a program. All variables defined in the `main` function become inactive when a function is called and are reactivated when the control returns to `main`. By the same token, all formal parameters and variables defined inside a function are active only during the time that function is executing. What this means is that an actual parameter and its corresponding formal parameter are never active at the same time. Thus there is no confusion as to which memory location to access even if corresponding parameters have the same name. More on scope will be presented in the next lesson set.

Now compare the function prototype with the function heading.

Prototype	**Function heading**
`void paycheck(float, int);`	`void paycheck(float rate, int time)`

1. The prototype has a semicolon at the end and the heading does not.
2. The prototype normally lists only the data type of the parameters and not their name. However, the prototype could list both and thus be exactly like the heading except for the semicolon. Some instructors tell students to copy the prototype without the semicolon and paste it to form the function heading.

Let us look at all three parts: prototype, call, and heading.

1. The heading *must* have both data type and name for all its **formal parameters**.
2. The prototype must have the data type and could have the name for its **formal parameters**.
3. The call *must* have the name but *must not* have the data type for its **actual parameters**.

Pass by Reference

Suppose we wanted the `paycheck` function to only compute the gross pay and then pass this value back to the calling function rather than printing it. We would need another parameter, not to get information from the call but to give information back to the calling function. This particular parameter could not be **passed by value** since any change made in a function to a *pass by value formal parameter* has no effect on its corresponding actual parameter. Instead, this parameter would be **passed by reference**, which means that the calling function will give the called function the location of its actual parameter instead of a copy of the value that is stored in that location. This allows the called function to go in and change the value of the actual parameter.

Example: Assume that I have a set of lockers each containing a sheet of paper with a number on it. Making a copy of a sheet from a particular locker and giving that sheet to you will ensure that you will not change my original copy. This is pass by value. On the other hand, if I give you a spare key to a particular locker, you could go to that locker and change the number on the sheet of paper located there. This is pass by reference.

How does the program know whether a parameter is passed by value or by reference? In C++ this is done with the & symbol. All parameters are passed by value unless they have the character & listed after the data type, which indicates a pass by reference.

Sample Program 6.1b

```
#include <iostream>
#include <iomanip>
using namespace std;

// Function prototypes
void description();                    // prototype for a parameter-less function
void paycheck(float, int, float&);     // prototype for a function with 3 parameters
                                       // The first two are passed by value.
                                       // The third is passed by reference.

int main()
{
   float payRate;
   float grossPay;
   float netPay;
   int hours;

   cout << setprecision(2) << fixed;

   cout << "Welcome to the Payroll Program." << endl;

   description();                      // call to the description function

   cout << "Please input the pay per hour." << endl;
   cin  >> payRate;

   cout << endl << "Please input the number of hours worked." << endl;
   cin  >> hours;
   cout << endl << endl;

   paycheck(payRate, hours, grossPay);  // call to the paycheck function
   netPay = grossPay - (grossPay * .15);

   cout << "The net pay is " << netPay << endl;
   cout << "We hope you enjoyed this program." << endl;

   return 0;
}
```

continues

```
/*******************************************************
 *                    description                      *
 * This function prints a program description.         *
 *******************************************************/

void description()
{
  cout << "***********************************************" << endl << endl;
  cout << "This program takes two numbers (pay rate and hours)" << endl;
  cout << "and outputs net pay. "<< endl;
  cout << "***********************************************" << endl << endl;
}

/*******************************************************
 *                    paycheck                         *
 * This function computes gross pay, using values      *
 * passed into its rate and time parameters. The       *
 * result is placed in a reference parameter.          *
 *******************************************************/

void paycheck(float rate, int time, float& gross)
{
   gross = rate * time;
}
```

Notice that the function `paycheck` now has three parameters. The first two, `rate` and `time`, receive values passed by value while the third has an & after its data type, indicating that it is a reference parameter able to access the actual parameter passed to it. The actual parameter `grossPay` is paired with `gross` since they both are the third parameter in their respective lists. Since this pairing is pass by reference, these two names refer to the *same* memory location. Whatever changes the function makes to its formal parameter `gross` changes the value of `grossPay`. After the `paycheck` function calculates and places a value in `gross`, control goes back to the `main` function that now has this value in `grossPay`. Even though the change to `grossPay` actually occurred during the execution of the `paycheck` function, since the calling function has this new value for the variable when control returns to it, we often say that the function has "passed back" the reference parameter. Study this latest revision of the program very carefully. You will be working with it again in one of the lab exercises.

PRE-LAB WRITING ASSIGNMENT

Fill-in-the-Blank Questions

1. The word _______________ precedes the name of every function prototype and heading that does not return a value back to the calling routine.
2. Pass by _______________ indicates that a copy of the actual parameter is placed in the memory location of its corresponding formal parameter.
3. _______________ parameters are found in the call to a function.
4. A prototype must give the _______________ of its formal parameters and may give their _______________.
5. A _______________ after a data type in the function heading and in the prototype indicates that the parameter will be passed by reference.

6. Functions that do not return a value are often called ________________ in other programming languages.
7. Pass by ______________ indicates that the location of an actual parameter, rather than just a copy of its value, is passed to the called function.
8. A call must have the ______________ of its actual parameters and must *not* have the _________________ of those parameters.
9. ______________ refers to the region of a program where a variable is active.
10. ______________ parameters are found in the function heading.

LESSON 6.1A

LAB 6.1 Functions with No Parameters

Retrieve program `proverb.cpp` from the Set 6.1 folder. The code follows.

```
// This program prints the proverb
// "Now is the time for all good men to come to the aid of their party."
// in a function (procedure) called by the main function.

// PLACE YOUR NAME HERE.

#include <iostream>
using namespace std;

void proverb();                    // prototype for the proverb function

int main()
{
   // Fill in the code to call the proverb function.
   return 0;
}

/*************************************************
 *                 proverb                       *
 * This function prints a proverb.               *
 *************************************************/

void proverb()
{  // Fill in the body of the function that will print to the screen
   // the proverb listed in the comments at the beginning of the program.
}
```

Exercise 1: Complete the code as directed so that the program will print out the proverb listed in the comments at the beginning of the program. The proverb will be printed by the `proverb` function, which is called by the `main` function.

LAB 6.2 Pass by Value

Retrieve program `newproverb.cpp` from the Set 6.1 folder. The code follows.

```
// This program will allow the user to input from the keyboard
// whether the last word to the following proverb should be party or country.
// "Now is the time for all good men to come to the aid of their ________ .
// Inputting a 1 will use the word party. Any other number will use the
// word country.

// PLACE YOUR NAME HERE.

#include <iostream>
#include <string>
using namespace std;

// Fill in the prototype of the proverb function.

int main ()
{
     int wordCode;

     cout << "Given the phrase:" << endl;
     cout << "Now is the time for all good men to come to the aid of their ___"
          << endl;
     cout << "Input a 1 if you want the sentence to be finished with party."
          << endl;
     cout << "Input any other number for the word country." << endl;
     cout << "Please input your choice now." << endl;
     cin  >> wordCode;
     cout << endl;

     proverb(wordCode);

     return 0;
}

/*********************************************************************
 *                           proverb                                 *
 * This function takes number from the call.  If the number is a 1   *
 * it prints "Now is the time for all good men to come to the aid of *
 * their party." Otherwise it prints "Now is the time for all good   *
 * men to come to the aid of their country."                         *
 *********************************************************************/

void proverb (int number)
{
  // Fill in the body of the function to accomplish what is described above.
}
```

Exercise 1: Some people know this proverb as "Now is the time for all good men to come to the aid of their country" while others heard it as "Now is the time for all good men to come to the aid of their party." This program will allow the user to choose which way they want it printed. Complete the program as instructed to accomplish what is described in the program comments. Compile and run it. What happens if you enter a 1? What happens if you enter a 2? What happens if you inadvertently enter a float such as –3.97?

Exercise 2: Change the program so that an input of 1 from the user will print "party" at the end, a 2 will print "country", and any other number will be an invalid choice so that the user will need to repeat the choice.

Sample Run

```
Given the phrase:
Now is the time for all good men to come to the aid of their ___
Input a 1 if you want the sentence to be finished with party.
Input a 2 if you want the sentence to be finished with country.
Please input your choice now.
4
I'm sorry but that is an incorrect choice. Please input a 1 or 2.
2
Now is the time for all good men to come to the aid of their country.
```

Exercise 3: Change the previous program to allow the user to input the word to end the phrase. The string holding the user's input word will be passed to the proverb function instead of passing a number to it. Notice that this change requires you to change the proverb function heading and the proverb prototype as well as the call to the function.

Sample Run

```
Given the phrase:
Now is the time for all good men to come to the aid of their ____
Please input the word you would like to have finish the proverb.
family
Now is the time for all good men to come to the aid of their family.
```

LESSON 6.1B

LAB 6.3 Pass by Reference

Retrieve program `paycheck.cpp` from the Set 6.1 folder. This program is similar to Sample Program 6.1b that was given in the Pre-lab Reading Assignment. The code follows.

```
// This program takes two numbers (pay rate and hours) and multiplies them
// to get gross pay. It then calculates net pay by subtracting 15%.

// PLACE YOUR NAME HERE.

#include <iostream>
#include <iomanip>
using namespace std;

// Function prototypes
void description();
void paycheck(float, int, float&, _________ );
```

continues

```
int main()
{
   float payRate;
   float grossPay;
   float netPay;
   int hours;

   cout << setprecision(2) << fixed;

   cout << "Welcome to the Payroll Program." << endl;

   description();

   cout << "Please input the pay per hour: ";
   cin  >> payRate;

   cout << endl << "Please input the number of hours worked: ";
   cin  >> hours;
   cout << endl << endl;

   paycheck(payRate, hours, grossPay, _______ );

   // Write statements to print out both gross pay and net pay, with labels.
   cout << "We hope you enjoyed this program." << endl;

   return 0;
}

/*****************************************************
 *                    description                    *
 * This function prints a program description        *
 *****************************************************/

void description()
{
  cout << "**********************************************" << endl << endl;
  cout << "This program takes two numbers (pay rate and hours)" << endl;
  cout << "and outputs net pay. "<< endl;
  cout << "**********************************************" << endl << endl;
}

/*****************************************************
 *                    paycheck                       *
 * This function computes gross and net pay, placing *
 * the results in reference parameters.              *
 *****************************************************/

void paycheck(float rate, int time, float& gross, _______________)
{
   // Write an assignment statement to compute gross pay.
   // Write an assignment statement to compute net pay.
}
```

Exercise 1: Fill in the blanks and complete the indicated code (places in bold) so that the program will run correctly. The `paycheck` function will now have a fourth parameter, called `net`, that holds the net pay calculated by subtracting 15 percent from the gross pay. Make `net` a reference parameter. Since `gross` and `net` are both reference parameters, the values placed in them will have actually been placed in the `main` function's `grossPay` and `netPay` variables respectively. The `main` function will thus have these values, which were set by the `paycheck` function, available to print.

Exercise 2: Compile and run your program with the following data and make sure you get the output shown.

```
Please input the pay per hour.
9.50
Please input the number of hours worked.
40

The gross pay is $380.00
The net pay is $323.00
We hope you enjoyed this program.
```

Exercise 3: What do you think would happen if you had not made `net` a reference parameter? Remove the `&` after its data type in the `paycheck` function prototype and function header and see what happens when you run the program again. What value did the `main` function now print for `netPay`? ____________ Can you explain the result you got? Now change `net` back to a reference parameter.

LAB 6.4 Student-Generated Code Assignments

Option 1: Write a program that will read two floating-point numbers (the first read into a variable called `first` and the second read into a variable called `second`) and then call the function `swapNums` with the actual parameters `first` and `second`. The `swapNums` function having formal parameters `number1` and `number2` should swap the value of the two variables. Note: This is similar to a program you did in Lesson Set 1; however, it had a logic error that needed to be corrected before the swap would work correctly. Also, now you are required to use a function. You may want to look at `logicprob.cpp` from Lesson Set 1.

Sample Run

```
Enter a number: 70
Enter a second number: 80

You input the numbers as 70 and 80.
After swapping, the values of the two numbers are 80 and 70.
```

Compile the program and correct it if necessary until you get no syntax errors. Run the program with the sample data above and make sure you get the same results. The `swap` parameters must be passed by ______________. Why?

Option 2: Write a program that will input miles traveled and hours spent in travel. The program will determine miles per hour. This calculation must be done in a `mph` function called by `main`; however, `main` will print the returned result. The function will thus have 3 parameters: `miles`, `hours`, `milesPerHour`. Which parameter(s) should be pass by value and which must be pass by reference? The output should be fixed with two decimal point precision.

Sample Run

```
Input the miles traveled: 275
Input the hours traveled: 4.5
Your speed is 61.11 miles per hour.
```

Option 3: Write a program that uses and calls a `convert` function to convert hours and minutes to hours. The `main` function should prompt for the hours and minutes, pass them to the function, and print the result.

Sample Run

```
This program will convert hours and minutes to hours.
Input hours: 3
Input minutes: 12
Total hours = 3.2
```

Option 4: Combine options 2 and 3 to determine miles per hour when the time traveled is input in hours and minutes. Once the miles, hours, and minutes have been input, your program should call the `convert` function to convert hours and minutes to hours. The value returned from that function can then be passed, along with miles traveled, to the `mph` function. As before, all printing should be done in the `main` function.

Sample Run

```
Input the miles traveled: 275
Input the hours traveled: 4
Input the minutes traveled: 30
Your speed is 61.11 miles per hour.
```

LESSON SET

6.2 Functions That Return a Value

PURPOSE

1. To introduce the concept of scope
2. To understand the difference between static, local, and global variables
3. To introduce the concept of functions that return a value
4. To introduce the concept of overloading functions

PROCEDURE

1. Students should read the Pre-lab Reading Assignment before coming to lab.
2. Students should complete the Pre-lab Writing Assignment before coming to lab.
3. In the lab, students should complete labs assigned to them by the instructor.

Contents	Prerequisites	Approximate completion time	Page number	Check when done
Pre-lab Reading Assignment		20 min.	88	
Pre-lab Writing Assignment	Pre-lab reading	10 min.	96	
LESSON 6.2A				
Lab 6.5 Scope of Variables	Basic understanding of scope rules and of parameter passing	25 min.	96	
Lab 6.6 Static and Local Variables	Basic understanding of parameters and local variables	25 min.	98	
LESSON 6.2B				
Lab 6.7 Value Returning and Overloaded Functions	Understanding of value-returning and overloaded functions	30 min.	99	
Lab 6.8 Student-Generated Code Assignments	Basic understanding of pass by reference and value	30 min.	103	

PRE-LAB READING ASSIGNMENT

Scope

As mentioned in Lesson Set 6.1, the scope of an identifier (variable, constant, function, etc.) is an indication of where it can be accessed in a program. There can be certain portions of a program where a variable or other identifier is out of scope and cannot be accessed. The header (the portion of the program before `main`) has often been referred to as the global section. Any identifier defined in this area is said to have **global scope** (and any variable defined here is referred to as a **global variable**), meaning it can normally be accessed at any time by any function during the execution of the program. In fact, any identifier defined outside the bounds of all the functions has global scope. Although most constants and all functions are defined globally, the use of global variables is not considered good programming practice and should normally be avoided.

Local scope refers to identifiers defined within a block. They are active only within the bounds of that particular block. In C++ a **block** begins with a left brace { and ends with a right brace }. Since all functions (including `main`) begin and end with a pair of braces, the body of a function is a block. Variables defined within functions are called **local variables**. They normally can be accessed anywhere within that function from the point they are defined. However, blocks can be defined within other blocks, and the scope of an identifier defined in such an inner block would be limited to that inner block. A function's formal parameters (Lesson Set 6.1) have the same scope as local variables defined in the outermost block of that function. That means that the scope of a formal parameter of a function is the entire function.

The following example illustrates some of these scope rules. The braces nested within the outer braces of `main()` indicate another block in which `square` is defined. The variable `square` is active only within the bounds of the inner braces, while `circle` is active for the entire `main` function. Neither of these are active when the `heading` function is executing. The variable `triangle` is a local variable of the `heading` function and is active only when that function is active. `PI`, being a global identifier, is active everywhere.

Sample Program 6.2a

```
#include <iostream>
using namespace std;

const PI = 3.14;

void heading();

int main()
{
   float circle;
   cout << "circle has local scope that extends the entire main function."
        << endl;
   {
      float square;
      cout << "square has local scope active for only a portion of main." << endl;
      cout << "Both square and circle can be accessed here "
           << "as well as the global constant PI." << endl;
   }
```

continues

```
   cout << "circle is active here, but square is not." << endl;

   heading();

   return 0;
}

void heading()
{
    int triangle;

    cout << "The global constant PI is active here "
         << "as well as the local variable triangle." << endl;
}
```

What happens if two identifiers have the same name? For example, in the previous program could the `heading` function also define a variable named `circle`? The answer is yes, but it would be a different memory location than the one defined in the `main` function. `main`'s `circle` variable would be local to `main()` and `heading`'s `circle` variable would be local to `heading()`. What about a local variable having the same name as a global variable or as another local variable in an outer block it is nested in? Even this is not a problem. Rules of **name precedence** handle cases like this and determine which memory location is active when two or more variables have the same name. The basic rule is that the most recently defined variable has precedence over any other variable with the same name. So within a block in which a local variable is active, it takes precedence over any variable with the same name that is global or that is defined in an outer block. For example, if there were a global constant or variable named `triangle`, the `heading` function would not be able to access it, since any reference it makes to that name would be to its own local variable `triangle`.

Lifetime is related to the scope of a variable. It refers to the time during a program that an identifier has storage assigned to it.

Scope Rules

1. The scope of a global identifier, any identifier defined outside all functions, is the entire program (though such identifiers are not accessible to blocks having their own identifier with the same name).
2. Functions are defined globally. That means any function can call any other function at any time.
3. The scope of a local identifier is from the point of its definition to the end of the block in which it is defined. This includes any nested blocks that may be contained within it, unless the nested block has a variable defined in it that has the same name.
4. The scope of a function's formal parameters is the same as the scope of local variables defined at the beginning of that function.

Why are variables almost never defined globally? Since global variables can be changed by any function, they are not considered "safe." One function may change a global variable's value when another function needed that value to remain unchanged. This problem can occur even more readily in large projects, where more than one programmer may be working on the same program. Thus good structured programming avoids the use of global variables and requires that all communication between functions be explicit through the use of parameters.

Static Local Variables

One of the biggest advantages of a function is the fact that it can be called multiple times to perform its job. This eliminates much redundant code and saves time and memory space. Memory is saved in part because once a function is exited the memory space used by its local variables is released. But this means that the values assigned to the local variables of a function are lost once the function is finished executing. The next time the function is called, new memory is assigned for these variables and they start "fresh" in terms of their initial value. There may be times, however, when a function needs to retain the value of a variable between calls. This can be done by defining it to be a **static variable**, which means it is initialized only once and its memory space is retained even after the function in which it is defined has finished executing. Thus the lifetime of a static variable is different than a normal local variable. Static variables are defined by placing the word `static` before the data type and name of the variable, as shown here.

```
static int totalOrders = 0;
```

Default Arguments

Actual parameters (parameters used in the call to a function) are often called **arguments**. Normally the number of these actual parameters, or arguments, must equal the number of formal parameters found in the function heading. It is considered good programming practice to do this. It is possible, however, to assign default values to some or all formal parameters so that the calling instruction does not have to pass values for all the arguments. Although these default values can be specified in the function heading, they are usually defined in the prototype. Certain arguments can be left out; however, if an argument is left out, then all the following arguments must also be left out. For this reason, if default argument values are being used, pass by reference arguments should be placed first (since by their very nature they must be included in the call).

Sample Program 6.2b

```
#include <iostream>
#include <iomanip>
using namespace std;

void netPay(float& net, int hours = 40, float rate = 6.00);
// Function prototype with default arguments specified
// If the 3rd argument is omitted, 6.00 will be passed to netPay.
// If the 2nd and 3rd arguments are omitted, 40 and 6.00 will be passed.

int main()
{
   int hoursWorked = 20;
   float payRate = 5.00;
   float pay;         // net pay amt. calculated by the netPay function

   cout << setprecision(2) << fixed << showpoint;
```

continues

```
   netPay(pay);                    // call with only 1 parameter
   cout << " The net pay is $" << pay << endl;

   return 0;
}


void netPay (float& net, int hours, float rate)
{
   net = hours * rate;
}
```

What would happen if `pay` were also not listed in the calling instruction? An error would occur that states that the function cannot take 0 arguments. The reason for this is that the formal parameter called `net` does not have a default value and so the call must have at least one argument. Of course the call can have more than one argument since a default value is used only when that argument is omitted.

The following calls would all be legal in the sample program. Fill in the values that the `netPay` function receives for `hours` and `rate` in each case. Also fill in the value that you expect net pay to have for each call.

```
netPay(pay);
   netPay receives the value of ______ for hours and _____ for rate.

   The net value "sent back" to main by netPay is $__________

netPay(pay, hoursWorked);
   netPay receives the value of ______ for hours and _____ for rate.

   The net value "sent back" to main by netPay is $__________

netPay(pay, hoursWorked, payRate);
   netPay receives the value of ______ for hours and _____ for rate.

   The net value "sent back" to main by netPay is $__________
```

The following would not be correct. List what you think causes the error in each case.

```
netPay(pay, payRate);
netPay(hoursWorked, payRate);
netPay(payRate);
netPay();
```

Functions That Return a Value

The functions discussed in the previous lesson set are not "true functions" because they do not return a value to the calling function. They are often referred to as procedures in computer science jargon. True functions, or value-returning functions, are modules that return exactly one value to the calling routine. In C++ they do this with a `return` statement. This is illustrated by the `cubeIt` function shown in the following example.

```
int cubeIt(int x);       // prototype for a user defined function
                         // that returns the cube of the value passed to it.
....

int main()
{
   int x = 2;
   int cube;

   cube = cubeIt(x);     // This is the call to the cubeIt function.
   ......
   return 0;
}

int cubeIt(int x)        // Function type is int rather than void.
{
   int num;

   num = x * x * x;      // We could also say num = pow(x,3);
   return num;
}
```

The function `cubeIt` receives the value of `x`, which in this case is 2, and finds its cube, which it places in a local variable `num`. It then returns the value stored in `num` to the function call `cubeIt(x)`. The value 8 replaces the entire function call and is assigned to `cube`. That is, `cube = cubeIt(x)` is replaced with `cube = 8`. It is not actually necessary to place the value to be returned in a local variable before returning it. The entire `cubeIt` function could have been written as follows:

```
int cubeIt(int x)
{   return x * x * x;
}
```

Value-returning functions replace the word `void` with the data type of the value that is returned. Since these functions are intended to return just one value (the one sent back by the `return` statement), nothing should be "sent back" to the calling function through parameters. To ensure this, all parameters of this type of function should be pass by value, *not* pass by reference. Nothing in C++ actually prevents the programmer from using pass by reference in value-returning functions; however, it is good programming practice not to do so.

The `net pay` program, Sample Program 6.2b, has a module that calculates the net pay when given the hours worked and the hourly pay rate. Since it calculates only one value that is needed by the call, it could easily be implemented as a value-returning function, instead of by having `pay` passed by reference. Sample Program 6.2c, which follows, modifies Program 6.2b in this manner.

Sample Program 6.2c

```
#include <iostream>
#include <iomanip>
using namespace std;
```

continues

```
float netPay(int hours, float rate);

int main()
{
  int hoursWorked = 20;
  float payRate = 5.00;
  float pay;

  cout << setprecision(2) << fixed << showpoint;

  pay = netPay(hoursWorked, payRate);
  cout << " The net pay is $" << pay << endl;

  return 0;
}

float netPay(int hours, float rate)
{
   return hours * rate;
}
```

Notice how this function is called.

```
pay = netPay(hoursWorked, payRate);
```

The call to the function is not a stand-alone statement, but rather part of an assignment statement. The call is used in an expression. In fact, the function will return a floating-point value that replaces the entire right-hand side of the assignment statement. This is the first major difference between the two types of functions (`void` functions and value-returning functions). A `void` function is called by just listing the name of the function along with its arguments. A value-returning function is called within a portion of some fundamental instruction (the right-hand side of an assignment statement, condition of a selection or loop statement, argument of a `cout` statement, etc.). As mentioned earlier, another difference is that in both the prototype and function heading the word `void` is replaced with the data type of the value that is returned. A third difference is the fact that a value-returning function *must* have a `return` statement. It is usually the very last instruction of the function. The following is a comparison between the `netPay` implementation as a procedure (`void` function) and as a value-returning function.

	Value-Returning Function	**Procedure**
PROTOTYPE	`float netPay(int hours, float rate);`	`void netPay(float& net, int hours,` `float rate);`
CALL	`pay = netPay(hoursWorked, payRate);`	`netPay(pay, hoursWorked, payRate);`
HEADING	`float netPay(int hours, float rate)`	`void netPay(float& net, int hours,` `float rate)`

BODY	`{`
	`return hours * rate;`
	`}`
		`{`
		`net = hours * rate;`
		`}`

You may have noticed that the `main` functions we have been using are declared as `int main()` and that their last instruction is `return 0;` This means that `main` is treated as a value-returning function. The 0, which is returned to the operating system, indicates that the program ran without any major complications. You may sometimes see the heading of `main` as `void main()`. In such cases there is no `return` statement at the end because `main` is treated as a procedure, or `void` function.

Overloaded Functions

Uniqueness of identifier names is a vital concept in programming languages. The convention in C++ is that every variable, function, constant, etc. name within the same scope needs to be unique. However, there is an exception. Two or more functions may have the same name as long as their parameters differ in quantity or data type. For example, a programmer could have two functions with the same name that do the exact same thing on different data types.

Example: Look at the following prototypes of functions all having the same name. Yet all could be included in the same program because each one differs from all the others either by the number of parameters or the data types of the parameters.

```
int   add(int a, int b, int c);
int   add(int a, int b);
float add(float a, float b, float c);
float add(float a, float b);
```

When the `add` function is called, the actual parameter list in the call will be used to determine ***which*** `add` function to call.

Stubs and Drivers

Many IDEs (Integrated Development Environments) have software debuggers which are used to help in the location of logical errors; however, programmers often use the concept of stubs and drivers to test and debug programs that use functions and procedures. A **stub** is nothing more than a dummy function that is called instead of the actual function that will replace it later. It usually does little more than write a message to the screen indicating that it was called with certain arguments. In structured design, the programmer often wants to delay the implementation of certain details until the overall design of the program is complete. The use of stubs makes this possible.

Sample Program 6.2d

```
#include <iostream>
using namespace std;

int squarert(int x);    // prototype for a user defined function that
                        // returns the square root of the number passed to it
int main()
{
   int number1;

   cout << "Input the number whose square root you want." << endl;
   cout << "Input a -99 when you would like to quit." << endl;
   cin  >> number1;

   while (number1 != -99)
   {
      cout << "The square root of your number is " << squarert(number1) << endl;
```

continues

```
      cout << "Input the number whose square root you want." << endl;
      cout << "Input a -99 when you would like to quit." << endl;
      cin  >> number1;
   }
   return 0;
}

int squarert(int x)
{
   cout << "squarert function was called with " << x << " as its argument.\n";
   return 0;
} // This bold section is the stub.
```

This example shows that the programmer can test the execution of `main` and the call to, and return from, the function without having yet written the function to find the square root. This allows the programmer to concentrate on one component at a time. Although a stub is not really needed in this simple program, stubs are very useful for larger programs.

A **driver** is a module that tests a function by simply calling it. While one programmer may be working on the `main` function, another programmer could be developing the code for a particular function. In this case the programmer would not be so concerned with the calling of the function but rather with the body of the function itself. In such a case a driver (call to the function) could be used just to see if the function performs properly.

Sample Program 6.2e

```
#include <iostream>
#include <cmath>
using namespace std;

int squarert(int x);     // prototype for a user defined function that
                         // returns the square root of the number passed to it
int main()
{
   int number1;

   cout << "Calling squarert function with a 4" << endl;
   cout << "The result is " << squarert(4) << endl;

   return 0;
}

int squarert(int x)
{
    return sqrt(x);
}
```

In this example, the `main` function is used solely as a tool (driver) to call the `squarert` function to see if it performs properly.

PRE-LAB WRITING ASSIGNMENT

Fill-in-the-Blank Questions

1. Normally local variables _______________ (do / do not) retain their value between calls to the function in which they are defined.
2. In order for a variable defined in a function to retain its value between calls to the function, the variable should be defined to be a _______________ variable.
3. Default arguments are usually defined in the _______________ of the function.
4. A function returning a value should not use pass by _______________ parameters.
5. Every function that begins with a data type in the heading, rather than the word `void`, must have a(n) _______________ statement somewhere, usually at the end, in its body of instructions.
6. A(n) _______________ is a program that tests a function by simply calling it.
7. In C++ a block boundary is defined within a pair of _______________.
8. A(n) _______________ is a dummy function that just indicates that a function was called properly.
9. Default values should not be used for pass by _______________ parameters.
10. _______________ functions are functions that have the same name but a different parameter list.

LESSON 6.2A

Lab 6.5 Scope of Variables

Retrieve program `scope.cpp` from the Set 6.2 folder. The code follows.

```
// This program demonstrates scope rules.
// PLACE YOUR NAME HERE.

#include <iostream>
#include <iomanip>
using namespace std;

// _____________ variable definitions
int sum1 = 0,
    sum2 = 0;

// Function prototype
void studyScope(int);

int main()
{  // ______________ variable definition
   int number = 10;
```

continues

```
   cout << "Starting in main, the value of number is "
        << number << endl;
   cout << "Starting in main, the value of sum1 is    "
        << sum1 << endl;
   cout << "Starting in main, the value of sum2 is    "
        << sum2 << endl << endl;

   studyScope(number);

   cout << "Back in main, the value of number is "
        << number << endl;
   cout << "Back in main, the value of sum1 is    "
        << sum1 << endl;
   cout << "Back in main, the value of sum2 is    "
        << sum2 << endl << endl;

   return 0;
}

/********************************************************
 *                   studyScope                         *
 * This function exists to illustrate scope rules.      *
 ********************************************************/

void studyScope(int myParameter)
{  // ___________ variable definition in studyScope's outer block
   int number = 5;

   {// ___________ variable definition in studyScope's inner block
      int number = 1;

      number++;
      cout << "In studyScope's inner block number is now "
           << number << endl;
      sum1 += myParameter;
      sum2 += number;
   }

   number++;
   cout << "In studyScope's outer block number is now "
        << number << endl << endl;
   sum2 += number;
}
```

Exercise 1: BEFORE you run the program, examine each variable in the program and replace each fill-in-the-blank underline with either the word `Local` or the word `Global`.

Exercise 2: BEFORE you run the program, study the scope of each variable and determine what will be printed by each output statement in the program. That is, which variable is being referenced and what value will be printed by each output statement. Use this information to complete the **Expected** column in the following table.

	Expected	**Observed**
`Starting in main, the value of number is`	________	________
`Starting in main, the value of sum1 is`	________	________
`Starting in main, the value of sum2 is`	________	________
`In studyScope's inner block number is now`	________	________
`In studyScope's outer block number is now`	________	________
`Back in main, the value of number is`	________	________
`Back in main, the value of sum1 is`	________	________
`Back in main, the value of sum2 is`	________	________

Exercise 3: Now run the program and complete the **Observed** column above. If you were incorrect in any of your expectations, re-examine the code and see why you got the observed results you did.

Lab 6.6 Static and Local Variables

Retrieve program `money.cpp` from the Set 6.2 folder. The code follows.

```
// This program illustrates the use of local variables vs.
// static local variables. It also illustrates the use of a
// default parameter.

// PLACE YOUR NAME HERE.

#include <iostream>
#include <iomanip>
using namespace std;

// Function prototype
void totalMoney(float amount __________); // Uses a default value of 1.00 if
                                          // no value is passed to the function
int main()
{
   cout << setprecision(2) << fixed << showpoint;

   cout << "\nAdding $2.50 \n";
   // Fill in the code to call the totalMoney function and pass it 2.50.

   cout << "\nAdding $1.25 \n";
   // Fill in the code to call the totalMoney function and pass it 1.25.

   cout << "\nAdding default amount of $1.00\n";
   // Fill in the code to call the totalMoney function and use the
   // default argument value, rather than passing a value to the function.

   cout << "The correct total should now be $4.75 \n\n";

   return 0;
}
```

continues

```
/*****************************************************************
 *                        totalMoney                              *
 * This function is passed an amount of money, which it adds to two  *
 * accumulators — one is a local variable and the other is a static  *
 * local variable. It then prints out the two totals to illustrate   *
 * the difference in the two kinds of variables.                     *
 *****************************************************************/

void totalMoney(float amount)
{
   float regularTotal = 0;        // Define a regular local float variable
   ____________ staticTotal = 0;  // Define a static float variable

   // Fill in the code to add the amount passed in to regularTotal.
   // Fill in the code to add the amount passed in to staticTotal.

   // Display the new totals
   cout << "\nThe total of all amounts so far is: \n";
   cout << "Regular Total: $" << regularTotal << endl;
   cout << "Static  Total: $" << staticTotal  << endl;
}
```

Exercise 1: Fill in the blanks and complete the program code as directed by the comments in the program. Then run the program. The final "Regular" total should be $1.00. The final "Static" total should be $4.75.

Exercise 2: Explain why the two totals were different. Clearly "Regular" total is wrong, but why did it end up with the particular value ($1.00) it did?

LESSON 6.2B

Lab 6.7 Value-Returning and Overloaded Functions

Retrieve program `convertmoney.cpp` from the Set 6.2 folder. The code follows.

```
// This program will convert American dollars to euros, pesos, and yen.
// PLACE YOUR NAME HERE.

#include <iostream>
#include <iomanip>
using namespace std;

// Function prototypes
void convertToEuros(double dollars, double& euros);
void convertToPesos(double dollars, double& pesos);
void convertToYen  (double dollars, double& yen);

// Global constant CONVERSION RATES
const double NUM_EUROS =    .8681,     // number of euros to the dollar
             NUM_PESOS =   7.76023,    // number of pesos to the dollar
             NUM_YEN   = 119.82;       // number of yen to the dollar
```

continues

```
int main ()
{
   double dollars,
          euros,
          pesos,
          yen;

   cout << "Input the amount of American Dollars \n"
        << "you want converted to foreign currency: ";
   cin  >> dollars;

   // Perform the conversions
   convertToEuros(dollars, euros);
   convertToPesos(dollars, pesos);
   convertToYen  (dollars, yen);

   // Display the results
   cout << fixed << showpoint << setprecision(2);
   cout << "\n$" << dollars << " = \n"
        << setw(17) << euros << " euros \n"
        << setw(17) << pesos << " pesos \n"
        << setw(17) << yen   << " yen \n\n";

   return 0;
}


/*********************************************************************
 *                          convertToEuros                           *
 * This function converts dollars to euros and places the result in *
 * a reference parameter so the result will be known to main.       *
 *********************************************************************/

void convertToEuros (double dollars, double& euros)
{
   euros = dollars * NUM_EUROS;

}

/*********************************************************************
 *                          convertToPesos                           *
 * This function converts dollars to pesos and places the result in *
 * a reference parameter so the result will be known to main.       *
 *********************************************************************/

void convertToPesos (double dollars, double& pesos)
{
   pesos = dollars * NUM_PESOS;

}
```

continues

```
/*****************************************************************
 *                          convertToYen                          *
 * This function converts dollars to yen and places the result in *
 * a reference parameter so the result will be known to main.     *
 *****************************************************************/

void convertToYen (double dollars, double& yen)
{
   yen = dollars * NUM_YEN;

}
```

Exercise 1: Run the program and observe how it works. Print out the results.

Exercise 2: Modify the program to make the three conversion functions all value-returning functions. To do this you will need to make the following changes:

- Change the return type in each function prototype and header from `void` to `double`.
- Change the parameter list in each function prototype and header so that there will be just one value parameter (rather than one value parameter and one reference parameter). Now that the function is passing back the converted value through a `return` statement, no reference parameter is needed.
- Replace the assignment statement in each conversion function with a `return` statement. Instead of calculating a result and placing it in a reference parameter, each conversion function will now calculate a result and return it.
- Revise the documentation for each function to describe what it now does.
- Revise the 3 function calls in `main` with calls that pass only one argument (the dollar amount to be converted), rather than two.
- Revise the code in `main` so that the value returned by each function call will be assigned to the correct variable for later printing.

Run your revised program. You should get the same results you got from running the original code in Exercise 1.

Exercise 3: Revise the `main` function of your Exercise 2 program to place the calls to the three conversion functions in the `cout` statement. That is, instead of assigning the result of each function call to a variable for later printing, the values returned by the function calls will be printed immediately. When this is done, `main` will no longer even need the three local variables `euros`, `pesos`, and `yen`.

Now retrieve program `overloaded.cpp` from the Set 6.2 folder. Its code follows. This program also converts dollars to foreign currencies, however, it converts dollars to multiple currencies at once. Note its use of overloaded functions.

```
// overloaded.cpp
// This program will input American money and convert it to foreign
// currency. It illustrates the use of overloaded functions.
// PLACE YOUR NAME HERE.

#include <iostream>
#include <iomanip>
using namespace std;

// Function prototypes
void  multiConversion (double dollars, double& euros, double& pesos);
void  multiConversion (double dollars, double& euros, double& pesos, double& yen);

// global constant CONVERSION RATES
const double NUM_EUROS =     .8681,    // number of euros to the dollar
             NUM_PESOS =    7.76023,   // number of pesos to the dollar
             NUM_YEN   = 119.82;       // number of yen to the dollar

int main ()
{
   double dollars,
          euros = 0,
          pesos = 0,
          yen = 0;

   cout << fixed << showpoint << setprecision(2);
   cout << "Input the amount in American Dollars to \n"
        << "convert to euros and pesos: $" ;
   cin  >> dollars;

   // Fill in the code to call the multiConversion function that
   // converts dollars to euros and pesos.  Note that it requires
   // 3 arguments.  Be sure to place them in the correct order.

   cout << "\n$" << dollars << " equals " << euros << " euros and "
        << pesos << " pesos.\n\n";

   cout << "Input the amount in American Dollars to \n"
        << "convert to euros, pesos, and yen: $" ;
   cin  >> dollars;

   // Fill in the code to call the multiConversion function that
   // converts dollars to euros, pesos, and yen.  Note that it requires
   // 4 arguments.  Be sure to place them in the correct order.

   cout << "\n$" << dollars << " equals " << euros << " euros, "
        << pesos << " pesos, and " << yen << " yen.\n\n";

   return 0;
}
```

continues

```
/*******************************************************************
 *                       multiConversion                           *
 * This version of the overloaded multiConversion function converts *
 * dollars to euros and pesos.  It has 3 parameters.               *
 *******************************************************************/

void multiConversion(double dollars, double& euros, double& pesos)
{
   // Currently this function is just a stub.  Remove the cout statement
   // below and replace it with the code needed to complete this function.
   cout << "\nThe 3-parameter multiConversion function was called \n"
        << "with the value " << dollars << " passed to it.\n";
}

/*******************************************************************
 *                       multiConversion                           *
 * This version of the overloaded multiConversion function converts *
 * dollars to euros, pesos, and yen. It has 4 parameters.          *
 *******************************************************************/

void multiConversion(double dollars, double& euros, double& pesos, double& yen)
{
   // Currently this function is just a stub.  Remove the cout statement
   // below and replace it with the code needed to complete this function.
   cout << "\nThe 4-parameter multiConversion function was called \n"
        << "with the value " << dollars << " passed to it.\n";
}
```

Exercise 4: Complete the code as directed and run the program.

Sample Run

```
Input the amount in American Dollars to
convert to euros and pesos: 10.00

$10.00 equals 8.68 euros and 77.60 pesos.

Input the amount in American Dollars to
convert to euros, pesos, and yen: 200.35

$200.35 equals 173.92 euros, 1554.76 pesos, and 24005.94 yen.
```

Exercise 5: Remove the constant definitions from the global section of `overloaded.cpp` and have the program read in those conversion rates from a file. Be sure to include an error message if the file cannot be found and opened.

Lab 6.8 Student-Generated Code Assignments

Option 1: Write a program that will convert miles to kilometers and kilometers to miles. The user will indicate both a number (representing a distance) and a choice of whether that number is in miles to be converted to kilometers or kilometers to be converted to miles. Each conversion is done with value-returning functions. You can use the following conversions.

1 kilometer = .621 miles
1 mile = 1.61 kilometers

Sample Run

```
          Menu
*************************
1 Convert miles to kilometers
2 Convert kilometers to miles
3 Quit
*************************
1
Miles to be converted: 120
120 miles = 193.2 kilometers.

          Menu
*************************
1 Convert miles to kilometers
2 Convert kilometers to miles
3 Quit
*************************
2
Kilometers to be converted: 235
235 kilometers = 145.935 miles.

          Menu
*************************
1 Convert miles to kilometers
2 Convert kilometers to miles
3 Quit
****************************
3
```

Option 2: Write a program that uses the number of wins and losses a baseball team acquired during a complete season to calculate their percentage of wins. The program should be organized as a `main` function and three value-returning functions. The first is a parameter-less function that inputs the number of wins and returns this number to the `main` function. The second is a similar function that does the same thing for the losses. The third function should be passed the wins and losses, which it will use to calculate and return the percentage of wins (number of wins / total games) to the `main` function. `main` should print the result to two decimal places.

Sample Run

```
Number of wins:   80
Number of losses: 40
The percentage of wins is 66.67%
```

Option 3: Write a program that produces a dentist bill. For members of a dental plan, the bill consists of the service charge (for the particular procedure performed), and test fees, input to the program by the user. To non-members the charges consist of the above services plus medicine (also input by the user). The program first asks if the patient is a member of the dental plan. The program uses two overloaded functions to calculate the total bill. Both are value-returning functions that return the total charge.

Sample Run 1

```
Dental Plan member?
1 = yes
2 = no
1

Input the service charge: 7.89
Input test charges: 89.56
The total bill is $97.45
```

Sample Run 2

```
Dental Plan member?
1 = yes
2 = no
2

Input the service charge: 75.84
Input test charges: 49.78
Input medicine charges: 40.22
The total bill is $165.84
```

LESSON SET

7.1 Structures

PURPOSE

1. To introduce the concept of an abstract data type
2. To introduce the concept of a structure
3. To use hierarchical (nested) structures
4. To use structures as parameters

PROCEDURE

1. Students should read the Pre-lab Reading Assignment before coming to lab.
2. Students should complete the Pre-lab Writing Assignment before coming to lab.
3. In the lab, students should complete labs assigned to them by the instructor.

PRE-LAB READING ASSIGNMENT

So far we have learned of data types such as `float`, `int`, `char`, etc. In some applications the programmer needs to create a data type. A programmer-defined data type can be simple like the structures introduced below, or can be a more complex type in which the programmer must decide which values are valid for the data type and which operations may be performed on the data type. It may even be necessary for the programmer to design new operations to be applied to the data. This more complex programmer-defined data type, which we will study in Lesson Set 7.2, is called an **abstract data type (ADT)**.

Structures

The C++ programmer-defined data type studied in this lab is the **structure**, a useful data type that allows the programmer to group together data that logically belong together. To see how this might be used, consider what a student must do to register for a college course. The following is an example of a course you may choose:

```
CHEM 310            Physical Chemistry            4 Credits
```

There are four items related to this course: the course discipline (CHEM), the course number (310), the course title (Physical Chemistry), and the number of credit hours (4). We could define variables as follows:

Variable Definition	**Information Held**
`char discipline[5]`	4-letter abbreviation for discipline
`int courseNumber`	integer-valued course number
`char courseTitle[21]`	first 20 characters of course title
`short credits`	number of credit hours

Because all of these variables are related, and together describe a course, it makes sense to package them together into a structure. Notice that they do not have to be of the same data type to do this. Here is the declaration:

```
struct CourseInfo
{
     char  discipline[5];
     int   courseNumber;
     char  courseTitle[21];
     short credits;
};                          // note the required semicolon here
```

The **tag** is the name of the structure—`CourseInfo` in this case. The tag is used like a data type name. Inside the braces we have the declarations of the four data items that are the **members** of the structure: `discipline`, `courseNumber`, `courseTitle`, and `credits`.

It is important to understand that the above structure declaration does not actually define any variables or cause any memory to be allocated for them. It just lets the compiler know what a `CourseInfo` structure is composed of. When we do, later, define a variable to be a `CourseInfo` structure (i.e., defined with `CourseInfo` as its data type), it will have these four data members.

We can now define variables of type `CourseInfo` as follows:

```
CourseInfo pChem;
CourseInfo colonialHist;
```

Both `pChem` and `colonialHist` now exist as separate **instances** of the `CourseInfo` structure, each with its own memory to hold its four data members.

Accessing Structure Members

To access a data member of a structure we have to indicate which structure variable and which data member of that structure we want to access. In C++ this is done with the **dot operator (.)** as illustrated below.

```
pChem.credits = 4;

colonialHist.credits = 3;
```

Now let us put all of these ideas together into a program. Sample Program 7.1a uses the `CourseInfo` structure just described. This interactive program allows a student to add requested courses and keeps track of the total number of credit hours for which they have enrolled. The execution is controlled by a `do-while` loop.

Sample Program 7.1a

```
#include <iostream>
#include <cctype>
using namespace std;

struct CourseInfo
{
   char  discipline[5];
   int   courseNumber;
   char  courseTitle[21];
   short credits;
};

int main()
{
   CourseInfo nextClass;            // nextClass is a CourseInfo structure
   int  totalCredits = 0;
   char addClass;

   do
   {
      cout << "Enter the 4 letter course discipline code: ";
      cin  >> nextClass.discipline;

      cout << "Enter the course number: ";
      cin  >> nextClass.courseNumber;

      cout << "Enter the course title: ";
      cin.ignore();                    // necessary for the next line
      cin.getline(nextClass.courseTitle, 21);

      cout << "Enter the number of credit hours: ";
      cin  >> nextClass.credits;
```

continues

```
      totalCredits = totalCredits + nextClass.credits;

      // output the selected course and pertinent information
      cout << endl << "You have been registered for the following: " << endl;
      cout << nextClass.discipline << "      " << nextClass.courseNumber
           << "      " << nextClass.courseTitle
           << "      " << nextClass.credits << " credits" << endl <<endl;

      cout << "Would you like to add another class (Y/N)? ";
      cin  >> addClass;
      cout << endl;

   } while(toupper(addClass) == 'Y');

   cout << "The total number of credit hours you registered for is: "
        << totalCredits << endl;

   return 0;
}
```

Make sure that you understand the logic of this program and, in particular, how structures are used. Notice the line at the end of the `while` loop that reads

```
while(toupper(addClass) == 'Y');
```

What do you think the purpose of `toupper` is?

As a second example, suppose we would like a simple program that computes the area and circumference of two circles input by the user. Although we can easily do this using previously developed techniques, let us see how this can be done using structures. We will also determine which circle's center is further from the origin.

Sample Program 7.1b

```
#include <iostream>
#include <cmath>                   // necessary for the pow function
#include <iomanip>
using namespace std;

struct Circle                      // declares a structured data type named
{                                  // Circle which has 6 data members
   int   center_x;                 // x coordinate of center
   int   center_y;                 // y coordinate of center
   float radius;
   float area;
   float circumference;
   float distanceFromOrigin;       // distance of center from origin
};

const double PI = 3.14159;
```

continues

```
int main()
{
   Circle circ1, circ2;  // defines variables circ1 and circ2. The data
                         // type of each is a Circle structure.

   // Get basic information about the first circle
   cout << "Enter the radius of the first circle: ";
   cin  >> circ1.radius;
   cout << "Enter the x-coordinate of its center: ";
   cin  >> circ1.center_x;
   cout << "Enter the y-coordinate of its center: ";
   cin  >> circ1.center_y;

   // Calculate other values for the first circle
   circ1.area = PI * pow(circ1.radius, 2);
   circ1.circumference = 2 * PI * circ1.radius;
   circ1.distanceFromOrigin =
            sqrt( pow(circ1.center_x, 2) + pow(circ1.center_y, 2) );
   cout << endl << endl;

   // Get basic information about the second circle
   cout << "Enter the radius of the second circle: ";
   cin  >> circ2.radius;
   cout << "Enter the x-coordinate of its center: ";
   cin  >> circ2.center_x;
   cout << "Enter the y-coordinate of its center: ";
   cin  >> circ2.center_y;

   // Calculate other values for the second circle
   circ2.area = PI * pow(circ2.radius, 2);
   circ2.circumference = 2 * PI * circ2.radius;
   circ2.distanceFromOrigin =
            sqrt( pow(circ2.center_x, 2) + pow(circ2.center_y, 2) );
   cout << endl << endl;

   cout << setprecision(2);
   cout << fixed << showpoint;

   // Display information about the first circle
   cout << "The area of the first circle is: " << circ1.area << endl;
   cout << "The circumference of the first circle is: "
        << circ1.circumference << endl;
   cout << "Its center is at (" << circ1.center_x << ','
        << circ1.center_y << ")\n\n";

   // Display information about the second circle
   cout << "The area of the second circle is: " << circ2.area << endl;
   cout << "The circumference of the second circle is: "
        << circ2.circumference << endl;
   cout << "Its center is at (" << circ2.center_x << ','
        << circ2.center_y << ")\n\n";
```

continues

```
    // Determine and report which circle's center is closer to the origin.
    if (circ1.distanceFromOrigin > circ2.distanceFromOrigin)
    {
       cout << "The first circle is further from the origin.\n\n";
    }
    else if (circ1.distanceFromOrigin < circ2.distanceFromOrigin)
    {
       cout << "The first circle is closer to the origin.\n\n";
    }
    else
    cout << "The two circles are equidistant from the origin.\n\n";

    return 0;
}
```

Initializing Structures

We have already seen numerous examples of initializing variables at the time of their definition. Members of structures can also be initialized in a similar manner when they are defined using an **initialization list**, providing they contain no string objects. This is why the structure examples used in this lesson set use C-strings. Later you will learn how to initialize a structure that contains string objects. Suppose we have the following structure declaration in our program:

```
struct CourseInfo
{
     char discipline[5];
     int courseNumber;
     char courseTitle[21];
     short credits;
};
```

A structure variable `colonialHist` can be defined and initialized as follows:

```
CourseInfo colonialHist = {"HIST",302,"Colonial History",3};
```

The values in this list are assigned to `colonialHist`'s data members in the order they appear. Thus, the string `"HIST"` is assigned to `colonialHist.discipline`, the integer `302` is assigned to `colonialHist.courseNumber`, the string `"Colonial History"` is assigned to `colonialHist.courseTitle`, and the short int value `3` is assigned to `colonialHist.credits`. It is not necessary to initialize all the members of a structure variable. For example, we could initialize just the first member:

```
CourseInfo colonialHist = {"HIST"};
```

This statement leaves the last three members uninitialized. We could also initialize only the first two members:

```
CourseInfo colonialHist = {"HIST",302};
```

There is one important rule, however, when initializing structure members. If one structure member is left uninitialized, then all structure members that follow it must be left uninitialized also. In other words, we cannot skip members of a structure during the initialization process.

It is also worth pointing out that you cannot initialize a structure member in the declaration of the structure. The following is an illegal declaration:

```
// illegal structure declaration
struct CourseInfo
{
     char discipline[5] = "HIST";              // illegal
     int courseNumber = 302;                   // illegal
     char courseTitle[21] = "Colonial History"; // illegal
     short credits = 3;                        // illegal
};
```

If we recall what a structure declaration does, it is clear why the previous code is illegal. A structure declaration simply lets the compiler know what a structure is composed of. That is, the declaration creates a new data type (called `CourseInfo` in this case), but the structure declaration does not define any variables. Hence there is nothing that can be initialized there.

We have just seen that initialization lists do not allow you to skip members during the initialization process and they may not allow you to initialize string objects (depending on your compiler). An alternate approach that avoids these limitations is to use a **constructor** in the structure declaration. A constructor is a special type of function that will allow a programmer to initialize a structure. The constructor name must be the same as the name of the structure tag. In addition, the constructor is not a value returning function.

As an example, let us return to the `CourseInfo` structure. Suppose that the History department at the University of Structville is currently using Sample Program *7.1a* and that all of their courses are 3 credits. In this case the `discipline` and `credits` members will be the same for every `CourseInfo` structure variable. Only the `courseNumber` and `courseTitle` members will vary with each course. To handle this we could add a constructor to the structure declaration as follows:

```
struct CourseInfo
{
     string discipline;
     int courseNumber;
     string courseTitle;
     short credits;

     CourseInfo()                    // Constructor
     {
          discipline = "HIST";
          credits = 3;
     }
};
```

Observe that the `discipline` and `courseTitle` members are now string objects rather than character arrays. We are also able to initialize the first and last members even though the middle two are not initialized. Only data that is unique to each `CourseInfo` structure variable is needed. For example, consider the following code:

```
CourseInfo colonialHist;

colonialHist.courseNumber = 302;
colonialHist.courseTitle = "Colonial History";
```

After this portion of code is executed, all of the members of the colonialHist structure variable have the desired values.

In this example two of the structure members never change values, regardless of the course. However, in many applications each new structure variable has a unique set of data values. In such cases data must be passed to the constructor for each new variable to be properly initialized. To accomplish this we can use constructors that accept arguments. Let us return to the CourseInfo structure, but now assume that the entire University of Structville is using the program. Certainly there will be multiple disciplines at this university as well as courses of varying numbers of credits. The following structure declaration with a constructor that accepts arguments could be used:

```
struct CourseInfo
{
     string discipline;
     int courseNumber;
     string courseTitle;
     short credits;

     CourseInfo(string d, int cn, string ct, short c)
     {
          discipline = d;
          courseNumber = cn;
          courseTitle = ct;
          credits = c;
     }
};
```

Now CourseInfo variables can be created and initialized as follows:

```
CourseInfo pChem("CHEM",310, "Physical Chemistry",4);
CourseInfo abstAlgebra("MATH",441, "Abstract Alegebra",3);
```

Each variable will be initialized with the data it passes to the constructor when it is created.

Hierarchical (Nested) Structures

Often it is useful to nest one structure inside another. The following sample program illustrates this. Notice how a nested structure is declared, how its members are referenced, and how a nested structure variable can be initialized at the time it is defined.

Sample Program 7.1c

```
#include <iostream>
using namespace std;

struct Dimension
{
       int length,          // dimensions are to the nearest inch
       width,
       height;
};

struct Package
{
    int weight;             // weight is to the nearest ounce
    Dimension size;         // A Dimension struct is nested
};                          // inside a Package struct

int main()
{
    // Define and initialize a structure variable
    Package box = {18, {12, 8, 2} };

    // Print out the information
    cout << "Weight = " << box.weight << " ounces \n";
    cout << "Length = " << box.size.length << " inches \n";
    cout << "Width  = " << box.size.width  << " inches \n";
    cout << "Height = " << box.size.height << " inches \n";
    cout << "Volume = "
         << box.size.length * box.size.width * box.size.height
         << " cubic inches \n\n";

    return 0;
}
```

Notice that when we want to access a member of an inner nested structure, we must use two dot operators. For example, note that the box's length is referenced as

```
box.size.length
```

The first dot operator allows us to access the box's `size` member, but that is another structure. We need a second dot operator to access the `length` member of this structure.

Structures and Functions

Just as we can use other variables as function arguments, structure members may also be used as function arguments. Consider the following structure declaration:

```
struct Circle
{
     int center_x;    // x coordinate of center
```

continues

```
          int center_y;    // y coordinate of center
          float radius;
          float area;
     };
```

Suppose we also have the following function definition in the same program:

```
float computeArea(float r)
{
     return PI * r * r;     // PI must have previously been defined
                            // as a constant float.
}
```

If `firstCircle` were a variable of the `Circle` structure type, the following function call would pass `firstCircle.radius` into `r`. The return value would be stored in `firstCircle.area`:

```
firstCircle.area = computeArea(firstCircle.radius);
```

It is also possible to pass an entire structure variable to a function rather than just an individual member. This is illustrated in Sample Program 7.1d.

Sample Program 7.1d

```
#include <iostream>
using namespace std;

struct CourseInfo
{  char  discipline[5];
   int   courseNumber;
   char  courseTitle[21];
   short credits;
};

// Function prototype
void displayInfo(CourseInfo);

int main()
{
   // Create and initialize a Course structure variable named pChem.
   CourseInfo pChem = {"CHEM", 310, "Physical Chemistry", 4};

   displayInfo(pChem);  // Pass pChem to the displayInfo function.
   return 0;
}

/*********************************************************************
 *                          displayInfo                              *
 * Displays the information in the CourseInfo structure passed to it*
 *********************************************************************/
void displayInfo(CourseInfo c) // receives an entire CourseInfo structure
{
    cout << c.discipline  << "  " << c.courseNumber << "    "
         << c.courseTitle << "  " << c.credits << endl;
}
```

Note that `pChem` was passed by value to the `displayInfo` function. If that function had made any changes to the four member variables, they would have been made to a local copy and would not have affected the data in the main function's `pChem` variable. This safeguards the data. Another way to safeguard a structure's member data when it is not to be altered is to pass the structure as a constant reference.

```
void displayInfo(const CourseInfo &c)
```

This is often done with large structures to avoid making a copy of them while still ensuring that the data in the structure cannot be changed by the function.

Modularizing programs through the use of functions has many advantages, one of which is to reduce, or eliminate, redundant code. When you first examined Sample Program 7.1b, you may have noticed how repetitious it was, with identical code repeated to input data, perform calculations, and display results for each of the two circles. However, by passing structures to functions we can create a modular version of that program. The code to perform each task appears only once, in an appropriately named function, and each `Circle` variable is simply passed to the functions that need to operate on it. Notice how this is done in Sample Program 7.1e, which is a modular version of Sample Program 7.1b.

Sample Program 7.1e

```
// This program is a modular version of Sample Program 7.1b

#include <iostream>
#include <cmath>                    // necessary for the pow function
#include <iomanip>
using namespace std;

struct Circle                       // declares a structured data type named
{                                   // Circle which has 6 data members
   int   center_x;                  // x coordinate of center
   int   center_y;                  // y coordinate of center
   float radius;
   float area;
   float circumference;
   float distanceFromOrigin;        // distance of center from origin
};

// Function prototypes
void getData(Circle&, int);
void calcCircleStats(Circle&);
void printStats(Circle, int);
void compareOrigins(Circle, Circle);

// global constant declaration
const double PI = 3.14159;

int main()
{
```

continues

```
   Circle circ1, circ2;  // defines variables circ1 and circ2. The
                         // data type of each is a Circle structure

   // Get circle size and location information
   getData(circ1, 1);
   getData(circ2, 2);

   // Calculate circle statistics
   calcCircleStats(circ1);
   calcCircleStats(circ2);

   // Set print formats and print report heading
   cout << fixed << showpoint << setprecision(2);
   cout << "\n\n************ Circle Statistics ************\n\n";

   // Print circle statistics
   printStats(circ1, 1);
   printStats(circ2, 2);

  // Print information on relative distance from the origin
   compareOrigins(circ1, circ2);

   return 0;
}

/*********************************************************************
 *                             getData                               *
 *  This function inputs the radius and x and y center coordinates *
 *  of the circle passed to it by reference.                         *
 *********************************************************************/

void getData(Circle& aCircle, int number)
{
   cout << "\nPlease input the following information for circle "
        << number << endl;
   cout << "Radius: ";
   cin  >> aCircle.radius;
   cout << "Center x-coordinate: ";
   cin  >> aCircle.center_x;
   cout << "Center y-coordinate: ";
   cin  >> aCircle.center_y;
}

/*********************************************************************
 *                         calcCircleStats                           *
 *  This function calculates the area, circumference, and distance *
 *  from the origin of the circle passed to it by reference.        *
 *********************************************************************/
```

continues

```
void calcCircleStats(Circle& aCircle)
{
   aCircle.area = PI * pow(aCircle.radius, 2);
   aCircle.circumference = 2 * PI * aCircle.radius;
   aCircle.distanceFromOrigin =
           sqrt( pow(aCircle.center_x, 2) + pow(aCircle.center_y, 2) );
}

/*****************************************************************
 *                          printStats                           *
 *  This function prints information about the circle passed to it.*
 *****************************************************************/

void printStats(Circle aCircle, int number)
{
   cout << "Circle " << number << endl;
   cout << "Area: " << aCircle.area;
   cout << "   Circumference: " << aCircle.circumference << endl;
   cout << "Center is located at (" << aCircle.center_x << ','
        << aCircle.center_y << ")\n\n";
}

/*****************************************************************
 *                        compareOrigins                         *
 *  This function indicates which of the two Circle structures   *
 *  passed to it is closer to the origin.                        *
 *****************************************************************/

void compareOrigins(Circle circleA, Circle circleB)
{
   if (circleA.distanceFromOrigin > circleB.distanceFromOrigin)
   {
      cout << "The first circle is further from the origin.\n\n";
   }
   else if (circleA.distanceFromOrigin < circleB.distanceFromOrigin)
   {
      cout << "The first circle is closer to the origin.\n\n";
   }
   else
      cout << "The two circles are equidistant from the origin.\n\n";
}
```

PRE-LAB WRITING ASSIGNMENT

Fill-in-the-Blank Questions

1. The name of a structure is called the ______________.
2. The variables declared inside the structure declaration are called the ______________ of the structure.
3. One structure inside of another structure is an example of a ___________________.
4. Members of a structure ______________ (do / do not) all have to have the same data type.
5. When initializing structure members, if one structure member is left uninitialized, then all the structure members that follow must be ___________________.
6. The ______________________ allows the programmer to access structure members.
7. You may not initialize a structure member in the ____________________.
8. Like variables, structure members, or even entire structures, may be used as ___________________ to functions.

LESSON 7.1A

LAB 7.1 Working with Basic Structures

Bring in program `rect_struct.cpp` from the Set 7.1 folder. The code follows.

```
// This program uses a structure to hold data about a rectangle.
// PLACE YOUR NAME HERE.

#include <iostream>
#include <iomanip>
using namespace std;

// Fill in the code to declare a structure named Rectangle which has
// 4 float members: length, width, area, and perimeter.

int main()
{
   // Fill in the code to define a Rectangle variable named box.

   cout << "Enter the length of a rectangle: ";
   // Fill in the code to read in the length of box.
   cout << "Enter the width of a rectangle: ";
   // Fill in the code to read in the width of box.

   // Fill in the code to compute the area of box.
   // Fill in the code to compute the perimeter of box.

   cout << fixed << showpoint << setprecision(2);
   // Fill in the code to output the area with an appropriate message.
   // Fill in the code to output the perimeter with an appropriate message.

   return 0;
}
```

Exercise 1: Complete the above program as instructed.

Exercise 2: Add code to the program above so that the modified program will determine and report whether or not the rectangle entered by the user is a square.

Sample Run

```
Enter the length of a rectangle: 7
Enter the width of a rectangle: 6
The area of the rectangle is 42.00
The perimeter of the rectangle is 26.00
The rectangle is not a square.
```

Lab 7.2 Initializing Structures

Bring in program `init_struct.cpp` from the Set 7.1 folder. The code follows.

```
// This program demonstrates partially initialized structure variables.
// PLACE YOUR NAME HERE.

#include <iostream>
using namespace std;

struct TaxPayer
{
   char name[25];              // uses a C-string, rather than a string object
   long int SSNum;             // social security number
   double taxRate;
   double income;
   double taxes;
};

int main()
{
   // Fill in the code to define and initialize a TaxPayer structure variable named
   // citizen1 with the first 3 members initialized as follows:
   // name is Tim McGuiness, SSNum is 255871234, and taxRate is .35

   // Fill in the code to define and initialize a TaxPayer structure variable named
   // citizen2 with the first 3 members initialized as follows:
   // name is John Kane, SSNum is 278990582, and taxRate is .29

   cout.precision(2);          // works the same as cout << setprecision(2);
   cout << fixed << showpoint;

   // Fill in the code to prompt the user to enter this year's income for citizen1.
   // Fill in the code to read this income into citizen1's appropriate structure member.

   // Fill in the code to calculate taxes for citizen1 and store it in his appropriate
   // structure member.

   // Fill in the code to repeat the same three steps for citizen2.
```

continues

```
   cout << "Name: " << citizen1.name << endl;
   cout << "Social Security Number: " << citizen1.SSNum << endl;
   cout << "Taxes due for this year: " << citizen1.taxes << endl << endl;

   // Fill in the code to print out the same information for citizen2.

   return 0;
}
```

Exercise 1: Complete the above program as instructed. This program uses an initialization list to initialize the structure.

Sample Run

```
Enter this year's income for Tim McGuiness: 30000
Enter this year's income for John Kane: 60000

Name: Tim McGuiness
Social Security Number: 255871234
Taxes due for this year: $10500.00

Name: John Kane
Social Security Number: 278990582
Taxes due for this year: $17400.00
```

Bring in program `con_struct.cpp` from the Set 7.1 folder. The code follows.

```
// This program demonstrates partially initialized structure variables
// PLACE YOUR NAME HERE.

#include <iostream>
#include <string>
using namespace std;

struct taxPayer
{
   string name;        // uses a string object, rather than a C-string
   long int SSNum;     // social security number
   double taxRate;
   double income;
   double taxes;
   taxPayer()
   {
      name = "";
      SSNum = 000000000;
      taxRate = 0;
   }

   // Fill in the code to create another constructor that has the
   // parameters:  n, id and rate. name will be set to the value of n
   // SSNum will be set with the value of id and taxRate will be set
   // with the value of rate.

};
```

continues

```
int main()
{
   // Fill in the code to define and initialize (through the use of a
   // a constructor) a taxpayer structure variable name citizen1
   // with the first 3 members initialized as follows:
   // name is Tim McGuiness, SSNum is 255871234, and taxRate is .35

   // Fill in the code to define and initialize (to the default values)
   // a taxpayer structure variable named citizen2.


   cout.precision(2); // works the same as cout << setprecision(2);
   cout << fixed << showpoint;

   // Fill in the code to prompt the user to enter this year's income
   // for citizen1.
   // Fill in the code to read this income into citizen1's appropriate
   // structure member.

   // Fill in the code to calculate taxes for citizen1 and store it
   // in his appropriate structure member.

   // Fill in the code to repeat these same three steps for citizen2.

   cout << "Name: " << citizen1.name << endl;
   cout << "Social Security Number: "  << citizen1.SSNum << endl;
   cout << "Taxes due for this year: " << citizen1.taxes << endl
                                       << endl;

   // Fill in the code to print out the same information for citizen2.

   return 0;
}
```

Exercise 2: Complete the program as instructed. This program uses constructors to initialize the structure.

Run the program so it produces the following output:

Please input the yearly income for Tim McGuiness

3000

Please input the yearly income for John Brown

9000

Name: Tim McGuiness
Social Security Number: 255871234
Taxes due for this year: 1020.00

continues

Name: John Brown

Social Security Number: 0

Taxes due for this year: 0.00

LAB 7.3 Nested Structures

Bring in program `nestedRect_struct.cpp` from the Set 7.1 folder. This code is very similar to the rectangle program from Lab 7.1. However, this time you will complete the code using nested structures. The code follows.

```
// This program uses a structure to hold data about a rectangle.
// PLACE YOUR NAME HERE.

#include <iostream>
#include <iomanip>
using namespace std;

// Fill in the code to declare a structure named Dimension that contains 2 float members,
// length and width.

// Fill in the code to declare a structure named Rectangle that contains 3 members:
// area, perimeter, and size. The first two should be floats but
// size should be a Dimension structure variable.

int main()
{
   // Fill in the code to define a Rectangle variable named box.

   cout << "Enter the length of a rectangle: ";
   // Fill in the code to read in the length and store it in the appropriate box location.
   cout << "Enter the width of a rectangle: ";
   // Fill in the code to read in the width and store it in the appropriate box location.

   // Fill in the code to compute the box area and store it in the appropriate
   // box location.
   // Fill in the code to compute the box perimeter and store it in the appropriate
   // box location.

   cout << fixed << showpoint << setprecision(2);
   cout << "The area of the rectangle is " <<        // Fill this in.
   cout << "The perimeter of the rectangle is " <<   // Fill this in.

   return 0;
}
```

Exercise 1: Complete the above program as instructed.

Exercise 2: Modify the program by adding a third structure named `Results` which has two members, `area` and `perimeter`. Adjust the `Rectangle` structure so that both of its members are now structure variables.

Exercise 3: Modify the program further by adding value-returning functions that compute the `area` and `perimeter`. The necessary structure variables should be passed as arguments to the functions.

Sample Run

```
Enter the length of a rectangle: 9
Enter the width of a rectangle : 6
The area of the rectangle is 54.00
The perimeter of the rectangle is 30.00
```

LESSON 7.1B

LAB 7.4 Student-Generated Code Assignment

Write a program to input and display information on champion dogs. Information on each dog should be kept in a `Dog` structure with the following structure members: `name`, `breed`, `gender`, `firstPlaceWins`, `secondPlaceWins`, and `bestOfShow`. These last three items keep track of the total number of wins a dog has had in each of the three categories. You decide on the appropriate data type for each member.

The `main` function should create 3 `Dog` structure variables and pass each one in turn to a `void getInfo` function which will prompt for and input the information. The structure variable must be passed by reference so that the information can be correctly written into the `Dog` variable belonging to the `main` function.

The `main` function should then pass each of the 3 `Dog` variables, in turn, to a `void displayInfo` function that will display the fields of information with appropriate labels, plus display a total number of wins (in all 3 categories combined) for that dog. Does the structure variable passed to this function need to be passed by reference, or can it be passed by value or constant reference?

You may wish to just use one-word names for the dogs and the breeds (i.e., no embedded spaces) so that you can input them using simple `cin >>` statements.

Once your program is correctly working, create another structure named `Awards`. It should have 3 members: `firstPlace`, `secondPlace`, and `bestOfShow`. Modify the `Dog` structure so that instead of having 3 individual data members to keep track of the dog's wins it instead has a member named `wins` that is of type `Awards`. Modify the code in your `getInfo` and `displayInfo` functions to correctly work with the revised `Dog` structure it is passed.

Sample Run

```
Input dog name: Champion
Input dog breed: terrier
Input dog gender (m for male or f for female): m
Enter the number of this dog's first place wins : 1
Enter the number of this dog's second place wins: 2
Enter the number of this dog's Best of Show wins: 1
```

This prompting and input repeats for dogs 2 and 3.

```
Dog name : Champion   breed: terrier    gender: m
Wins—First place :    1
     Second place:    2
     Best of Show:    1
       TOTAL WINS:    4
```

This output repeats for dogs 2 and 3.

LESSON SET

7.2 Introduction to Classes and OOP

PURPOSE

1. To introduce object-oriented programming
2. To introduce the concept of classes
3. To introduce class member variables and member functions
4. To introduce constructors and destructors

PROCEDURE

1. Students should read Chapter 7 of the text.
2. Students should read the Pre-lab Reading Assignment before coming to lab.
3. Students should complete the Pre-lab Writing Assignment before coming to lab.
4. In the lab, students should complete labs assigned to them by the instructor.

Contents	Prerequisites	Approximate completion time	Page number	Check when done
Pre-lab Reading Assignment		20 min.	128	
Pre-lab Writing Assignment	Pre-lab reading	10 min.	138	
LESSON 7.2A				
Lab 7.5 Money Exchange	Basic understanding of structures and classes	35 min.	138	
Lab 7.6 `Square` as a Class	Basic understanding of structures and classes	15 min.	141	
LESSON 7.2B				
Lab 7.7 Constructors Used in the `Circles` Class	Understanding of constructors, destructors and overloading	35 min.	142	
Lab 7.8 Student-Generated Code Assignment	Completion of the above labs	homework	145	

PRE-LAB READING ASSIGNMENT

Introduction to Object-Oriented Programming

Up until now, we have been using the procedural programming method for writing all our programs. A procedural program has data stored in a collection of variables and has a set of functions that perform certain operations. The functions and data are treated as separate entities. Although operational, this method has some serious drawbacks when applied to many large real-world situations. Even though this process is modularized (broken into a set of functions), in a large complex program the number of functions can become overwhelming and difficult to modify or extend. This can create a level of complexity that is difficult to understand.

Object-oriented programming (OOP) helps control this complexity by creating **classes** of **objects** which model real-world entities. The classes act as prototypes for the objects. The objects are similar to nouns in that they can simulate persons, places, or things that exist in the real world. In addition to helping simplify and manage complexity, OOP enhances code reusability (reuse of existing code or classes). Object-oriented programming is not learned in one lesson. This lab gives a brief introduction to this very important programming paradigm.

Classes and objects are often confused with one another; however, there is an important difference as explained by the following example. A plaster of Paris mold consists of the design for a particular figurine. When the plaster is poured into the mold and hardened, we have the creation of the figurine itself. A class is analogous to the mold, for it holds the definition of an object. The object is analogous to the figurine, for it is an **instance** of the class. Just as we can create many figurines from the same mold, many objects (instances of the class) can be created from the same class. A class then is a prototype (template) for a set of objects. An object is a single instance of a class in much the same way that a variable is an instance of a particular data type.

When you examine the declaration of a class you will notice that it is much like the declaration of a structure except that classes encapsulate functions as well as data.[1] They also normally designate the functions and data items belonging to them as being either **public** or **private**, an indication of who can access them. Functions and data which are declared to be `public` can be directly accessed by code outside the class, while `private` functions and data can normally be accessed only by functions belonging to the class. Classes generally safeguard important data members by making them `private` and requiring outside access to them to be done through a carefully defined `public` interface.

A class consists of a name (its identity), its member data (what it is), and its member functions (what it does). For example, a circle, in order to be drawn, must have a radius and a center (an *x* and a *y* coordinate). In practical terms these three things (`radius`, `center_x`, and `center_y`) make up its member data, or member variables. We can also describe a set of member functions that can perform certain actions relating to the circle. These actions consist of such things as giving values to the three member variables and finding the circumference and area of the circle. A class thus combines data and functions in one package. Notice how this is done in the following example, which defines a C++ `Circles` class.

[1] Actually, structures can also contain functions, but usually do not, whereas classes always contain them.

```
class Circles    // Circles is the name of the class (its identity).
                 // The following is the declaration of the Circles class.
{
   public:
   // The following are labeled as public.
   // Usually member functions are declared public
   // so they can be called by code outside the class.
   // Member functions describe what the class can do.

   void setCenter(int x, int y);
   // This procedure receives the center coordinates of a Circles
   // object and places them in the appropriate member variables.

   void setRadius(float r);
   // This procedure receives the radius of a Circles object and
   // places it in the appropriate member variable.

   double calcArea();
   // This function calculates and returns the area of a Circles object.

   double calcCircumference();
   // This function calculates and returns the circumference of a Circles object.

   void printStats();
   // This procedure prints out the radius and center coordinates
   // of a Circles object.


private:
// The following are labeled as private.
// Usually member variables are defined as private
// so they can ONLY be accessed by functions that belong to the class.
// Member variables describe the attributes of the class.

  float  radius;
  int    center_x;
  int    center_y;
};                       // Notice the closing brace and the semicolon at the end.
```

The user programs that create and use `Circles` objects do not need to know anything about the inner workings of the `Circles` class, just as it is not necessary for someone to understand how a television remote control works in order to change the television stations or the volume. The user of the remote only needs to know which buttons to push (the interface) in order to accomplish a certain task. The user of an object only needs to understand how to call the member functions (the **interface**) in order to use the object. The **implementation**, which contains the details of how the functions accomplish what they do, is normally in a separate file hidden from the user. Not only does this simplify the use of the object, but the fact that programs and users of the object do not "see" what they do not need to see makes the object more accessible to a greater number of programs. This concept is known as **data hiding**.

User of an object ⟶ Public Interface ⟶ Private Internal Data (`radius, center_x, center_y`) Implementation of the member functions

Types of Objects

Objects are either general purpose or application-specific. General purpose objects are designed to create a specific data type such as currency or date. They are also designed to perform common tasks such as input verification and graphical output. Application-specific objects are created to handle specific limited operations for some organization or task. A student class, for example, may be created for an educational institution.

Creation and Use of Objects

As noted, the class declaration acts very much like a prototype or data type for an object. An object is defined much like a variable except that it uses the class name as the data type. This definition creates an **instance** (actual occurrence) of the class. `Circles`, described previously, is a class and `sphere1` and `sphere2`, defined below, are two instances of that class.

```
Circles sphere1,sphere2;     // sphere1 and sphere2 are
                             // two Circles class objects.
```

`sphere1` has its own `radius`, `center_x`, and `center_y` whose values are possibly different from the `radius`, `center_x`, and `center_y` of `sphere2`.

Member functions are sometimes called **methods**. To access a particular member function, or method, of an object we use the dot operator, just as we did to access data members of structures.

Examples:

```
sphere1.setCenter(9,10);  // Notice we have associated a particular object
                          // with the call to its setCenter function.
sphere1.setRadius(20);

cout << "The area of the circle is " << sphere1.calcArea() << endl;
```

Since `calcArea` must have the radius of the object before it can do the calculation, the user must be sure to have the object call `setRadius` before it calls `calcArea`. It is not good programming practice, however, to assume that a user will remember to do this necessary initialization. Later in this lesson we will look at how to use constructors to solve this problem.

The following is a complete `main` function that creates and uses a `Circles` object.

```
int main()
{
   Circles  sphere1;      // sphere1 is defined to be a Circles class object.

   sphere1.setCenter(9,10);
   sphere1.setRadius(20);

   cout << "The area of the circle is " << sphere1.calcArea() << endl;
   cout << "The circumference of the circle is "
        << sphere1.calcCircumference() << endl;

   sphere1.printStats();

   return 0;
}
```

Implementation of Member Functions

As previously noted, the implementation of the member functions can be hidden from the users (clients) of the objects. However, they must be implemented by someone, somewhere. Usually classes are defined in a **header file**, the code to implement member functions is stored in an **implementation file**, and the user functions that create and use objects are stored in a **client file**, though all three could be located in three different sections of the same file. If placed in different files, these files are often bound together in a project. Various development environments have different means of creating and storing related files in a project.[2] The following shows the implementation of the `Circles` member functions. Note that the name of the class followed by a `::` symbol, called the **scope resolution operator**, precedes the name of each function.

```
void Circles::setRadius(float r)
```

Note also that the `calcArea` and `calcCircumference` functions do not have to be passed the radius to work with since `radius` is a class member variable that they can directly access.

```
/***************************************************************
 *                         setCenter                           *
 * This procedure receives the center coordinates of a Circles*
 * object and places them in the appropriate member variables.*
 ***************************************************************/
void Circles::setCenter(int x, int y)
{
   center_x = x;
   center_y = y;
}

/***************************************************************
 *                         setRadius                           *
 * This procedure receives the radius of a Circles object and *
 * places it in the appropriate member variable.              *
 ***************************************************************/
void Circles::setRadius(float r)
{
   radius = r;
}

/***************************************************************
 *                         calcArea                            *
 * This function calculates and returns the area of            *
 * a Circles object.                                           *
 ***************************************************************/
double Circles::calcArea()
{
   return PI * radius * radius;
}
```

continues

---

[2] Check with the instructor for the environment used in your class.

```
/*************************************************************
 *                   calcCircumference                       *
 * This function calculates and returns the circumference of *
 * a Circles object.                                         *
 *************************************************************/
double Circles::calcCircumference()
{
   return 2 * PI * radius;
}

/*************************************************************
 *                        printStats                         *
 * This procedure prints out the radius and center coordinates*
 * of a Circles object.                                      *
 *************************************************************/
void Circles::printStats()
{
   cout << "The radius of the circle is " << radius << endl;
   cout << "The center of the circle is " << center_x
        << "   " << center_y << endl;
}
```

Complete Program

The following code shows the class declaration, the member function implementations, and the use (client) of the `Circles` class.

```
#include <iostream>
using namespace std;

// Class declaration section   (header file)
class Circles    // Circles is the name of the class (its identity).
                 // The following is the declaration of the Circles class.
{
  public:
  // The following are labeled as public.
  // Usually member functions are declared public
  // so they can be called by code outside the class.
  // Member functions describe what the class can do.

  void setCenter(int x, int y);
  // This procedure receives the center coordinates of a Circles
  // object and places them in the appropriate member variables.

  void setRadius(float r);
  // This procedure receives the radius of a Circles object and
  // places it in the appropriate member variable.

  double calcArea();
  // This function calculates and returns the area of a Circles object.
```

continues

```
  double calcCircumference();
  // This function calculates and returns the circumference of a Circles object.

  void printStats();
  // This procedure prints out the radius and center coordinates
  // of a Circles object.

  private:
  // The following are labeled as private.
  // Usually member variables are defined as private
  // so they can ONLY be accessed by functions that belong to the class.
  // Member variables describe the attributes of the class.

  float  radius;
  int    center_x;
  int    center_y;
};

//________________________________________________________________________
// Implementation section or file

const double PI = 3.14;

/***************************************************************
 *                          setCenter                          *
 * This procedure receives the center coordinates of a Circles*
 * object and places them in the appropriate member variables.*
 ***************************************************************/
void Circles::setCenter(int x, int y)
{
   center_x = x;
   center_y = y;
}

/***************************************************************
 *                          setRadius                          *
 * This procedure receives the radius of a Circles object and *
 * places it in the appropriate member variable.              *
 ***************************************************************/
void Circles::setRadius(float r)
{
   radius = r;
}

/***************************************************************
 *                          calcArea                           *
 * This function calculates and returns the area of           *
 * a Circles object.                                           *
 ***************************************************************/
double Circles::calcArea()
{
   return PI * radius * radius;
}
```

continues

```
/*************************************************************
 *                   calcCircumference                       *
 * This function calculates and returns the circumference of *
 * a Circles object.                                         *
 *************************************************************/
double Circles::calcCircumference()
{
   return 2 * PI * radius;
}

/*************************************************************
 *                        printStats                         *
 * This procedure prints out the radius and center coordinates*
 * of a Circles object.                                      *
 *************************************************************/
void Circles::printStats()
{
   cout << "The radius of the circle is " << radius << endl;
   cout << "The center of the circle is " << center_x
        << "   " << center_y << endl;
}
```

```
// Client section or file

int main()
{
   Circles  sphere1;      // sphere1 is defined as an object of Circles class

   sphere1.setCenter(9,10);
   sphere1.setRadius(20);

   cout << "The area of the circle is " << sphere1.calcArea() << endl;
   cout << "The circumference of the circle is "
        << sphere1.calcCircumference() << endl;

   sphere1.printStats();

   return 0;
}
```

Inline Member Functions

Sometimes the implementation of a member function is so short and simple it can be defined inside a class declaration using something called an **inline member function**. In the above `Circles` class, `calcArea` and `calcCircumference` are so simple that they could be defined this way. Notice that when the implementation of a member function is located within the class declaration, the class name and scope resolution operator do not precede the function name.

```
const double PI = 3.14;

class Circles
{
private:
```

continues

```
    float  radius;
    int    center_x;
    int    center_y;

public:

    void setCenter(int x, int y);
    void setRadius(float r);
    double calcArea()    { return PI * radius * radius; }
    double calcCircumference() { return 2 * PI * radius; }
    void printStats();
};
```

Constructors

Of the five member functions, `setCenter`, `setRadius`, `calcArea`, `calcCircumference`, and `printStats`, one of these must be called before some of the other functions can be called. Can you figure out which one? By its very definition, a circle must have a radius. Once an object of type `Circles` is defined, the user *must* call `setRadius`. What happens if the user forgets and tries calling the function `calcArea` without first calling `setRadius`? The program will try to find the area of a circle that has an undefined radius. The creator of the class should never rely on the user to initialize essential data.

C++ provides a mechanism, called a **constructor**, to guarantee the initialization of an object. A constructor is a member function that is *implicitly* invoked whenever a class instance is created (e.g., whenever an object is defined). A constructor is unique from other member functions in three ways:

1. It has the same name as the class itself.
2. It does not have a data type (or the word `void`) in front of it.
3. It is never allowed to return a value.

The main purpose of a constructor is to initialize an object's data. Recall that in Lesson Set 7.1 we used constructors to initialize structure variables. The following shows the `Circles` class using two constructors that replace the `setRadius` function.

```
class Circles
{
public:

    void setCenter(int x, int y);
    double calcArea();
    double calcCircumference();
    void printStats();
    Circles(float r); // Constructor allowing a user to input the radius
    Circles();        // Constructor using a default value for the radius

private:

    float  radius;
    int    center_x;
    int    center_y;
};
```

A class may have many constructors. Recall from Lesson Set 6.2 that two or more functions can have the same name as long as their parameters differ in quantity or data type. Since all constructors have the same name as the class, when there is more than one constructor they must be differentiated by their parameter lists. The **default constructor**, which has no parameters, is used to initialize member variables to default values. The other constructors, if any, pass initial values to member variables. A class can have many constructors, but only one default constructor.

The `Circles` class shown above includes two constructors. The first constructor has one parameter through which it receives an initial value for the radius. The second constructor, which has no parameters, is the default constructor. Like all member functions, constructors are defined either by in-line functions within the class declaration; in a function implementation section, which normally follows the class declaration; or in a separate implementation file.

Constructor Definitions

The function definitions of the two constructors in the previous example are as follows:

```
Circles::Circles(float r)         // Sets radius to the value passed in
{
     radius = r;
}

Circles::Circles()                // Sets radius to a default value
{
     radius = 1;
}
```

The first constructor allows the user to input a value for `radius` at the time an object is created (shown later in the lab). The second constructor (the default constructor) sets `radius` to 1 whenever the object is created with no radius specified. With the use of these constructors, every object of class `Circles` will have a value for `radius`.

Invoking a Constructor

Although a constructor is a member function, it is never invoked using the dot notation. Instead it is automatically invoked when an object (an instance of the class) is created.

Example:
```
Circles sphere1(8);
Circles sphere2;
```

In this example, `sphere1` is an object of the `Circles` class that has its radius initialized to 8. Since it has a parameter, it activates the constructor that has a parameter. The object `sphere2` is created without a parameter so the default constructor is activated and `sphere2`'s radius is initialized to 1. Note that when an object is created using the default constructor, no parentheses `()` follow the object name.

Destructors

A **destructor**, if defined for a class, is automatically invoked when an object of that class ceases to exist, such as when a program returns from the function in which the object is defined. The purpose of the destructor is to handle any "clean-up" tasks associated with an object's going out of existence. As with constructors, this special member function has the same name as the class; however, it is preceded by a tilde (~). Like constructors, destructors do not have a data type (or the word `void`) in front of them and they cannot return a value. However, unlike constructors, destructors can have no parameters, and therefore each class can have only one destructor.

The following example shows how constructors and destructors operate.

Example:

```
#include <iostream>
using namespace std;

class Demo          // class declaration
{
public:
   Demo();          // Default constructor
   ~Demo();         // Destructor
};
```

```
Demo::Demo()        // Implementation of class functions
{
   cout << "The constructor has been invoked." << endl;
}

Demo::~Demo()
{
   cout << "The destructor has been invoked." << endl;
}
```

```
int main()          // User program that uses the class
{
   Demo demoObj; // demoObj is created which invokes the default constructor

   cout << "The program is now running." << endl;

   return 0;
}

// Now that the main program is over, the object demoObj ceases to exist
// which causes the destructor to be invoked.
```

What 3 statements will this program print and in what order will they be printed?

PRE-LAB WRITING ASSIGNMENT

Fill-in-the-Blank Questions

1. ____________________ programming combines both data and functions that operate on the data together in one package.
2. A(n) _____________ is an instance of a class.
3. Member functions are sometimes called _____________.
4. To access a member function of an object, write the name of the object and the name of the function separated from each other by _____________.
5. _____________ member data of an object can be accessed only by functions belonging to that object.
6. _____________ hiding allows programmers to create objects with hidden complex logic that have a simple interface that is easy to understand and use.
7. A(n) ____________________ is a member function that is implicitly (i.e., automatically) called when an object is created.
8. A(n) ____________________ is a member function that is implicitly (i.e., automatically) called when an object ceases to exist.
9. A(n) ____________________ initializes an object's member variables to default values.
10. A constructor has the same name as _____________ .
11. A(n) _____________ precedes the destructor name.
12. Neither the word _____________ nor a data type precedes the definition of a constructor or a destructor.

LESSON 7.2A

LAB 7.5 Money Exchange

Retrieve program `moneyconverter.cpp` from the Set 7.2 folder. This program is a simplified object-oriented version of a program you worked with in Lab 6.7. The code follows.

```
// moneyconverter.cpp
// This program converts dollars to euros and pesos.
// It uses inline functions.
// PLACE YOUR NAME HERE.

#include <iostream>
#include <iomanip>
using namespace std;

const double DOLLAR_TO_EUROS  = 0.8681;  // number of Euros per dollar
const double DOLLAR_TO_PESOS  = 7.76023; // number of Mexican pesos per dollar

class MoneyConverter
{
public:
```

continues

```
    // default constructor
    MoneyConverter()
    {   // Fill in the code to initialize the totalConverted
         // private class member to zero.
    }

    double convertToEuros(double dollars)
    {   // Fill in the code to add dollars to the totalConverted accumulator.
        // Fill in the code to return the number of euros equal to dollars.
    }

    double convertToPesos(double dollars)
    {    // Fill in the code to add dollars to the totalConverted accumulator.
         // Fill in the code to return the number of pesos equal to dollars.
    }

    double amountConverted()
    {   // Fill in the code to return the value stored in the totalConverted
        // accumulator.
    }

private:

    // Fill in the code to declare a double member variable named totalConverted.

}; // End of MoneyConverter class declaration


// Implementation Section
// Since all functions are defined within the class declaration
// as inline functions, there is no separate class function
// implementation section or file


// Client code that uses the MoneyConverter class

int main()
{   double dollars,
           euros,
           pesos;
    char   more;

    // Fill in the code to create a MoneyConverter object named myMoney.

    cout << fixed << showpoint << setprecision(2);
    cout << "***Dollars to Euros Conversion***\n";
    do
    {
       cout << "\nInput number of dollars to be converted to euros: $";
       cin  >> dollars;
```

continues

```
      euros = // Fill in the code to call the myMoney function that
              // converts dollars to euros.  Pass dollars to it.
      cout << '$' << dollars << " = " << euros << " euros.\n\n";
      cout << "Convert more dollars to euros (y/n)? ";
      cin  >> more;
   } // Fill in the code to loop while more equals 'y' or 'Y'.

   cout << "\n***Dollars to Pesos Conversion***\n";
   do
   {
      cout << "\nInput number of dollars to be converted to pesos: $";
      cin  >> dollars;
     // Fill in the code for an assignment statement that calls the
     // myMoney function that converts dollars to pesos.  Pass dollars
     // to it and assign the value it returns to the pesos variable.
      cout << '$' << dollars << " = " << pesos << " pesos.\n\n";
      cout << "Convert more dollars to pesos (y/n)? ";
      cin  >> more;
   } // Fill in the code to loop while more equals 'y' or 'Y'.

   cout << "\nThe total amount of dollars converted to "
        << "foreign currency is $"
        << // Fill in the code that calls the myMoney function that
           // returns the total amount of money converted.
        << endl;

   return 0;
}
```

Exercise 1: Complete the code as instructed and run the program with the following data to get the results shown.

```
***Dollars to Euros Conversion***

Input number of dollars to be converted to euros: $100.50
$100.50 = 87.24 euros.

Convert more dollars to euros (y/n)? y

Input number of dollars to be converted to euros: $200.00
$200.00 = 173.62 euros.

Convert more dollars to euros (y/n)? n

***Dollars to Pesos Conversion***

Input number of dollars to be converted to pesos: $500.00
$500.00 = 3880.12 pesos.

Convert more dollars to pesos (y/n)? n

The total amount of dollars converted to foreign currency is $800.50
```

Exercise 2: Change the `convertToEuros` and `convertToPesos` functions to not be inline functions. Only their prototypes should be placed within the `MoneyConverter` class declaration. The definition for these two functions should be placed in the implementation section. Remember to precede the function name with the class name and scope resolution operator. Update the program documentation to correspond to the modified program. Run the program to get the same results as those shown for Exercise 1.

LAB 7.6 `Square` as a Class

Retrieve program `square.cpp` from the Set 7.2 folder. The code follows.

```
// This program defines a class Square and uses member functions to find
// the perimeter and area of the square.
// PLACE YOUR NAME HERE.

#include <iostream>
using namespace std;

// Fill in the code to define the class called Square. The member variable and
// member functions that need to be included in it can be determined
// by looking at the implementation section below.

//________________________________________________________________________
//Implementation section         Member function implementation

/***************************************************************
 *                          setSide                            *
 * This function stores the length passed to it in the side    *
 * member variable.                                            *
 ***************************************************************/

void Square::setSide(float length)
{
   side = length;
}

/***************************************************************
 *                         calcArea                            *
 * This function calculates and returns the square's area.     *
 ***************************************************************/

float Square::calcArea()
{
   return (side * side);
}

/***************************************************************
 *                      calcPerimeter                          *
 * This function calculates and returns the square's perimeter.*
 ***************************************************************/
```

continues

```
float Square::calcPerimeter()
{
   return (4 * side);
}
//______________________________________________________________________________
// Client file

int main()
{
   Square  box;          // box is defined as an object of Square class.
   float   side;         // side holds the length of a side of the square.

   // Fill in the code to prompt the user for the length of the square's
   // side and then to input this value and store it in the side variable.

   // Fill in the code that calls setSide to set the value of
   // box's side member variable.

   // Fill in the code that calls a Square member function to return
   // box's area and which then prints out that value to the screen.

   // Fill in the code that calls a Square member function to return
   // box's perimeter and which then prints out that value to the screen.

   return 0;
}
```

Exercise 1: This program asks you to fill in the class declaration and client code based on the implementation of the member functions. Complete these as instructed so that the following input and output will be generated:

```
Please input the length of the side of a square
8
The area of the square is 64
The perimeter of the square is 32
```

LESSON 7.2B

LAB 7.7 Constructors Used in the `Circles` Class

Retrieve program `circle.cpp` from the Set 7.2 folder. This is similar to the program given in the Pre-lab Reading Assignment. The code follows.

```
// This program defines a class for a circle that has member functions to set
// the center, find the area, find the circumference and display these attributes.
// The program as written does not allow the user to input data, but rather has
// the values of the circles (spheres in the program) initialized when the circles
// are created or set by a function.

// PLACE YOUR NAME HERE.
```

continues

```
#include <iostream>
using namespace std;

// class declaration section   (header file)

class Circles
{
public:
   void setCenter(int x, int y);
   double calcArea();
   double calcCircumference();
   void printStats();      // This outputs the radius and center of the circle.
   Circles (float r);      // constructor
   Circles();              // default constructor
private:
   float  radius;
   int    center_x;
   int    center_y;
};

//____________________________________________________________________________
// Implementation section     Member function implementation

const double PI = 3.14;

Circles::Circles()
{
   radius = 1;
}

Circles::Circles(float r)
// This procedure will take the radius of the circle from the user and place
// it in the appropriate member variable.
{
     radius = r;
}

double Circles::calcArea()
// This function will calculate and return the area of the circle.
{
  return PI * radius * radius;
}

double Circles::calcCircumference()
// This function will calculate and return the circumference of the circle.
{
   return 2 * PI * radius;
}
```

continues

```
void Circles::printStats()
// This procedure prints out the radius and center coordinates of the circle.
{
   cout << "The radius of the circle is " << radius << endl;
   cout << "The center of the circle is " << center_x
        << "   " << center_y << endl;
}

void Circles::setCenter(int x, int y)
// This procedure will take the coordinates of the center of the circle from
// the user and place them in the appropriate member variables.
{
   center_x = x;
   center_y = y;
}

//________________________________________________________________________
// Client section

int main()
{
   Circles sphere(8);
   sphere.setCenter(9,10);
   sphere.printStats();

   cout << "The area of the circle is " << sphere.calcArea() << endl;
   cout << "The circumference of the circle is " << sphere.calcCircumference()
        << endl;

   return 0;
}
```

Exercise 1: Alter the code to eliminate the `setCenter` function and, instead, to set the center of the circle at the time the object is created. This means that the constructors will take care of this initialization. The default constructor should place the center at point (0,0) and keep the default radius as 1. The other constructor will now have three parameters instead of one and will set `center_x` and `center_y`, as well as `radius`, to the values passed to it. In the main function replace the two lines of code that create the sphere and that set its center coordinates with a single line of code that creates the sphere with radius 8 and center coordinates (9,10). When the revised program is run, the following output should be produced.

```
The radius of the circle is 8
The center of the circle is 9   10
The area of the circle is 200.96
The circumference of the circle is 50.24
```

Exercise 2: As noted in the Pre-lab Reading Assignment, there can be several constructors as long as each one has a different number of parameters. Exercise 1 has two constructors: a default constructor (no arguments) and a constructor that lets the client program specify the radius and center coordinates or a newly created sphere (3 arguments). Add two more constructors. One should allow the client code to specify just the radius (1 argument) and should use a default value of 0 for both center coordinates. The other should allow the client code to specify just the two center coordinates (2 arguments) and should use a default value of 1 for the radius. Alter the client portion (`main`) to create an object `sphere1` by giving just the radius of 2 and using the default center, an object `sphere2` by giving neither the radius nor the center (it uses all the default values), and an object `sphere3` by giving the center coordinates (15,16) and using the default radius. That is, `sphere1` will be created using the 1-parameter constructor, `sphere2` will be created using the default (i.e. no parameter) constructor, and `sphere3` will be created using the 2-parameter constructor. Print out the vital statistics for these new objects (area and circumference). The output from running your modified program should look like the following sample output.

```
The radius of the circle is 2
The center of the circle is 0   0
The area of the circle is 12.56
The circumference of the circle is 12.56

The radius of the circle is 1
The center of the circle is 0   0
The area of the circle is 3.14
The circumference of the circle is 6.28

The radius of the circle is 1
The center of the circle is 15   16
The area of the circle is 3.14
The circumference of the circle is 6.28
```

Exercise 3: Add a destructor to the code that prints the message **This concludes a Circles object.** for each object when it is destroyed. How many times is this printed? Why?

LAB 7.8 Student-Generated Code Assignment (Homework)

Part 1: Create a `SavingsAccount` class and write a program that uses it, by carrying out the following steps.

Create a C++ class declaration for the `SavingsAccount` class which has the following private member data:

```
long dollars,
     cents;
```

and which has public member functions to do the following things.

1. A default constructor to create an account with an initial balance of 100 dollars and 0 cents.
2. A constructor to create an account with the initial dollars and cents passed to it.
3. A function that makes a deposit. This adds the dollars and cents passed to it onto the balance.
4. A function that makes a withdrawal. Providing the balance is greater than or equal to the amount to be withdrawn, the dollars and cents

passed to it are subtracted from the balance; otherwise an *insufficient funds* message is printed.

5. A function to return the balance converted to dollars. That is, if dollars is 95 and cents is 2, it would return 95.02

Write the implementation code for all the member functions. Be sure to perform normalization on cents. This means that if `cents` is 100 or more, it must increment `dollars` by the appropriate amount. Example: if cents is 234, then dollars must be increased by 2 and cents reduced to 34. Be sure also that your program can correctly handle actions like withdrawing 10 dollars and 85 cents from a balance of 135 dollars and 12 cents.

Write the code for a `main` function that creates an object of your class called `acct1` with an initial balance of $200.50. Deposit $40.50. Withdraw $100.98. Get and print the balance. These amounts may be hard coded into the program. The output should display with 2 decimal points and look like the following.

```
Balance: $140.02
```

Part 2: Modify the program to have the user input the initial balance and all deposit and withdrawal amounts. Place the deposit statements in a loop and the withdrawal statements in another loop so that users can make as many deposits and then as many withdrawals as they wish. After all deposits and withdrawals have been made, the final balance should be displayed.

Sample Run

```
Input the initial dollars: 402
Input the initial cents: 78

Would you like to make a deposit (Y or y for yes)? y
Input the dollars to be deposited: 35
Input the cents to be deposited: 67

Would you like to make a deposit (Y or y for yes)? y
Input the dollars to be deposited: 19
Input the cents to be deposited: 150

Would you like to make a deposit (Y or y for yes)? n

Would you like to make a withdrawal (Y or y for yes)? y
Input the dollars to be withdrawn: 28
Input the cents to be withdrawn: 8

Would you like to make a withdrawal (Y or y for yes)? n
Balance: $ 430.87
```

Part 3: Have your program generate a second object, `acct2`. Add code to make a series of deposits and withdrawals for `acct2` and then print its balance (similarly to what you have already done for `acct1`).

Can you think of a way to modularize your program to avoid repeating code to handle the deposits and withdrawals for `acct2`?

LESSON SET

8 Arrays

PURPOSE

1. To introduce and work with one-dimensional arrays
2. To introduce and work with two-dimensional arrays
3. To pass arrays to functions
4. To work with arrays of structures and class objects

PROCEDURE

1. Students should read the Pre-lab Reading Assignment before coming to lab.
2. Students should complete the Pre-lab Writing Assignment before coming to lab.
3. In the lab, students should complete labs assigned to them by the instructor.

Contents	Prerequisites	Approximate completion time	Page number	Check when done
Pre-lab Reading Assignment		20 min.	148	
Pre-lab Writing Assignment	Pre-lab reading	10 min.	156	
LESSON 8A				
Lab 8.1 Working with One-Dimensional Arrays	Basic understanding of one-dimensional arrays	25 min.	157	
Lab 8.2 Working with Two-Dimensional Arrays	Basic understanding of two-dimensional arrays	35 min.	159	
LESSON 8B				
Lab 8.3 Working with Arrays of Structures	Understanding of structures and arrays	20 min.	164	
Lab 8.4 Working with Arrays of Class Objects	Understanding of class objects and arrays	25 min.	165	
Lab 8.5 Student-Generated Code Assignments	Basic understanding of arrays	homework	168	

PRE-LAB READING ASSIGNMENT

One-Dimensional Arrays

So far we have talked about a variable as a single location in the computer's memory. It is possible to have a collection of memory locations, all of which have the same data type, grouped together under one name. Such a collection is called an **array**. Like every variable, an array must be defined so that the computer can "reserve" the appropriate amount of memory. This amount is based upon the type of data to be stored and the number of locations, i.e., size of the array, each of which is given in the definition.

Example: Given a list of ages (from a file or input from the keyboard), find and display the number of people for each age.

The programmer would not know the ages to be read but would need a space for the total number of occurrences of each "legitimate" age. Assuming that ages 1, 2, . . . , 100 are possible, the following array definition could be used.

```
const int TOTALYEARS = 100;
int ageFrequency[TOTALYEARS];      // reserves memory for 100 ints
```

Following the rules of variable definition, the data type (integer in this case) is given first, followed by the name of the array (`ageFrequency`), and then the total number of memory locations enclosed in brackets. The number of memory locations must be an integer expression greater than zero and can be given either as a named constant (as shown in the above example) or as a literal constant (an actual number such as 100).

Each element of an array is accessed by giving the name of the array and a subscript which identifies its position within the array. In C++ this subscript, sometimes referred to as an index, is enclosed in square brackets. The numbering of the subscripts always begins at 0 and ends with one less than the total number of locations. Thus the elements in the `ageFrequency` array defined above would be referenced as `ageFrequency[0]` through `ageFrequency[99]`.

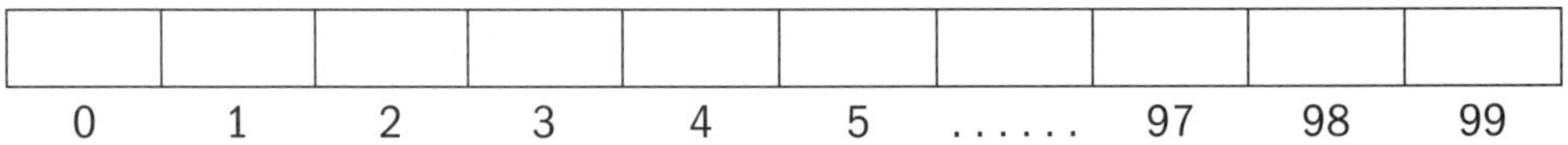

This means that the number of occurrences of age 1 would actually be placed in `ageFrequency[0]` since that is the first location. The number of occurrences of age 2 would be placed in `ageFrequency[1]` since that is the second location, etc. This odd way of numbering is often confusing to new programmers; however, it quickly becomes routine.[1]

[1] Some instructors have their students create the array with one more location than is needed and then ignore location 0, letting 1 be the first location used. In the above example, such a process would define the array as `int ageFrequency[101];` and then only use subscripts 1 through 100. In this case the number of occurrences of age 1 would be kept in `ageFrequency[1]`, of age 2 would be kept in `ageFrequency[2]`, etc. Our examples will use location 0. Your instructor will tell you which method to use.

Array Initialization

In our example, keeping track of how many people of each particular age exist in the data set would require reading in each age and then adding one to the location holding the count for that age. Of course it is important that all the counters start at 0. The following shows one way to initialize all of the elements in the array to 0.

```
for (int i = 0; i < TOTALYEARS; i++) // i acts as the array subscript
{
   ageFrequency[i] = 0;
}
```

A simple for loop will process the entire array, adding one to the subscript each time through the loop. Notice that the subscript (i) starts with 0. Why is the condition i < TOTALYEARS used instead of i <= TOTALYEARS? Remember that the last subscript is one less than the total number. The subscripts for this array go from 0 to 99. Notice also that i is the identifier name we have selected for the variable holding the subscript. In general more descriptive variable names are desirable, but the name i is sometimes used for a variable serving as an array index.

Array Processing

Arrays are generally processed inside loops so that the input/output processing of each element of the array can be performed with minimal statements. Our age frequency problem first needs to read in the ages from a file or from the keyboard. For each age read in, the "appropriate" element of the array (the one corresponding to that age) needs to be incremented by one. The following examples show how this can be accomplished. Assume that only valid data values are input.

from a file using `infile` as a logical name

```
int age;


infile >> age;

while (!infile.eof()) // while the eof has
{                     // not yet been read
   ageFrequency[age-1] += 1;

   infile >> age;
}
```

from a keyboard with –99 as sentinel data

```
int age;
cout << "Please input an age from one"
     << "to 100. Input -99 to stop." << endl;
cin  >> age;

while (age != -99)    // while the sentinel
{                     // has not yet been read
   ageFrequency[age-1] += 1;

   cout << "Please input an age from one"
        << "to 100. Input -99 to stop."
        << endl;
   cin  >> age;
}
```

In reading from a file or from the keyboard it is common to use a technique known as **priming the read**, which means the first value is read in before the test condition checks to see if the loop should be executed. The body of the loop processes the value just read in and then, as the last statement in the loop, the next value is read in. In the above examples, when we read an age, we increment the location in the array that keeps track of the amount of people in that age group. Since C++ arrays always start with 0, and we are choosing to use that location, the subscript will be one value less than the age read in. When the loop is exited, each element of the array will contain the total number of people of the given age. The following data is from a random sample run.

4	0	14	5	0	6		1	0
0 1 year	1 2 years	2 3 years	3 4 years	4 5 years	5 6 years	......	98 99 years	99 100 years

The next thing we need our sample program to do is display the total number of people for each age. However, we want to print out only those totals that have values greater than 0. The following code will do just that.

```
for (age = 0; age < TOTALYEARS; age++)
{
   if (ageFrequency[age] > 0)
   {  cout << "The number of people " << age + 1 <<" years old is "
           << ageFrequency[age] << endl;

   }

}
```

The `for` loop goes from 0 to one less than `TOTALYEARS` (0 to 99). This will test every element of the array. If that element has a value greater than 0, it will be output. What does outputting `age + 1` do? It gives the age we are dealing with at any given time, while the value of `ageFrequency[age]` gives the number of people in that age group.

The complete age frequency program will be given as one of the lab assignments.

Arrays as Arguments

So far you have learned to pass arguments to functions using either pass by value or pass by reference. Arrays also can be passed to functions, but they are passed using a method called **pass by pointer**. For now you need not be concerned with the details of this method, which will be dealt with in Lesson Set 10. You simply need to be aware that pass by pointer works like pass by reference in the sense that the original array, not a copy, is referenced by the function. This means that arrays, like pass by reference parameters, can be altered by the calling function. Note, however, that they never have the & symbol between the data type and name, as pass by reference parameters do. Sample Program 8.1 below illustrates how arrays are used and are passed as arguments to functions.

Sample Program 8.1

```
// Grade averaging program
// This program illustrates how one-dimensional arrays are used and how they are
// passed as arguments to functions. One function is called to input a set of
// grades and store them in an array. Another function is then called to find
// the average grade.

#include <iostream>
using namespace std;

// Function prototypes
void  getData(int grades[], int& size);
float findAverage(int grades[], int size);
```

continues

```
const int TOTALGRADES = 50; // TOTALGRADES is the maximum size of the array

int main()
{
   int   grades[TOTALGRADES];          // an array that holds up to 50 ints
   int   numberOfGrades = 0;           // the number of grades read in
   float average;

   getData(grades, numberOfGrades);  // getData function is called to read the
                                     // grades into the array and store how
                                     // many grades there are in numberOfGrades
   average = findAverage(grades, numberOfGrades);

   cout << endl <<"The average of the " << numberOfGrades
        << " grades read in is " << average << "." << endl << endl;

   return 0;
}

/****************************************************************
 *                          getData                             *
 * This function inputs and stores data in the grades array.   *
 ****************************************************************/

void getData(int grades[], int& size)
{
   int count = 0,                  // array index which starts at 0
       indGrade;                   // holds each individual grade read in

   cout << "Please input a grade or type -99 to stop: ";
   cin  >> indGrade;

   while (indGrade != -99)
   {
      grades[count] = indGrade;    // store grade read in next array location
      count++;                     // increment array index

      cout << "Please input a grade or type -99 to stop: ";
      cin  >> indGrade;
   }

   size = count;                   // Upon exiting the loop, count holds the
                                   // number of grades read in.
                                   // size send this value back to main.
}

/****************************************************************
 *                         findAverage                          *
 * This function finds and returns the average of the values   *
 * stored in the grades array.                                  *
 ****************************************************************/

float findAverage(int grades[], int size)
{   int sum = 0;

    for (int count = 0; count < size; count++)
    {   sum += grades[count];      // add grade in array position count to sum
    }

    return  float(sum)/size;       // return the average
}
```

Notice in Sample Program 8.1 how the array is indicated in the prototypes and in the headers of the functions that are passed the array. In both cases a set of empty brackets `[]` follows the parameter. Otherwise the syntax is the same as for passing simple variables. Notice that no brackets appear in the actual call to the functions that receive the array.

Remember that arrays in C++ are always passed in a way that allows the original array to be accessed, even though no & is used to designate this. This is why the `getData` function is able to store new values into the `grades` array, thus changing its contents. Since `numberOfGrades` is not an array, it has to be explicitly passed by reference (by using an &) to the `getData` function (which calls it `size`) so that the number of grades read in can be stored in it. `main` then passes this number as a value parameter to the `findAverage` function so it will know how many values to process. Frequently not every element of an array is used, so the size of an array given in its definition and the number of actual elements stored in it are often different. This is why passing the number of elements in an array to a function that uses the array is very common.

Even though all arrays are passed by pointer, there are times when we do not want a function to alter the values in the array. Inserting the word **const** before the data type in the formal parameter list and function header prevents the function from altering the array. In the previous sample program the `findAverage` function is not altering the array, but just using it to get a sum of all its values. The prototype and procedure heading could thus have been as follows:

```
float findAverage(const int grades[], int size); // prototype
float findAverage(const int grades[], int size)  // header
```

Of course the prototypes could also be written without named parameters.

```
float findAverage(const int [], int);            // prototype
```

Sometimes programmers prefer not to use brackets in function prototypes and headings. They can be avoided by using a **`typedef`** statement to declare a programmer-defined data type.

Example: `typedef int GradeType[50];`

This declares a data type, called `GradeType`, that is an array containing 50 integer memory locations. Since `GradeType` is a data type, it can be used in defining variables. The following defines `grades` as an integer array with 50 elements.

```
GradeType grades;
```

The following shows the revised code (in bold) for key parts of Sample Program 8.1 using `typedef`. The `grades` array has also been safeguarded from any changes by the `findAverage` function.

```
const int TOTALGRADES = 50;          // TOTALGRADES is the maximum array size

typedef int GradeType[TOTALGRADES];  // declares a new data type, a 50 int array

// Function prototypes
void  getData(GradeType grades, int& size);
float findAverage(const GradeType grades, int size);
```

continues

```
int main()
{
   GradeType grades;                // an array that holds up to 50 ints
       .
       .
   getData(grades, numberOfGrades);
   average = findAverage(grades, numberOfGrades);
       .
       .
   return 0;
}

void getData(GradeType grades, int& size)
{   .
    .
}

float findAverage(const GradeType grades, int size)
{   .
    .
}
```

This method used to eliminate brackets in function headings is especially useful for multi-dimensional arrays such as those introduced in the next section.

Two-Dimensional Arrays

The arrays we have worked with so far are **one-dimensional arrays**. That is, they consist of a set of values that can be thought of as a list, or a single column of values. They only require a single subscript to access an element. In many applications, however, the data is organized as a table with rows and columns. This is the case with the data below where each figure represents profit (in thousands) for a particular year and quarter.

	Quarter 1	Quarter 2	Quarter 3	Quarter 4
1999	72	80	10	100
2000	82	90	43	42
2001	10	87	48	53

In this case the data can most easily be stored and accessed using a **two-dimensional array**.

A two-dimensional array views data as a set of rows and columns. It thus takes two subscripts, or indices, to access a piece of data. The first indicates which row the desired item is in and the second indicates the column. We could create a two-dimensional array to hold the above data as follows.

```
float profit[3][4];
```

This allocates enough memory to hold 12 floating point values, three rows of four values each. Since C++ always uses 0 as the first subscript, the rows will be numbered 0 through 2 and the columns will be numbered 0 through 3. Thus the profit for 1999 quarter 1 (72) will be stored in `profit[0][0]` while the profit for 2001 quarter 4 (53) will be stored in `profit[2][3]`.

As with a one-dimensional array, we could have used a `typedef` statement to create a data type for a two-dimensional array and then have defined `profit` to be of that data type. This is illustrated in the following example, which reads in and stores the 12 values in the array. You will recall that we commonly use a loop to access, in turn, each element, of a one-dimensional array. Similarly we use a set of nested loops to access, in turn, each element of a two-dimensional array. In the example below, the outer loop is being used to index the row and the inner loop is being used to index the column so that each value can be input and stored in its correct array location.

Example:

```
const NO_OF_ROWS = 3;
const NO_OF_COLS = 4;

typedef float ProfitType[NO_OF_ROWS][NO_OF_COLS]; // declares a new data type, a
                                                   // 2-dimensional array of 12 floats
int main()
{
   ProfitType profit;                // defines profit as a 2-dimensional array

   for (int row = 0; row < NO_OF_ROWS; row++)
      for (int col = 0; col < NO_OF_COLS; col++)
      {
          cout << "Please input a profit" << endl;
          cin  >> profit[row][col];
      }

   return 0;
}
```

How many times will the code above ask for a profit? It processes the inner loop `NO_OF_ROWS * NO_OF_COLS` times, which is 12 times in this case.

Multi-Dimensional Arrays

C++ arrays can have any number of dimensions (although more than three is rarely used). To input, process, or output every item in an *n*-dimensional array, you need *n* nested loops.

Arrays of Characters

Any variable defined as **`char`** can hold only one character. To hold more than one character in a single variable, that variable needs to be an array of characters. A string (a group of characters used together that normally form meaningful names or words) is really just an array of characters. In Lesson Set 7.1 when we wanted to store a course title like `"Physical Chemistry"` in a variable we defined it as `char courseTitle[21];` In that case we were actually defining it to be an array of 21 characters (i.e., 21 contiguous memory locations each capable of storing one `char`).

Arrays of Structures

The `courseTitle` variable found in Lesson Set 7.1 was part of the following structure.

```
struct CourseInfo
{
   char  discipline[5];
   int   courseNumber;
   char  courseTitle[21];
   short credits;
};
```

Notice that its member variables consist of a mixture of data types. Suppose we wanted an array to hold a course record like the one above for each of the 178 courses our school offers. Could we do that? The answer is yes. C++ requires that all elements of an array be the same data type. But that data type can be a structure. If we defined `course` as follows

```
CourseInfo course[200];
```

`course` would be an array of 200 such structures, referenced as `course[0]` through `course[199]`. Notice we made the array a little bigger than required to allow additional records to be added later.

To access information in the array we would first use a subscript to identify which structure in the array we desired and would then use the dot operator to access the desired field within that structure. So, for example, to print out the information for the course stored in array location 5 we could use the following statement.

```
cout << course[5].discipline  << "   " << course[5].courseNumber << "   "
     << course[5].courseTitle << "   " << course[5].credits << endl;
```

Arrays of Class Objects

Arrays can also contain class objects. Recall the `Circles` class introduced in Lesson Set 7.2. Suppose we needed an entire array of circle objects. We could define one as shown in the following code.

```
Circles sphere[4];  // sphere is an array of 4 Circles class objects
```

Since this class has a default constructor, the default values are assigned to each element (object) of the array. The radius for each of the objects in the `sphere` array is equal to 1 since that is the default value assigned by the default constructor. Sample Program 8.2 shows the header file and client file for a program that uses `Circles` objects. (The implementation file for the `Circles` class can be found in Lesson Set 7.2.) Notice in this program how a member function for an object is called. First an object is accessed by giving its array name and position in the array and then, following the dot operator, the desired member function and any needed parameters are given.

Sample Program 8.2

```
#include <iostream>
using namespace std;

class Circles
{
public:
   void setCenter(int x, int y);
   double calcArea();
```

continues

```
      double calcCircumference();
      void printStats();
      Circles (float r);     // constructor
      Circles();             // default constructor
      ~Circles();            // destructor
   private:

      float  radius;
      int    center_x;
      int    center_y;
   };

   const double PI = 3.14;
   const int NUM_OBJECTS = 4;

   //_______________________________________________________________
   //Client file

   int main()
   {
      Circles sphere[NUM_OBJECTS];      // sphere is defined as an array of
                                        // objects of Circles class

      for (int pos = 0; pos < NUM_OBJECTS; pos++)
      {
         cout << "Stats for circle number " << pos+1 << endl << endl;
         sphere[pos].printStats();

         cout << "The area of the circle is " << sphere[pos].calcArea() << endl;
         cout << "The circumference of the circle is"
              << sphere[pos].calcCircumference() << endl << endl;
      }

      return 0;
   }
```

PRE-LAB WRITING ASSIGNMENT

Fill-in-the-Blank Questions

1. The first subscript of every array in C++ is _______________ and the last is _______________ less than the total number of locations in the array.
2. The amount of memory allocated to an array is based on the _______________ and the _______________ of locations, or size, of the array.
3. Array initialization and processing is usually done inside a _______________.
4. The _______________ statement can be used to declare a new data type such as an array type.
5. Multi-dimensional arrays are usually processed within _______________ loops.
6. An *n*-dimensional array will be processed within _______________ nested loops when accessing all members of the array.

7. Arrays used as arguments are always passed by _______________.
8. A string can be defined as an array of _______________.
9. Upon exiting a loop that reads values into an array, the variable used as a(n) _______________ to the array will contain the size of that array.
10. C++ _______________ (does / does not) allow arrays of structures and of class objects.

LESSON 8A

LAB 8.1 Working with One-Dimensional Arrays

Retrieve program `testscore.cpp` from the Set 8 folder. The code follows.

```
// This program reads in a group of test scores (positive integers from 1 to 100)
// from the keyboard and then calculates and outputs the average score as well as
// the highest and lowest score.  There will be a maximum of 100 scores.

// PLACE YOUR NAME HERE.

#include <iostream>
using namespace std;

typedef int GradeType[100]; //declares a new data type, a 100 element int array

float findAverage (const GradeType, int);  // finds average of all grades
int   findHighest (const GradeType, int);  // finds highest of all grades
int   findLowest  (const GradeType, int);  // finds lowest of all grades

int main()
{
    GradeType grades;                      // the array holding the grades
    int numberOfGrades;                    // the number of grades read
    int pos;                               // array index
    int aGrade;                            // a single grade read in
    float avgOfGrades;                     // contains the average of the grades
    int highestGrade;                      // contains the highest grade
    int lowestGrade;                       // contains the lowest grade

    // Read in the values and store them in the array.
    pos = 0;
    cout << "Please input a grade from 1 to 100 (or -99 to stop)" << endl;
    cin  >> aGrade;

    while (aGrade != -99)
    {
        // Fill in the lines of code to read in and store all the grades
        // in the array.
    }

    numberOfGrades = _________;  // Fill blank with appropriate identifier.
```

continues

```
    // call to the function to find average

    avgOfGrades = findAverage(grades, numberOfGrades);

    cout << endl << "The average of all the grades is " << avgOfGrades
         << endl;

    // Fill in the call to the function that calculates highest grade.
    // Assign the value it returns to the variable highestGrade.

    cout << endl << "The highest grade is " << highestGrade << endl;

    // Fill in the call to the function that calculates lowest grade.
    // Assign the value it returns to the variable lowestGrade.
    // Fill in the code to write the lowest grade to the screen.

    return 0;
}

/**************************************************************
 *                      findAverage                           *
 * This function receives an array of integers and its size.  *
 * It finds and returns the average of these numbers.         *
 **************************************************************/

float findAverage (const GradeType A, int size)
// A is the name of the formal parameter used to access the array.
{
   float sum = 0;

   for (int pos = 0; pos < size; pos++)
   {
      sum = sum + A[pos];
   }
   return (sum / size);                  // returns the average
}

/**************************************************************
 *                      findHighest                           *
 * This function receives an array of integers and its size.  *
 * It finds and returns the highest value in the array.       *
 **************************************************************/

int findHighest (const GradeType A, int size)
// A is the name of the formal parameter used to access the array.
{
    int highest = A[0];
```

continues

```
    for (int pos = 1; pos < size; pos++)
    {  if (A[pos] > highest)
           highest = A[pos];
    }
    return highest;
}

/*************************************************************
 *                     findLowest                            *
 * This function receives an array of integers and its size. *
 * It finds and returns the lowest value in the array.       *
 *************************************************************/

int findLowest (const GradeType A, int size)
// A is the name of the formal parameter used to access the array.
{
   // Fill in the code for this function.

}
```

Exercise 1: Complete this program as directed. Then run the program with the following data: 90 45 73 21 62 –99 and record the output here:

____

____

____

Exercise 2: Modify your program from Exercise 1 so that it reads the information from the `gradfile.txt` file, reading until the end of file is encountered, instead of inputting it from the keyboard until a –99 is encountered. You will need to first retrieve this file from the Set 8 folder and place it in the same folder as your C++ source code. If you do not remember how to use files, see Lab 3.5 for a review of basic file use. Examples on how to read from a file until the end of file is encountered are shown in the prelab reading for Lab 8, as well as in Section 5.6 of Chapter 5 of your textbook. Run the program. The output should be the same as what you observed for Exercise 1.

LAB 8.2 Working with Two-Dimensional Arrays

Look at the following table containing prices of certain items:

1.45	2.56	12.98
37.86	102.34	67.89

These numbers can be read into a two-dimensional array.

Retrieve `prices.cpp` from the Set 8 folder. The code follows.

```
// This program will read in prices and store them in a two-dimensional array.
// It will then print those prices in a table form.  It also will determine and
// print the highest and lowest price in the array.

// PLACE YOUR NAME HERE.
```

continues

```
#include <iostream>
#include <iomanip>
using namespace std;

const  MAXROWS = 10;
const  MAXCOLS = 10;

typedef float PriceType[MAXROWS][MAXCOLS];        // creates a new data type,
                                                  // a 2D array of floats

// Function prototypes
void getPrices(PriceType, int&, int&);            // gets the prices into the array
void printPrices(PriceType, int, int);            // prints the data as a table

int main()
{
   int rowsUsed;                                  // holds number of rows used
   int colsUsed;                                  // holds number of columns used

   PriceType priceTable;                          // 2D array holding the prices

   getPrices(priceTable, rowsUsed, colsUsed);     // calls getPrices to fill array
   printPrices(priceTable, rowsUsed, colsUsed); // calls printPrices to display array

   return 0;
}

/*******************************************************************
 *                          getPrices                              *
 * This procedure asks the user to input the number of rows and    *
 * columns used.  It then asks the user to input x number of prices *
 * (x = rows * columns).  This data is placed in the array.        *
 *******************************************************************/

void getPrices(PriceType table, int& numOfRows, int& numOfCols)
{
   cout << "Please input the number of rows from 1 to " << MAXROWS << ": ";
   cin  >> numOfRows;

   cout << "Please input the number of columns from 1 to " << MAXCOLS << ": ";
   cin  >> numOfCols;
   cout << endl;

   for (int row = 0; row < numOfRows; row++)
   {
      for (int col = 0; col < numOfCols; col++)
        // Fill in the code to read and store the next value in the array.
   }
}
```

continues

```
/*******************************************************************
 *                          printPrices                            *
 * This procedure prints the table of prices, using the information *
 * stored in the array.                                             *
 *******************************************************************/

void printPrices(PriceType table, int numOfRows, int numOfCols)
{
   cout << fixed << showpoint << setprecision(2);

   for (int row = 0;  row < numOfRows; row++)
   {
      for (int col = 0;  col < numOfCols; col++)
        // Fill in the code to print the table.
   }
}
```

Exercise 1: Fill in the code as directed to complete both functions `getPrices` and `printPrices`. Then run the program with the following data. The output should be formatted as shown in the following example.

```
Please input the number of rows from 1 to 10: 2
Please input the number of columns from 1 to 10: 3

Please input the price of an item with 2 decimal places: 1.45
Please input the price of an item with 2 decimal places: 2.56
Please input the price of an item with 2 decimal places: 12.98
Please input the price of an item with 2 decimal places: 37.86
Please input the price of an item with 2 decimal places: 102.34
Please input the price of an item with 2 decimal places: 67.89

    1.45        2.56       12.98
   37.86      102.34       67.89
```

Exercise 2: Why does `getPrices` have the parameters `numOfRows` and `numOfCols` passed by reference whereas `printPrices` has those parameters passed by value?

____

____

____

Exercise 3: The following code is a value-returning function that returns the highest price in the array. After studying it very carefully, place the function in the above program and have `main()` call it and print out the value it returns. Be sure to include its prototype in the global section.

```
// Function highestPrice returns the highest price in the array.
float highestPrice(PriceType table, int numOfRows, int numOfCols)
{
    float highest;            // local variable to hold the highest price

    highest = table[0][0];  // make first element the highest price
```

continues

```
        for (int row = 0;  row < numOfRows;  row++)
        {  for (int col = 0;  col < numOfCols; col++)
           {
               if ( highest < table[row][col] )
                  highest = table[row][col];
           }
        }
        return highest;
}
```

Exercise 4: Create a similar value-returning function that finds the lowest price in the array. Have `main()` call it and print the value it returns.

Exercise 5: After completing all the exercises above, run the program again with the values from Exercise 1 and record your results.

____

____

____

____

Exercise 6: (Optional) Look at the following table that contains quarterly sales transactions of a small company for three years. Each of the quarterly transactions are integers (number of sales) and the year is also an integer.

YEAR	Quarter1	Quarter2	Quarter3	Quarter4
2000	72	80	60	100
2001	82	90	43	98
2002	64	78	58	84

We could store this data in a two-dimensional array consisting of 3 rows and 5 columns. Even though there are only four quarters we need 5 columns because the first column, column 0, holds the year.

Retrieve `quartsal.cpp` from the Set 8 folder. The code follows.

```
// This program will read in the quarterly sales transactions for a given
// number of years.  It will print the year and transactions in a table format.

// PLACE YOUR NAME HERE.

#include <iostream>
#include <iomanip>
using namespace std;

const MAXYEAR = 10;
const MAXCOL = 5;

typedef int SalesType[MAXYEAR][MAXCOL]; // creates a new data type, a 2D int array

void getSales(SalesType, int&);         // places sales figures into the array
void printSales(SalesType, int);        // prints data as a table
void tableHeading();                    // prints table heading

int main()
{
   int yearsUsed;                       // holds the number of years
   SalesType sales;                     // 2D array holding the sales transactions
```

continues

```
   getSales(sales, yearsUsed);          // calls getSales to put data in array
   tableHeading();                      // calls procedure to print table heading
   printSales(sales, yearsUsed);        // calls printSales to display data table

   return 0;
}

/*************************************************************************
 *                          tableHeading                                 *
 * This procedure prints a report heading for the table display.         *
 *************************************************************************/

void tableHeading()
{  cout << endl;
   cout << setw(30) << "YEARLY QUARTERLY SALES" << endl << endl << endl;
   cout << setw(10) << "YEAR"      << "    "
        << setw(10) << "Quarter 1" << setw(10) << "Quarter 2"
        << setw(10) << "Quarter 3" << setw(10) << "Quarter 4" << endl;
}

/*************************************************************************
 *                            getSales                                   *
 * This procedure asks the user to input the number of years.  For each  *
 * of those years it then asks the user to input the year (e.g. 2002),   *
 * followed by the sales figures for each of the 4 quarters of that year.*
 * That data is placed in a 2-dimensional array.                         *
 *************************************************************************/

void getSales(SalesType table, int& numOfYears)
{
   cout << "Please input the number of years (1 - " << MAXYEAR << ')' << endl;
   cin  >> numOfYears;

   // Fill in the code to read and store the values in the array.

}

/*************************************************************************
 *                           printSales                                  *
 * This procedure prints out all the information in the array.          *
 *************************************************************************/

void printSales(SalesType table, int numOfYears)
{
   // Fill in the code to print the table.

}
```

Complete the code as directed for both getSales and printSales. This is similar to the prices.cpp program in Exercise 1; however, the code will be different. This is a table that contains something other than sales in the first column. Run the program so that the chart shown at the top of Exercise 6 is printed.

LESSON 8B

Lab 8.3 Working with Arrays of Structures

Bring in program array_struct.cpp from the Set 8 folder. The code follows.

```
// This program demonstrates how to use an array of structures
// PLACE YOUR NAME HERE.

// Put the necessary include statement here for cout and cin.
// Put the necessary include statement here to use formatted output.
using namespace std;

// Declare a structure called TaxPayer that has three members:
// taxRate, income, and taxes -- each of type float.

int main()
{
   // Fill in the code to define an array named citizen which holds 5 TaxPayer structures.

   cout.precision(2);
   cout << fixed << showpoint;

   cout << "Please enter the annual income and tax rate for 5 tax payers: "
        << endl << endl << endl;

   for(int count = 0; count < 5; count++)
   {
      cout << "Enter this year's income for tax payer " << (count+1) << ": ";
      // Fill in the code to read in the income to the appropriate place.

      cout << "Enter the tax rate for tax payer # " << (count+1) << ": ";
       // Fill in the code to read in the tax rate to the appropriate place.
       cout << endl;

      // Fill in the code to compute taxes for this citizen and store it in
       // the appropriate place.

   }
   cout << endl;
   cout << "Taxes due for this year: " << endl << endl;
```

continues

```
   // Fill in the code for the first line of a loop that will output the tax information.
   {
      cout << "Tax Payer # " << (index+1) << ": " << "$ "
           << setw(8) << citizen[index].taxes << endl;
   }
   return 0;
}
```

Exercise 1: Complete the program as instructed.

Exercise 2: In the code above we have the following statement:

```
cout << "Tax Payer # " << (index+1) << ": " << "$ "
     << setw(8) << citizen[index].taxes << endl;
```

Why do you think we need `(index+1)` in the first line but `index` in the second?

Sample Run

```
Enter this year's income for tax payer 1: 45000
Enter the tax rate for tax payer # 1: .19

Enter this year's income for tax payer 2: 60000
Enter the tax rate for tax payer # 2: .23

Enter this year's income for tax payer 3: 12000
Enter the tax rate for tax payer # 3: .01

Enter this year's income for tax payer 4: 104000
Enter the tax rate for tax payer # 4: .30

Enter this year's income for tax payer 5: 50000
Enter the tax rate for tax payer # 5: .22

Taxes due for this year:

Tax Payer # 1: $   8550.00
Tax Payer # 2: $  13800.00
Tax Payer # 3: $    120.00
Tax Payer # 4: $  31200.00
Tax Payer # 5: $  11000.00
```

LAB 8.4 Working with Arrays of Class Objects

Retrieve program `inventory.cpp` and `inventory.dat` from the Set 8 folder. The code follows.

```
// This program defines a class called Inventory that has two private data members:
// itemNumber (product ID) and quantity (quantity on hand of that product)
// The program will read these values from a file and store them in an array of
// Inventory class objects. It will then print these values to the screen.
```

continues

```
// Example: Given the following data file:
//      986 8
//      432 24
// This program reads these values into an array of objects and then prints
//      Item number 986 has 8 items in stock.
//      Item number 432 has 24 items in stock.

// PLACE YOUR NAME HERE.

#include <iostream>
#include <iomanip>
#include <fstream>
using namespace std;

const NUM_PRODUCTS = 10;     // This holds the number of products a store sells.

class Inventory
{
public:
  void setId(int item);      // This puts item in the private data member
                             // itemNumber of the object.
  void setAmount(int num);   // This puts num in the private data member
                             // quantity of the object.
  void displayInfo();        // This prints to the screen the value of
                             // itemNumber and quantity of the object.

  Inventory() { itemNumber = quantity = 0;}  // default constructor

private:
   int  itemNumber;          // id number of the product

   int  quantity;            // number of items in stock of that item
};

// implementation section

void Inventory::setId(int item)
{
   itemNumber = item;
}

void Inventory::setAmount(int num)
{
   // Write the line of code to copy num into quantity.
}

void Inventory::displayInfo()
{
   // Write the line of code to print out itemNumber and quantity.
}
```

continues

```
// client section
int main()
{
   ifstream infile;               // input file to read values into array
   infile.open("Inventory.dat");

   // Fill in the code that defines an array of objects of class Inventory
   // called product. The array should be of size NUM_PRODUCTS.

   int pos;                       // loop counter
   int id;                        // holds a product id number
   int total;                     // holds the total quantity for that product

   for (pos = _______ ; pos < ___________; pos++) // Fill in the blanks.
   {
      infile >> id >> total;      // reads in two data items from the file

     product[pos].setId(id);      // calls the setId function of the current product
                                  // to copy id into its private itemNumber variable.

      // Write the function call to copy total into the current product's quantity.
   }

   for (pos = _______ ; pos < ___________; pos++) // Fill in the blanks.
   {
      // Write the function call to displayInfo that causes it to display the
      // values for the current product.
   }

   return 0;
}
```

Exercise 1: Complete the program as instructed. The data file is as follows:

```
986   8
432   24
132   100
123   89
329   50
503   30
783   78
822   32
233   56
322   74
```

The output should be as follows:

```
Item number 986 has   8 items in stock.
Item number 432 has  24 items in stock.
Item number 132 has 100 items in stock.
Item number 123 has  89 items in stock.
Item number 329 has  50 items in stock
Item number 503 has  30 items in stock.
Item number 783 has  78 items in stock.
Item number 822 has  32 items in stock.
Item number 233 has  56 items in stock.
Item number 322 has  74 items in stock.
```

Exercise 2: Why was there no code for the constructor in the implementation section?

Lab 8.5 Student-Generated Code Assignments (Homework)

Option 1: Write the complete age population program given in the Pre-lab Reading Assignment.

Statement of the problem: Given a list of ages (1 to 100) input from the keyboard, the program will tally how many people are in each age group.

Sample Run

```
Please input an age from one to 100. Input -99 to stop.
5
Please input an age from one to 100. Input -99 to stop.
10
Please input an age from one to 100. Input -99 to stop.
100
Please input an age from one to 100. Input -99 to stop.
20
Please input an age from one to 100. Input -99 to stop.
5
Please input an age from one to 100. Input -99 to stop.
8
Please input an age from one to 100. Input -99 to stop.
20
Please input an age from one to 100. Input -99 to stop.
5
Please input an age from one to 100. Input -99 to stop.
9
Please input an age from one to 100. Input -99 to stop.
17
Please input an age from one to 100. Input -99 to stop.
-99
```

```
The number of people   5 years old is 3
The number of people   8 years old is 1
The number of people   9 years old is 1
The number of people  10 years old is 1
The number of people  17 years old is 1
The number of people  20 years old is 2
The number of people 100 years old is 1
```

Option 2: Write a program that will input temperatures for consecutive days. The program will store these values into an array and call a function that will return the average of the temperatures. It will also call a function that will return the highest temperature and a function that will return the lowest temperature. The user will input the number of temperatures to be read. There will be no more than 50 temperatures. Use `typedef` to declare the array type. The average should be displayed to two decimal places.

Sample Run

```
Please input the number of temperatures to be read: 5
Input temperature 1: 68
Input temperature 2: 75
Input temperature 3: 36
Input temperature 4: 91
Input temperature 5: 84

The average temperature is 70.80
The highest temperature is 91.00
The lowest temperature is 36.00
```

Option 3: Write a program that will input letter grades (A, B, C, D, F), the number of which is input by the user (a maximum of 50 grades). The grades will be read into an array. A function will be called five times (once for each letter grade) and will return the total number of grades in that category. The function must be passed 3 parameters: the array, the number of elements in the array, and the letter to be searched for and counted (A,B, C, D or F). The program will print the number of each grade.

Sample Run

```
Please input the number of grades to be read in. (1-50): 6
All grades must be upper case A B C D or F

Input a grade: A
Input a grade: C
Input a grade: A
Input a grade: B
Input a grade: B
Input a grade: D

Number of As = 2
Number of Bs = 2
Number of Cs = 1
Number of Ds = 1
Number of Fs = 0
```

LESSON SET

9 Searching and Sorting Arrays

PURPOSE

1. To introduce the concept of a search routine
2. To introduce the linear and binary searches
3. To introduce the concept of a sorting algorithm
4. To introduce the bubble and selection sorts

PROCEDURE

1. Students should read the Pre-lab Reading Assignment before coming to lab.
2. Students should complete the Pre-lab Writing Assignment before coming to lab.
3. In the lab, students should complete labs assigned to them by the instructor.

Contents	Prerequisites	Approximate completion time	Page number	Check when done
Pre-lab Reading Assignment		30 min.	172	
Pre-lab Writing Assignment	Pre-lab reading	20 min.	182	
LESSON 9A				
Lab 9.1 Working with the Linear Search	Understanding of character arrays	15 min.	183	
Lab 9.2 Working with the Binary Search	Understanding of integer arrays	20 min.	185	
Lab 9.3 Working with Sorts	Understanding of arrays	20 min.	187	
LESSON 9B				
Lab 9.4 Student-Generated Code Assignments	Understanding of arrays	50 min.	191	

PRE-LAB READING ASSIGNMENT

Search Algorithms

A search algorithm is a procedure for locating a specific piece of data from a collection of data. For example, suppose you want to find the phone number for Wilson Electric in the phonebook. You would open the phonebook to the business section under W and then look for all the entries that begin with the word Wilson. There would most likely be many such entries, so you would then look for the one(s) that end with Electric. This is an example of a **search algorithm**. Since each section in the phonebook is alphabetized, this is a particularly easy search. Of course, there are numerous types of "collections of data" that one could search. In this section we will focus on searching strings and arrays. Two algorithms, the linear and binary searches, will be studied. We will see that each algorithm has its advantages and disadvantages.

Linear Search

The easiest array search to understand is probably the **linear search**. This algorithm starts at the beginning of the string or array and then steps through the elements sequentially until either the desired value is found or the last value is reached. For example, suppose we want to find the first occurrence of the letter 'o' in the word "Harpoon." We can visualize the corresponding string of characters as follows:

0	1	2	3	4	5	6	7
H	a	r	p	o	o	n	\0

In C++ we can define and initialize the string in either of the following ways:

```
string word = "Harpoon";          // word is a string object
char word[8] = "Harpoon";         // word is a char array
```

In either case, the individual characters of the string can now be accessed by indexing into the string. For example, `word[0] = 'H'`, `word[1] = 'a'`, and so forth. If we are using a character array, C++ places a `'\0'` in `word[7]` to mark the end of the string. If we are using a string object, C++ may use a different method of marking the end of the string.

To perform a linear search looking for 'o' we first check `word[0]` which is not equal to `'o'`. So we then move to `word[1]` which is also not equal to `'o'`. We continue until we get to `word[4]='o'`. At this point the subscript 4 is returned, indicating the position in the array that contains the first occurrence of the letter `'o'`. What would happen if we searched for `'z'`? We would step through the array until we reached the end and not find any occurrence of `'z'`. In this case the search algorithm should return something that signals the desired item was not found. It is customary to use –1 as this signal since this is not a valid subscript. Here is the complete program that performs the linear search on a string. We have stored the string in a character array, but it could just as easily have been implemented by placing the characters in a string object. In either case, notice that when `searchList` is called it is passed the `word` string to be searched, `SIZE-1` (which is the actual number of characters to be searched through), and `ch`, the character to search for.

Sample Program 9.1

```
// This program performs a linear search on a character array.

#include <iostream>
using namespace std;

// Function prototype
int searchList( char[], int, char);

const int SIZE = 8;

int main()
{
   char word[SIZE] = "Harpoon";
   int found;
   char ch;

   cout << "Enter a letter to search for: " ;
   cin >> ch;

   found = searchList(word, SIZE-1, ch);

   if (found == -1)
      cout << "The letter " <<ch <<" was not found in the list." << endl;
   else
      cout << "The letter " << ch << " is in position " << found + 1
           << " of the list." << endl;

   return 0;
}

/*******************************************************
 *                   searchList                        *
 * This function performs a linear search, looking for *
 * a character that matches desiredValue.              *
 *******************************************************/

int searchList( char list[], int numElems, char desiredValue)
{                                            // The for loop steps through the
   for(int count = 0; count < numElems; count++) // array so one element at a time
   {                                         // can be compared to desiredValue

      if (list[count] == desiredValue)       // If the desired value is found,
        return count;                        // count, the array subscript, is
                                             // returned to indicate its
                                             // location in the array.
   }
                                             // -1 is returned as a signal
   return -1;                                // that desiredValue was not found
}
```

If we use Sample Program 9.1 to search the word `"Harpoon"` for the letter `'o'`, the `searchList` function returns a 4, as mentioned before, since that is the index of the array where `'o'` was found. Notice, however, that the main function then outputs a 5, since we want to output the character's position within the string rather than its storage location in the `word` array. Also notice that `searchList` stopped its search after finding the first occurrence of the letter `'o'`, so it did not find or report that there was another `'o'` in the word `"Harpoon"`. We could create an algorithm to find all occurrences of a particular item in an array, but that would be a different search algorithm. The linear search algorithm always quits after finding the first occurrence of the item it is looking for.

One advantage of the linear search is its simplicity. It is easy to step sequentially through an array and check each element for a designated value. Another advantage is that the elements of the array do not need to be in any order to implement the algorithm. For example, to search either of the integer arrays

First Array	23	45	12	456	99
Second Array	12	29	45	23	456

for the integer 99, the linear search will work. It will return 4 for the first array and –1 for the second. The main disadvantage of the linear search is that it is time consuming for large arrays. If the desired piece of data is not in the array, then the search has to check every element of the array before it knows it is not there and returns –1. Even if the desired piece of data is in the array, there is a good chance that a significant portion of the array will need to be checked to find it. So we need a more efficient search algorithm for large arrays.

Binary Search

A more efficient algorithm for searching an array is the **binary search**, which eliminates half of the array every time it does a check. The drawback is that the data in the array must be ordered to use a binary search. If we are searching an array of integers, then the values stored in the array must be arranged in either ascending order (from smallest to largest) or descending order (from largest to smallest).

Examples: Consider the following three integer arrays:

1)	19	15	13	13	11	6	-1	-3
2)	19	15	16	13	13	11	-1	-3
3)	-3	0	1	1	12	14	18	25

Arrays 1 and 3 could be searched using a binary search since the values in array 1 are arranged largest to smallest and those in array 3 are arranged smallest to largest. However, array 2 could not be searched using a binary search because not all of its elements are in order.

The binary search works as follows. Let us assume for the moment that the elements in the array being searched through are integers arranged in descending order as illustrated here

22	19	17	14	12	10	9	3	1
0	1	2	3	4	5	6	7	8

and that the integer we are searching for, stored in the `desiredValue` variable, is 19. We first find the middle element of the array, making sure the algorithm that does this can handle arrays with both odd and even numbers of elements. The middle element in this case is the one in array position 4. If the value of the element at the middle position (in this case 12) equals `desiredValue`, then we are done. However, it does not. This means that `desiredValue` must be either less than or greater than the middle value. Since `desiredValue` (19) is greater than the middle value (12) and the array is in descending order, we know we must look to the left of the middle to find our value. So we can now ignore the right half of the array and restrict the search to those array locations to the left of the middle. If `desiredValue` had been less than the middle value we would have known to ignore the left half of the array and restrict the search to those array locations to the right of the middle. In either case there are now only half as many locations to search through.

The process is repeated using just the "active" part of the array, the part we are continuing to look in. In our previous example, the active part of the array is now the array locations 0 through 3. We find the middle element of these, which is computed to be element 1. Any time there are an even number of elements the algorithm calculates the middle element as the first of the middle pair. The value in element 1, 19, is thus compared to `desiredValue`. Since they match, the desired value has been found and binary search will return 1, the array subscript indicating where the item is found. If it had not been found yet, the search procedure would continue, halving the size of the active part of the array each time, either until the desired item was found or until there were no more items to search through, meaning that the desired value is not in the array.

The following program implements the steps described above, performing a binary search on an array of integers ordered from largest to smallest. Notice that once an item has been found, and its array position returned to `main` to be stored in the variable `found`, `main` prints out `found + 1`, rather than `found`. This is because we want to output the item's relative position within the array rather than its actual storage location. If we want to print out its actual storage location, the program could be modified to print out `found`.

Sample Program 9.2

```
// This program performs a binary search on an ordered integer array.
#include <iostream>
using namespace std;

// Function prototype
int binarySearch(int [], int, int);

const int SIZE = 16;
```

continues

```
int main()
{
   int found, value;
   int array[] = {34,19,19,18,17,13,12,12,12,11,9,5,3,2,2,0}; // array to be
                                                               // searched
   cout << "Enter an integer to search for: ";
   cin  >> value;

   found = binarySearch(array, SIZE, value); // call to the binarySearch function
                                             // to search in array for value.
                                             // found will be set to the index
                                             // returned by the function.

   if (found == -1)                          // signal that item was not found
      cout << "The value " << value << " is not in the list." << endl;
   else
   {
      cout << "The value " << value << " is in position number "
           << found + 1 << " of the list." << endl;
   }
   return 0;
}

/*******************************************************************
 *                          binarySearch                           *
 * This function uses the binary search algorithm to search through an *
 * array, looking for a desired value.  If it is found, its array     *
 * position is returned.  If it is not found, -1 is returned.          *
 *******************************************************************/

int binarySearch(int array[], int numElems, int desiredValue)
{
   int first = 0;                    // index of the first element in the
                                     // part of the array still being searched,
                                     // initially 0

   int last = numElems - 1;          // index of the last element in the
                                     // part of the array still being searched,
                                     // initially numElems - 1

   int middle;                       // index of the middle element in the
                                     // part of the array still being searched,

   while (first <= last)             // If this ever becomes false it will mean
   {                                 // there are no more array elements to be
                                     // searched through and the desired value
                                     // was not found.

      middle = (first + last) / 2;   // middle is set to the index
                                     // of the middle array element.
```

continues

```
      if (array[middle] == desiredValue)      // If the value stored in the middle
                                              // element = desiredValue we are done
         return middle;                       // and the function returns the array
                                              // position where it was found.

      else if (array[middle] < desiredValue) // If the value stored in the middle
                                              // element < desiredValue we need to
         last = middle - 1;                   // look to the "left" of middle,
                                              // i.e. in array locations between
                                              // first and middle-1.

      else                                    // else the value in the middle
                                              // element must be > desiredValue so
         first = middle + 1;                  // we need to look to the "right" of
                                              // middle, i.e. in array locations
   }                                          // between middle+1 and last.

   return -1;                                 // desiredValue is not in the array.
}
```

If you run this program and search for 2, the output indicates that 2 is in position 14 of the list. Since 2 is in both positions 14 and 15, we see that the binary search found the first occurrence of 2 in this particular data set. However, in Lab 9.2 you will see that there are other possibilities for which occurrence of a duplicated value is found.

Sorting Algorithms

We have just seen how to search an array for a specific piece of data, However, what if we do not like the order in which the data is stored in the array? For example, if a collection of numerical values is not in order, we might wish to put it in order so we can use a binary search to find a particular value. Or, if we have a list of names, we may want them put in alphabetical order. To order data stored in an array, one uses a **sorting algorithm**. In this section we will consider two such algorithms, the bubble sort and the selection sort.

Bubble Sort

The **bubble sort** is a simple algorithm used to arrange data in either ascending (lowest to highest) or descending (highest to lowest) order. To see how this sort works, let us arrange the array below in ascending order.

9	2	0	11	5
`Element 0`	`Element 1`	`Element 2`	`Element 3`	`Element 4`

The bubble sort begins by comparing the first two array elements. If `Element 0 > Element 1`, which is true in this case, then these two pieces of data are exchanged. The array is now the following:

2	9	0	11	5
`Element 0`	`Element 1`	`Element 2`	`Element 3`	`Element 4`

Next Elements 1 and 2 are compared. Since `Element 1 > Element 2`, another exchange occurs:

2	0	9	11	5
Element 0	Element 1	Element 2	Element 3	Element 4

Now Elements 2 and 3 are compared. Since 9 < 11, there is no exchange at this step. Next Elements 3 and 4 are compared and exchanged:

2	0	9	5	11
Element 0	Element 1	Element 2	Element 3	Element 4

At this point we are at the end of the array. Note that the largest value is now in the last position of the array. We have completed one **pass** of the sort. Now we go back to the beginning of the array and repeat the entire process over again. Elements 0 and 1 are compared. Since 2 > 0, an exchange occurs:

0	2	9	5	11
Element 0	Element 1	Element 2	Element 3	Element 4

Next Elements 1 and 2 are compared. Since 2 < 9, no swap occurs. However, when we compare Elements 2 and 3 we find that 9 > 5 and so they are exchanged. Since Element 4 contains the largest value (from the previous pass), we do not need to make any more comparisons in this pass. The final result is:

0	2	5	9	11
Element 0	Element 1	Element 2	Element 3	Element 4

The data is now arranged in ascending order though the algorithm requires one more pass, during which no exchanges will take place, before the algorithm realizes the data is sorted and terminates. Note that the smaller values seem to rise "like bubbles" to the "top," or beginning positions, of the array as the sort progresses.

Also note how the first pass through the array positioned the largest value at the end of the array. This is always the case when bubble sort is used to sort a set of values in ascending order. Likewise, the second pass will position the second to largest value in the second position from the end of the array. The pattern continues with one more value being placed in order on each pass until the array is fully sorted. Subsequent passes have one less array element to check than their immediate predecessor. We know the array is fully sorted when no swaps took place during the preceding pass. Using a bubble sort it takes, at most, $n - 1$ passes to sort n pieces of data. Sample Program 9.3, which follows, demonstrates a bubble sort.

Sample Program 9.3

```
// This program uses a bubble sort to arrange an array of integers in
// ascending order.

#include <iostream>
using namespace std;

// Function prototypes
```

continues

```
void bubbleSortArray(int[], int);
void displayArray(int[], int);

const int SIZE = 5;

int main()
{
   int values[SIZE] = {9,2,0,11,5};

   cout << "The values before the bubble sort is performed are:" << endl;
   displayArray(values,SIZE);

   bubbleSortArray(values,SIZE);

   cout << "The values after the bubble sort is performed are:" << endl;
   displayArray(values,SIZE);

   return 0;
}

/*****************************************************************
 *                        displayArray                           *
 * This function displays the contents of the array.             *
 *****************************************************************/

void displayArray(int array[], int elems) // displays the array
{
   for (int count = 0; count < elems; count++)
      cout << array[count] << "  ";
   cout << endl << endl;
}

/*****************************************************************
 *                     bubbleSortArray                           *
 * This function uses a bubble sort to sort the array contents   *
 * in ascending order.                                           *
 *****************************************************************/

void bubbleSortArray(int array[], int elems)
{  bool swap;
   int  temp;
   int  bottom = elems - 1;       // bottom is the end part of the array where
                                  // the largest values have settled in order.

   do                             // Start a new pass.
   {
      swap = false;               // There have been no swaps yet on this pass.
      for (int count = 0; count < bottom; count++)
      {
         if (array[count] > array[count+1])
```

continues

```
            {
                temp = array[count];            // These three lines swap 2 values.
                array[count] = array[count+1];
                array[count+1] = temp;
                swap = true;                    // Let swap indicate a swap occurred.
            }
        }                                       // bottom is decremented by 1 since
        bottom--;                               // each pass through the array puts
                                                // one more value in order.  Only
                                                // array locations at and "above"
                                                // bottom still need to be sorted.

    } while(swap == true);                      // The loop repeats until no swaps
}                                               // occur on a pass through the array.
```

Although the bubble sort algorithm is fairly simple, it is inefficient for large arrays since each pass places only one data value in order and a pass often requires many swaps.

Selection Sort

A generally more efficient algorithm for large arrays is the **selection sort**. As before, let us assume that we want to arrange numerical data in ascending order. The idea of the selection sort algorithm is to first locate the smallest value in the array and move that value to the beginning of the array (i.e., Element 0). Then the next smallest element is located and put in the second position (i.e., Element 1). This process continues until all the data is ordered. Even though only one value is placed in its correct position during each pass of the sort, an advantage of the selection sort is that only one swap occurs during each pass. Thus, for n data elements only $n - 1$ moves are required. The disadvantage is that to sort n elements, $n(n-1)/2$ comparisons are always required. To see how this sort works, let us consider the array we arranged using the bubble sort:

9	2	0	11	5
`Element 0`	`Element 1`	`Element 2`	`Element 3`	`Element 4`

In pass one, the smallest value is located. It is 0, so the contents of `Element 0` and `Element 2` are swapped:

0	2	9	11	5
`Element 0`	`Element 1`	`Element 2`	`Element 3`	`Element 4`

Next we look for the second smallest value. We do not need to check `Element 0` again since we know it already contains the smallest data value. So pass two starts by looking at `Element 1`. Since the second smallest value, 2, is already in `Element 1`, no data values are swapped on this pass. Pass three starts by looking at `Element 2`, and compares it to the remaining elements. Since `Element 4` holds the smallest of the remaining values, the contents of `Element 2` and `Element 4` are swapped:

0	2	5	11	9
`Element 0`	`Element 1`	`Element 2`	`Element 3`	`Element 4`

Finally, in pass four, the contents of `Element 3` and `Element 4` are compared. Since 11 > 9, the contents are swapped, leaving the array ordered as desired:

0	2	5	9	11
Element 0	Element 1	Element 2	Element 3	Element 4

Sample Program 9.4, which follows, uses a selection sort.

Sample Program 9.4

```
// This program uses selection sort to arrange an array of integers in
// ascending order.

#include <iostream>
using namespace std;

// Function prototypes
void selectionSortArray(int [], int);
void displayArray(int[], int);

const int SIZE = 5;

int main()
{
   int values[SIZE] = {9,2,0,11,5};

   cout << "The values before the selection sort is performed are:" << endl;
   displayArray(values,SIZE);

   selectionSortArray(values,SIZE);
   cout << "The values after the selection sort is performed are:" << endl;
   displayArray(values,SIZE);

   return 0;
}

/*****************************************************************
 *                      displayArray                             *
 * This function displays the contents of the array.             *
 *****************************************************************/

void displayArray(int array[], int elems) // displays array
{
   for (int count = 0; count < elems; count++)
      cout << array[count] << "  ";
   cout << endl;
}

/*****************************************************************
 *                  selectionSortArray                           *
 * This function uses selection sort to sort the array contents *
 * in ascending order.                                           *
 *****************************************************************/

void selectionSortArray(int array[], int elems)
{
   int seek;                     // array position currently being put in order
   int minCount;                 // array location of smallest value found
   int minValue;                 // holds the smallest value found
```

continues

```
    for (seek=0; seek < (elems-1); seek++) // outer loop performs the swap
    {                                      // and then increments seek
      minCount = seek;
      minValue = array[seek];
      for(int index = seek + 1; index < elems; index++)
      {
        if(array[index] < minValue)        // inner loop searches through array
        {                                  // starting at array[seek] searching
                                           // for the smallest value. When the
          minValue = array[index];         // value is found, the value is
                                           // stored in minValue and the
          minCount = index;                // subscript is stored in minCount.
        }
      }
                                           // exchange value of element currently
      array[minCount] = array[seek];       // needing smallest value found in the
      array[seek] = minValue;              // pass (indicated by seek) with the
                                           // smallest value found (located in
    }                                      // minValue)
}
```

PRE-LAB WRITING ASSIGNMENT

Fill-in-the-Blank Questions

1. The binary search is ______________ (simpler / more complex) than the linear search.
2. The binary search is ______________ (faster / slower) than the linear search.
3. In order to use a ______________ (linear / binary) search, the data must be in order.
4. After 3 passes of a binary search, assuming the desired item has not yet been found, only about ____________ (1/2   1/8   1/10) of the array still needs to be searched.
5. To put numbers in order from largest to smallest one would perform a(n) ____________ (ascending / descending) sort.
6. The bubble sort and the selection sort each place only ________ element(s) in order on each pass.
7. The bubble sort normally moves __________ (one / a few / many) element(s) during each pass.
8. The selection sort always moves __________ (one / a few / many) element(s) during each pass.
9. If the bubble sort was used to sort the following array from smallest to largest, show what the contents of the array would look like after pass 1, 2, and 3 have been completed. Remember that the array may not yet be fully sorted after just 3 passes.

	Element 0	Element 1	Element 2	Element 3	Element 4
Starting Array:	19	2	65	0	-7
After Pass 1:					
After Pass 2:					
After Pass 3:					

10. If the selection sort was used to sort the following array from smallest to largest, show what the contents of the array would look like after pass 1, 2, and 3 have been completed. Remember that the array may not yet be fully sorted after just 3 passes.

	Element 0	Element 1	Element 2	Element 3	Element 4
Starting Array:	19	2	65	0	-7
After Pass 1:					
After Pass 2:					
After Pass 3:					

LESSON 9A

LAB 9.1 Working with the Linear Search

Bring in program `linear_search.cpp` from the Set 9 folder. This is Sample Program 9.1 from the Pre-lab Reading Assignment. The code follows.

```
// This program performs a linear search on a character array.
// PLACE YOUR NAME HERE.

#include <iostream>
using namespace std;

// Function prototype
int searchList( char[], int, char);

const int SIZE = 8;
```

continues

```
int main()
{
   char word[SIZE] = "Harpoon";
   int found;
   char ch;

   cout << "Enter a letter to search for: " ;
   cin >> ch;

   found = searchList(word, SIZE-1, ch);

   if (found == -1)
      cout << "The letter " <<ch <<" was not found in the list." << endl;
   else
      cout << "The letter " << ch << " is in position " << found + 1
           << " of the list." << endl;

   return 0;
}

/*******************************************************
 *                     searchList                      *
 * This function performs a linear search, looking for *
 * a character that matches desiredValue.              *
 *******************************************************/

int searchList( char list[], int numElems, char desiredValue)
{                                                  // The for loop steps through the
   for(int count = 0; count < numElems; count++)   // array so one element at a time
   {                                               // can be compared to desiredValue

      if (list[count] == desiredValue)             // If the desired value is found,
        return count;                              // count, the array subscript, is
                                                   // returned to indicate its
                                                   // location in the array.
   }
                                                   // -1 is returned as a signal
   return -1;                                      // that desiredValue was not found
}
```

Exercise 1: Modify the program so it will print out the string being searched before the user is asked for a letter.

Exercise 2: Place a bottom test loop in the `main` function of your Exercise 1 program so that the user can continue inputting characters and having them searched for until they choose to quit, as illustrated in the following sample run.

Sample Run

```
Search string: Harpoon

Enter a letter to search for: a
The letter a is in position 2 of the list.
```

```
Search again (y/n) ?  y

Enter a letter to search for: w
The letter w was not found in the list.

Search again (y/n) ? n
```

Exercise 3: Revise the program you completed in Exercise 2 so that it searches an array of integers rather than characters. Define and initialize the array as

```
int nums[SIZE] = {3, 6, -19, 5, 5, 0, -2, 99};
```

Be sure to update the program documentation, prompts, output labeling and formatting, and function prototypes and headers, as well as the code to reflect the change. Test your revised program, searching for integers that are in the list and for others not in it. Can it find 99? If not, you have a bug. Search for 5. Which of the two occurrences of 5 did the program find? __________ . Why was that particular occurence the one found?

LAB 9.2 Working with the Binary Search

Bring in program `binary_search.cpp` from the Set 9 folder. This is Sample Program 9.2 from the Pre-lab Reading Assignment. The code follows.

```
// This program performs a binary search on an ordered integer array.
// PLACE YOUR NAME HERE.

#include <iostream>
using namespace std;

// Function prototype
int binarySearch(int [], int, int);

const int SIZE = 16;

int main()
{
   int found, value;
   int array[] = {34,19,19,18,17,13,12,12,12,11,9,5,3,2,2,0}; // array to be
                                                              // searched
   cout << "Enter an integer to search for: ";
   cin  >> value;

   found = binarySearch(array, SIZE, value); // call to the binarySearch function
                                             // to search in array for value.
                                             // found will be set to the index
                                             // returned by the function.
```

continues

```
   if (found == -1)                          // signal that item was not found
      cout << "The value " << value << " is not in the list." << endl;
   else
   {
      cout << "The value " << value << " is in position number "
           << found + 1 << " of the list." << endl;
   }
   return 0;
}

/*******************************************************************
 *                          binarySearch                           *
 * This function uses the binary search algorithm to search through an *
 * array, looking for a desired value.  If it is found, its array      *
 * position is returned.  If it is not found, -1 is returned.          *
 *******************************************************************/

int binarySearch(int array[], int numElems, int desiredValue)
{
   int first = 0;                       // index of the first element in the
                                        // part of the array still being searched,
                                        // initially 0

   int last = numElems - 1;             // index of the last element in the
                                        // part of the array still being searched,
                                        // initially numElems - 1

   int middle;                          // index of the middle element in the
                                        // part of the array still being searched,

   while (first <= last)                // If this ever becomes false it will mean
   {                                    // there are no more array elements to be
                                        // searched through and the desired value
                                        // was not found.

     middle = first + last) / 2;             // middle is set to the index
                                             // of the middle array element.

     if (array[middle] == desiredValue)      // If the value stored in the middle
                                             // element = desiredValue we are done
        return middle;                       // and the function returns the array
                                             // position where it was found.

     else if (array[middle] < desiredValue) // If the value stored in the middle
                                             // element < desiredValue we need to
        last = middle - 1;                   // look to the "left" of middle,
                                             // i.e. in array locations between
                                             // first and middle-1.
```

continues

```
      else                                // else the value in the middle
                                          // element must be > desiredValue so
         first = middle + 1;              // we need to look to the "right" of
                                          // middle, i.e. in array locations
   }                                      // between middle+1 and last.
   return -1;                             // desiredValue is not in the array.

}
```

Exercise 1: Modify the program so it will print out the contents of the array before the user is asked to input a number to search for.

Exercise 2: Place a bottom test loop in the `main` function of your Exercise 1 program, just as you did in Lab 9.1 so that users can continue inputting integers and having them searched for until they choose to quit.

Exercise 3: Modify the program you created in Exercise 2 to search for an integer located in an array that is in ascending order (lowest to highest). Change the array definition and initialization statement to the following.

```
int array[] = {2,3,5,9,11,12,12,12,13,17,18,19,19,34,35,38};
```

Be sure to modify the documentation to be consistent with the revised code.

Exercise 4: The variable `middle` is defined as an integer. The program contains the assignment statement `middle = (first + last) / 2;`

Is the right side of this statement necessarily an integer in computer memory? Explain how the `middle` value is determined if there are an even number of values. Remember that `first`, `last`, and `middle` refer to array positions, not to the values stored in those array positions.

Exercise 5: Use the program you created in Exercise 3 to search in the array for 19 and for 12. Record what the output is in each case.

____

____

____

Note that both 19 and 12 are repeated in the array. Which occurrence of 19 did the search find? _______________ Which occurrence of 12 did the search find? _______________ Can you explain why this happened?

Lab 9.3 Working with Sorts

Bring in either the program `bubble_sort.cpp` or `selection_sort.cpp` from the Set 9 folder. These are Sample Programs 9.3 and 9.4, respectively, from the Pre-lab Reading Assignment. The code for each follows.

`bubble_sort.cpp`

```
// This program uses a bubble sort to arrange an array of integers in
// ascending order.
// PLACE YOUR NAME HERE.

#include <iostream>
using namespace std;
```

continues

```
// Function prototypes

void bubbleSortArray(int [], int);
void displayArray(int[], int);

const int SIZE = 5;

int main()
{
   int values[SIZE] = {9,2,0,11,5};

   cout << "The values before the bubble sort is performed are:" << endl;
   displayArray(values,SIZE);

   bubbleSortArray(values,SIZE);

   cout << "The values after the bubble sort is performed are:" << endl;
   displayArray(values,SIZE);

   return 0;
}

/****************************************************************
 *                       displayArray                           *
 * This function displays the contents of the array.            *
 ****************************************************************/

void displayArray(int array[], int elems) // displays the array
{
   for (int count = 0; count < elems; count++)
      cout << array[count] << "  ";
   cout << endl << endl;
}

/****************************************************************
 *                    bubbleSortArray                           *
 * This function uses a bubble sort to sort the array contents  *
 * in ascending order.                                          *
 ****************************************************************/

void bubbleSortArray(int array[], int elems)
{  bool swap;
   int  temp;
   int  bottom = elems - 1;      // bottom is the end part of the array where
                                 // the largest values have settled in order.
```

continues

```
   do                              // Start a new pass.
   {
      swap = false;                // There have been no swaps yet on this pass.
      for (int count = 0; count < bottom; count++)
      {
         if (array[count] > array[count+1])
         {
            temp = array[count];          // These three lines swap 2 values.
            array[count] = array[count+1];
            array[count+1] = temp;
            swap = true;                  // Let swap indicate a swap occurred.
         }
      }                                   // bottom is decremented by 1 since
      bottom--;                           // each pass through the array puts
                                          // one more value in order.  Only
                                          // array locations at and "above"
                                          // bottom still need to be sorted.

   } while(swap == true);                 // The loop repeats until no swaps
}                                         // occur on a pass through the array.
```

selection_sort.cpp

```
// This program uses selection sort to arrange an array of integers in
// ascending order.
// PLACE YOUR NAME HERE.

#include <iostream>
using namespace std;

// Function prototypes
void selectionSortArray(int [], int);
void displayArray(int[], int);

const int SIZE = 5;

int main()
{
   int values[SIZE] = {9,2,0,11,5};

   cout << "The values before the selection sort is performed are:" <<endl;
   displayArray(values,SIZE);

   selectionSortArray(values,SIZE);
   cout << "The values after the selection sort is performed are:" << endl;
   displayArray(values,SIZE);

   return 0;
}

/*******************************************************************
 *                          displayArray                          *
 * This function displays the contents of the array.             *
 *******************************************************************/
```

continues

```
void displayArray(int array[], int elems) // displays array
{
   for (int count = 0; count < elems; count++)
      cout << array[count] << "  ";
   cout << endl;
}

/*************************************************************
 *                  selectionSortArray                       *
 * This function uses selection sort to sort the array contents *
 * in ascending order.                                        *
 *************************************************************/

void selectionSortArray(int array[], int elems)
{
   int seek;                    // array position currently being put in order
   int minCount;                // array location of smallest value found
   int minValue;                // holds the smallest value found

   for (seek=0; seek < (elems-1); seek++) // outer loop performs the swap
   {                                      // and then increments seek
      minCount = seek;
      minValue = array[seek];
      for(int index = seek + 1; index < elems; index++)
      {
         if(array[index] < minValue)      // inner loop searches through array
         {                                // starting at array[seek] searching
                                          // for the smallest value. When the
            minValue = array[index];      // value is found, the value is
                                          // stored in minValue and the
            minCount = index;             // subscript is stored in minCount.
         }
      }
                                          // exchange value of element currently
      array[minCount] = array[seek];      // needing smallest value found in the
      array[seek] = minValue;             // pass (indicated by seek) with the
                                          // smallest value found (located in
   }                                      // minValue)
}
```

Exercise 1: Re-write the sort program you chose so that it orders integers from largest to smallest rather than smallest to largest.

Exercise 2: Modify your program from Exercise 1 in the following way. It should still print out the original contents of the array before the sort begins. However, after each pass of the sort, it should also print out the pass number and the array contents after that pass. Before running your program, try sorting the array {9, 2, 0, 11, 5} by hand using whichever algorithm you chose. Write down the expected array contents after each pass. Then have your program do the sort. Does the output match what you did by hand?

Exercise 3: No matter which of the two sorts you chose, notice that it took 4 passes to sort the data even though it was completely in order after 3 passes. Why did the "unnecessary" fourth pass occur?

LESSON 9B

LAB 9.4 Student-Generated Code Assignments

Option 1: Working with an array of integers. Write a modular program that includes a sorting procedure (using either bubble sort or selection sort), a search procedure (using binary search), and a procedure to display the contents of the array. The program should do the following things:

Prompt the user to enter the size of an integer array and then to enter the array values one element at a time; sort the data in ascending order and print the final sorted array; allow the user to search for various values in the sorted array, outputting *the array location* at which the item is found, rather than its relative position in the set of values.

Option 2: Working with an array of CustomerRec structures. Write a program that does the same set of things listed in Option 1, but which uses an array of `CustomerRec` structures instead of an array of integers. Each structure should have 3 data members: `int custId;` `char name[10];` and `double balance;` The array should be sorted in ascending order by `custId`.

Option 3: Working with a `CustList` *class that owns and manipulates an array of* `CustomerRec` *structures.* Create a `CustList` class that has 2 private data members: a 100-element array of `CustomerRec` structures (as defined above) and a variable `numElts` which keeps track of how many items are currently stored in the array. Initially, of course, there are none. The class should have a default constructor to initialize all member variables appropriately. In addition, the class should provide the following public member functions:

`addCustomer` (to accept the three values for a new customer and place them into the next free structure in the array). The `CustList` object will keep track of which is the next "free" array location to use for the new record.

`findCustomer` (to search for a particular customer record when called with a `custId` passed to it). This function should print out the desired record, if it is found, or an appropriate message if it is not there. It should *not* report where in the list or in the array it was found since this type of information should be hidden from the user programs. In fact, they do not even need to know that the records are being stored in an array.

`sortCustomers` (to sort the array elements in ascending order by `custId`)

`printCustomerRecs` (to display all the elements).

Write the `CustList` class declaration, the implementation of all the class functions, and a user program that creates a `CustList` object and uses its functions to perform the operations described.

LESSON SET

10 Pointers

PURPOSE

1. To introduce pointer variables
2. To examine the relationship between pointers and arrays
3. To introduce dynamic variables
4. To work with pointers to structures and objects

PROCEDURE

1. Students should read the Pre-lab Reading Assignment before coming to lab.
2. Students should complete the Pre-lab Writing Assignment before coming to lab.
3. In the lab, students should complete labs assigned to them by the instructor.

Contents	Prerequisites	Approximate completion time	Page number	Check when done
Pre-lab Reading Assignment		30 min.	194	
Pre-lab Writing Assignment	Pre-lab reading	10 min.	205	
LESSON 10A				
Lab 10.1 Introduction to Pointer Variables	Basic understanding of pointer variables	15 min.	206	
Lab 10.2 Dynamic Memory	Basic understanding of dynamic memory, `new` and `delete` operators	25 min.	207	
Lab 10.3 Dynamic Arrays	Understanding of the relationship between arrays and pointers	20 min.	208	

continues

LESSON 10B			
Lab 10.4 Pointers to Structures	Understanding of pointers to structures	20 min.	210
Lab 10.5 Pointers to Objects	Understanding of pointers to objects	15 min.	212
Lab 10.6 Student-Generated Code Assignments	Completion of the above labs	homework	213

PRE-LAB READING ASSIGNMENT

Pointer Variables

It is important to make a distinction between a memory location's address and the data stored at that location. A street address like 119 Main St. is a location that is different than a description of what is at that location: the little red house of the Smith family. So far we have been concerned only with the data stored in a variable, rather than with its address (where in main memory the variable is located). In this lesson we will look at addresses of variables and at special variables, called **pointers**, which hold addresses.

You know, of course, that a statement like the following outputs the value stored in the variable `sum`.

```
cout << sum;            // This outputs the value stored in sum.
```

By preceding a variable name with the C++ **address operator (`&`)**, however, we get the address, rather than the value stored there.

```
cout << &sum;           // This outputs the address of the variable sum.
```

On most systems the above address will print as a hexadecimal value. Before this lesson where have you seen the & symbol in C++ programming? It is used in the prototype and the heading of a function for any parameter being passed by reference. We will talk more in the next section about reference parameters and what they have to do with addresses.

To define a variable to be a pointer, which means that it will hold a memory address, we precede it with a different symbol, an asterisk (*). The following statement defines the variable `ptr` to be a pointer to an `int`. This means it will hold the memory address of some integer variable.

```
int *ptr;
```

It is important to understand the distinction between a particular data type and a pointer to something of that data type. `ptr` is *not* an `int`. Instead it will hold the memory address of a location where an `int` value can be found. The following example illustrates this difference.

```
int someInt;            // someInt will hold an integer value.
int *intPtr;            // intPtr will hold an address where an integer
                        // value can be found.
```

By now there may be confusion between the symbols `*` and `&`, so let us clarify their use.

Using the & Symbol

The & symbol is basically used on two occasions.

1. The most frequent use we have seen is between the data type and the variable name of a pass by reference parameter in a function heading/ prototype. This is called a reference variable. The memory address of the argument (parameter) is sent to the function instead of the value at that address. When the parameter is used in the function, the compiler automatically **dereferences** the variable. Dereference means that the location of that reference variable (parameter in this case) is accessed to retrieve or store a value.

   We have looked at the swap function on several occasions. We revisit this routine to show that the & symbol is used in the parameters that need to be swapped. The reason is that these values need to be changed by the function and thus we give the address (location in memory) of those values so that the function can write their new values into them as they are swapped.

Example:

```
void swap(int &first, int &second) // The & indicates that the
{                          // parameters first and second are being
                           // being passed by reference.
   int temp;

   temp = first;           // Since first is a reference variable,
                           // the compiler can retrieve the value
                           // stored there and place it in temp.

   first = second;         // New values can be written directly into
   second = temp;          // the memory locations of first and second.
}
```

2. The & symbol is also used whenever we are interested in the *address* of a variable rather than its *contents.*

Example:

```
cout << total;             // This outputs the value stored in the
                           // variable total.
cout << &total;            // This outputs the address where
                           // total is stored in memory.
```

Using the & symbol to get the "address of" a variable comes in handy when we are assigning values to pointer variables (illustrated later in this lesson).

Using the * Symbol

The * symbol is also basically used on two occasions.

1. It is used to define pointer variables.

Example:

```
                  // ptr is defined to be a pointer
int *ptr;         // variable that will hold the address of a
                  // memory location where an int is stored.
```

2. It is also used whenever we are interested in the contents of the *memory location* pointed to by a *pointer variable,* rather than the address itself.

Example:

```
cout << *ptr;     // Since ptr is a pointer, the * dereferences
                  // the pointer.  The value stored at the
                  // location ptr points to will be printed.
```

When used this way `*` is called the **indirection operator**, or **dereferencing operator**.

Using * and & Together

In many ways `*` and `&` are the opposites of each other. The `*` symbol is used just before a pointer variable so that we may obtain data rather than the address of a variable. The `&` symbol is used on a non-pointer variable (every variable that we have studied prior to this lesson) so that the variable's address, rather than the data stored there, will be used. The following program demonstrates the use of pointers and illustrates how to make a pointer point to a particular variable.

Sample Program 10.1

```
#include <iostream>
using namespace std;

int main()
{
   int one = 10;       // one is a "normal" (non pointer) variable.
   int *ptr1;          // ptr1 is a pointer variable that points to an int.

   ptr1 = &one;        // &one indicates that the address, not the contents,
                       // of one is being assigned to ptr1. Remember that ptr1,
                       // being a pointer variable, can only hold an address.
                       // Since ptr1 now holds the address where the variable
                       // one is stored, we say that ptr1 "points to" one.

   cout << "The value of one is   " << one   << endl << endl;
   cout << "The value of &one is  " << &one  << endl << endl;
   cout << "The value of ptr1 is  " << ptr1  << endl << endl;
   cout << "The value of *ptr1 is " << *ptr1 << endl << endl;

   return 0;
}
```

What do you expect will be printed if the address of variable `one` is the hexadecimal value 006AF0F4? The following will be printed by the program:

Output	Comments
`The value of one is 10`	`one` is an integer variable, holding a 10.
`The value of &one is 006AF0F4`	`&one` is the "address of" variable one.
`The value of ptr1 is 006AF0F4`	`ptr1`, which can only hold an address, was assigned one's address.

```
The value of *ptr1 is 10
```

The * when used this way is the indirection, or dereferencing, operator which means `*ptr1` gives us the value of the variable `ptr1` is pointing at.

Arrays and Pointers

It was mentioned in Lesson Set 8 that when arrays are passed to functions they are passed by pointer. This is because an array name is actually a pointer to the beginning of the array. This makes sense when you think about it. Normal variables can hold just one value and so we can reference that value by just naming the variable. But arrays hold many values. We cannot reference all the array values by just naming the array. Pointers allow us to "get to" all the array elements. The array name is a pointer that holds the address of the first element in the array. When we use an array index it dereferences the pointer and gives us the contents of an array location. Thus if `scores` is an array of 5 integers, as shown here, `scores` is actually a pointer to the first location in the array, and `scores[0]` allows us to access the contents of that first location.

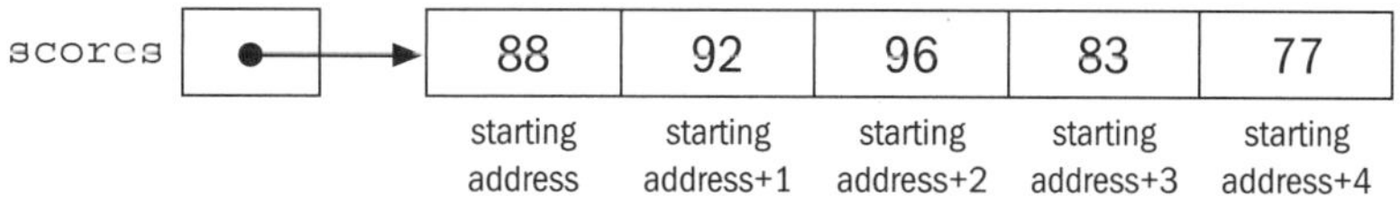

Of course we also could have dereferenced the pointer by using the * operator. The following two statements are equivalent. Both print out the contents of the first `scores` array location, an 88.

```
cout << scores[0];     // Output the value stored in the 1st array element.
cout << *scores;       // Output the value found at the address stored
                       // in scores (i.e., at the address of the 1st array element).
```

What is really going on behind the scenes when we use array indices is **pointer arithmetic**. We can access the second array location with `scores[1]`, the third location with `scores[2]`, and so on, because the indices allow us to move through memory to other addresses relative to the beginning address of the array. The +1 in the diagram means to move one array element forward from the starting address of the array. The +2 means to move two elements forward, and so forth. How far this is depends on how much memory was allocated for each element, and that depends of course on how the array was defined. Since `scores` was defined as an array of integers, if an integer on this particular machine is allocated 4 bytes, then +1 means to move forward 4 bytes from the starting address of the array, +2 means to move forward 8 bytes, etc. We don't really have to worry about any of this if we don't want to since the compiler will keep track of how far forward to move to find a desired element as long as we use array indices. So, for example, the following two statements are equivalent.

```
cout << scores[2];
cout << *(scores+2);
```

Both indicate it is the value located two elements forward from the starting address of the array, in this case 96, that should be printed. While many would agree it is easier to use the first of these two methods to access array elements, computer scientists need to also understand how to access memory through pointers. The following program illustrates how to use pointer arithmetic, rather than indexing, to access the elements of an array.

Sample Program 10.2

```
// This program illustrates how to use pointer arithmetic to access elements of
// an array.
#include <iostream>
using namespace std;

int main()
{
  int scores[] =                        // This defines and initializes an int
            {88, 92, 96, 83, 77};       // array.  Since scores is an array name,
                                        // it is really a pointer that holds
                                        // the starting address of the array.

  cout << "The first score is "         // The * before scores dereferences it
       << *scores << endl;              // so that the contents of array location 0,
                                        // 88, is printed instead of its address.

  cout << "The second score is "        // The same is done for array locations
       << *(scores + 1) << endl;        // 1 through 4. In each case, pointer
  cout << "The third score is "         // arithmetic gives us the address of the
       << *(scores + 2) << endl;        // next array element.  Then the indirection
  cout << "The fourth score is "        // operator * gives us the value of
       << *(scores + 3)<< endl;         // what is stored at that address.
  cout << "The fifth score is "
       << *(scores + 4) << endl;

   return 0;
}
```

What is printed by the program?

```
The first score is 88
The second score is 92
The third score is 96
The fourth score is 83
The fifth score is 77
```

Dynamic Variables

Another important use of pointers is that they allow programmers to use **dynamic variables**, which can be created and destroyed as needed within a program. We have studied scope rules, which define where a variable is active. Related to this is the concept of **lifetime**, the time during which a variable exists. The lifetime of dynamic variables is controlled by the program through explicit commands to allocate (i.e., create) and deallocate (i.e., destroy) them. In C++ the commands to do this are `new` and `delete`. With the other variables we have used in this course so far, the compiler keeps track of where in memory they are located. Therefore we can access their contents by just naming them. However, when a dynamic variable is created, neither we nor the compiler has any idea at which memory address it will be located. This is where pointers come in. When the `new` command is used to allocate memory for a dynamic variable, the system returns its address and we store it in a pointer variable. Through the pointer variable we can then access the memory.

Example:

```
int *one;                // one and two are defined to be pointer
int *two;                // variables that point to ints.

int result;              // int variable that will hold the sum of two values.

one = new int;           // These statements each dynamically allocate
two = new int;           // enough memory to hold an int and assign their
                         // addresses to pointer variables one and two
                         // respectively.

*one = 10;               // These statements assign the value 10 to the
*two = 20;               // memory location pointed to by one and 20
                         // to the memory location pointed to by two.

result = *one + *two;    // We are adding the contents of the memory
                         // locations pointed to by one and two.

cout << "result = " << result << endl;

delete one;              // These statements deallocate the dynamic
delete two;              // variables. Their memory is freed and they
                         // cease to exist.
```

Dynamic Arrays

Dynamic variables have many uses. One of these involves allocating an appropriate amount of memory to hold an array. Without dynamic allocation, the size of an array has to be given at the time of its definition, either explicitly or by providing an initialization list of elements (as shown in Sample Program 10.2) so the compiler will know how much memory must be allocated for the array. Thus the programmer must know, or estimate, the maximum number of elements that will be used by the array. This size is static and cannot change during the program execution. As a consequence, if the array is defined to be larger than needed, memory is wasted. If it is defined to be smaller than needed, there will not be enough memory to hold all the elements. Dynamic variables solve this problem. By using the `new` operator to create the array, we can wait until we know how big it needs to be before creating it.

The following program does just that. It first asks the user to input the number of grades to be processed. It then uses that number to allocate exactly enough memory to hold an array with the needed number of elements for the grades.

Sample Program 10.3

```
//  This program finds the average of a set of grades.
//  It dynamically allocates space for the array holding the grades.

#include <iostream>
#include <iomanip>
using namespace std;

// Function prototypes
void sortIt        (float* grades, int numOfGrades);
void displayGrades(float* grades, int numOfGrades);
```

continues

```
int main()
{
   float *grades;                    // a pointer that will be used to point to
                                     // the beginning of a float array

   float total = 0;                  // total of all grades
   float average;                    // average of all grades
   int numOfGrades;                  // the number of grades to be processed
   int count;                        // loop counter

   cout << fixed << showpoint << setprecision(2);

   cout << "How many grades will be processed " << endl;
   cin  >> numOfGrades;

   while (numOfGrades <= 0)    // validates that a legal value has been entered
   {
       cout << "There must be at least one grade.  Please reenter." << endl;
       cout << "How many grades will be processed " << endl;
       cin  >> numOfGrades;
   }

   grades = new float[numOfGrades];  // allocates memory for an array
                                     // new is the operator that is allocating
                                     // an array of floats with the number of
                                     // elements specified by the user.
                                     // grades is the pointer holding the
                                     // starting address of the array.

   if (grades == NULL)               // NULL is a special identifier predefined
   {                                 // to equal 0.  It indicates a non-valid
     cout                            // address.  If grades is 0 it means that
     <<"Error allocating memory!\n"; // the operating system was unable to
                                     // allocate enough memory for the array.
     return 1;                       // The program should output an appropriate
                                     // error message and return with a value
   }                                 // other than 0 to signal a problem.1
   cout << "Enter the grades below\n";
   for(count = 0; count < numOfGrades; count++) // reads in and stores the grades
   {
      cout << "Grade " << (count+1) << ": ";
      cin  >> grades[count];
      total = total + grades[count];
   }
   average = total / numOfGrades;
   cout << "Average Grade is " << average << "%" << endl;

   sortIt(grades, numOfGrades);            // calls function to sort the grades
   displayGrades(grades, numOfGrades);     // calls function to display the grades
```

continues

[1] Rather than returning NULL when there is a problem allocating memory, newer compilers handle this by having the operating system terminate the program with an error message.

```
   delete [] grades;                      // deallocates all the array memory
   return 0;                              // the [] indicates an array
}

/******************************************************
 *                     sortIt                         *
 * Function to sort a set of grades                   *
 ******************************************************/

void sortIt(float* grades, int numOfGrades)
{
    // Sort code goes here.
}

/******************************************************
 *                displayGrades                       *
 * Function to display the grades                     *
 ******************************************************/

void displayGrades(float* grades, int numOfGrades)
{
    // Code to output all the grades goes here.
}
```

Notice how the dynamic array is passed as a parameter to the `sortIt` and `displayGrades` functions. In each case, the call to the function simply passes the name of the array, along with its size, as an argument. The name of the array, highlighted below, holds the array's starting address.

`sortIt(`**`grades`**`, numOfGrades);`

In the function header, the formal parameter that will receive the array is defined to be a pointer data type so it can receive an address.

`void sortIt(`**`float* grades`**`, int numOfGrades)`

Since the compiler understands that an array name is a pointer, we could also have written the following function header. This is the method that was used in Chapter 8.

`void sortIt(`**`float grades[]`**`, int numOfGrades)`

In this program, dynamic memory was used to save memory. This is a minor consideration for the type of programs done in this course, but a major concern in professional programming environments where large fluctuating amounts of data are used. Pointers have many other practical applications also, especially when used with structures and classes.

Pointers to Structures

Pointer variables may point to structures as well as to primitive data types like `int` and `float`. Suppose we have the following structure declaration.

```
struct custRec
{
   int custId;
   string name;
   double balance;
};
```

We could define a pointer variable, let us call it `custPtr`, to be a pointer to a `custRec` by using the following statement: `custRec *custPtr;`

Note the difference between defining a variable to *be* a `custRec` structure and defining one to *be a pointer to* a `custRec` structure.

```
custRec customer;      // customer is a custRec structure.
custRec *custPtr;      // custPtr is a pointer to a custRec structure.

custPtr = &customer; // custPtr holds the address of customer so we
                       // say custPtr "points to" customer.
```

To access a data member of a structure through a pointer we need to first dereference the pointer and then use the dot operator to select the desired data item, as shown below. Note that parentheses are required to ensure that the dereferencing is done before the data member is accessed.

```
(*custPtr).custId = 999;
```

Because it is so common to use pointers to structures, C++ provides a special operator, the **structure pointer operator (`->`)**, that combines dereferencing the pointer and accessing the desired data member all in one step. The symbol for this operator is a hyphen followed by a greater-than symbol. Together they are meant to look like an arrow. Using this operator, we can rewrite the assignment statement as follows.

```
custPtr -> custId = 999;
```

Pointers to structures have many uses. They are most commonly used to access dynamically allocated structures. They are also sometimes used as a means of passing structures to functions. You recall that because array names are really pointers, when an array is passed to a function it is always passed "by pointer." In C++ any variable can be passed to a function through a pointer. A pointer must be dereferenced in order to access the value it points to. When a parameter is passed to a function *by reference,* an address is passed, but it is automatically dereferenced for the programmer. When a parameter is passed to a function *by address,* an address is passed, but the programmer must explicitly handle the dereferencing. While it is more common in C++ to pass structures to functions by reference, they are sometimes passed by pointer. Sample Program 10.4 illustrates how this is done. The address of the structure is passed to the function either by using a pointer variable holding the address or by using the address operator `&`. In either case, the formal parameter in the function heading is a pointer holding the address of the structure.

Sample Program 10.4

```
// This program illustrates passing a structure to a function by pointer,
// i.e. by passing the address of the structure and having the function
// access it through that address.
```

continues

```
#include <iostream>
using namespace std;

struct custRec
{
   int custId;
   char name[10];
   double balance;
};

// Function prototypes
void getCustInfo (custRec *);     // Each of these functions will receive
void displayCustInfo(custRec *); // a pointer to a custRec.

int main()
{
   custRec customer;          // customer is a custRec structure.
   custRec *custPtr;          // custPtr is a pointer to a custRec structure.
   custPtr = &customer;       // custPtr holds the address of customer so we
                              // say custPtr "points" to customer.

   getCustInfo(&customer);    // same as saying getCustInfo(custPtr);
   displayCustInfo(&customer);

   return 0;
}

/*****************************************************************************
 *                            getCustInfo                                    *
 * This function inputs customer information and places it in customer, which *
 * is a custRec structure. The structure is passed to the function by pointer *
 * (i.e., by sending an address) so that the function can modify its contents.*
 *****************************************************************************/

void getCustInfo(custRec *cust)
{
   cout << "Please enter customer ID: ";
   cin  >> cust->custId;
   cout << "Please input customer first name: ";
   cin  >> cust->name;
   cout << "Please input customer balance: ";
   cin  >> cust->balance;
}

/*****************************************************************************
 *                          displayCustInfo                                  *
 * This function displays the customer information.  Even though the function *
 * is not modifying the contents of the structure, it is passed by pointer    *
 * (i.e., address), rather than by value, to avoid having to make a copy of   *
 * the entire structure.                                                      *
 *****************************************************************************/
```

continues

```
void displayCustInfo(custRec *cust)
{
  // Code to display the data members of the customer structure would go here.
}
```

Pointers to Class Objects

Pointers can also be defined to point to class objects. If we were using the class `Circles`, introduced in Lesson Set 7.2, then the following statements would define `sphere` to be a `Circles` object and would define `circlePtr` to be a `Circles` pointer initialized to point to `sphere`.

```
Circles sphere;                 // sphere is a Circles object.
Circles *circlePtr = &sphere;   // circlePtr is a pointer to a
                                // Circles object.  It is assigned
                                // the address of sphere. Thus it
                                // "points to" sphere.
```

Data members of objects are accessed exactly like data members of structures. Assume for a moment that the `Circles` class has a member variable named `description` that we are authorized to access. To print `sphere`'s value for this variable we would say:

```
cout << sphere.description;
```

to access the member variable directly or

```
cout << circlePtr->description;
```

to access the variable through the pointer.

To access a member function through a pointer we use the same syntax shown above for accessing a member variable through a pointer except, like all functions, the function name must be followed by parentheses and any needed arguments. The following statement would invoke `sphere`'s `setCenter` function through the pointer.

```
circlePtr->setCenter(8, 5);
```

As with structures, pointers to class objects are most commonly used to access dynamically allocated objects. You will be working with pointers to objects in Lab 10.5.

Review of * and &

The * symbol is used to define pointer variables. In this case it appears in the variable definition statement between the data type and the pointer variable name. It indicates that the variable holds an address, rather than the data stored at that address. Note that spacing does not matter. It may be written any of the following ways.

Example 1: `int* ptr1;`   `int * ptr1;`   `int *ptr1;`

The * symbol is also used as a dereferencing operator. When placed in front of an already defined pointer variable, the data stored at the location the pointer points to will be used and *not* the address.

Example 2: `cout << *ptr1;`

Since ptr1 was defined as a pointer variable in Example 1, if we assume ptr1 has now been assigned an address, the output of Example 2 will be the data stored at that address. The * in this case dereferences the variable ptr1.

The & symbol is used in a procedure or function heading to indicate that a parameter is being passed by reference. It is placed between the data type and the parameter name of each parameter that is passed by reference.

The & symbol is also used before a non-pointer variable to indicate that the address, not the contents, of the variable is to be used.

Example 3:

```
int *ptr1;
int one = 10;                   // The value of variable one is 10.

ptr1 = &one;                    // This assigns the address of variable one
                                // to ptr1 because & means "address of."
cout << "The value of &one is  "
     << &one << endl;           // This prints an address.
cout << "The value of *ptr1 is "
     << *ptr1 << endl;          // This prints 10, because ptr1 points to one
                                // and * is the dereferencing operator.
```

PRE-LAB WRITING ASSIGNMENT

Fill-in-the-Blank Questions

1. The _______________ symbol means "address of."
2. When the * symbol appears before a variable name in a variable definition it means that the variable is a(n) _______________.
3. When the * symbol appears before an existing pointer variable it is called the _______________________ operator and means that we are referencing ____.
4. The name of an array, without any brackets, acts as a(n) _______________ to the first element of the array.
5. An operator that allocates a dynamic variable is _______________.
6. An operator that deallocates a dynamic variable is _______________.

Given the following information, fill the blanks with either "an address" or "3.75".

```
float * pointer;
float pay = 3.75;
pointer = &pay;
```

7. `cout << pointer;` will print _______________.
8. `cout << *pointer;` will print _______________.
9. `cout << &pay;` will print _______________.
10. `cout << pay;` will print _______________.

LESSON 10A

LAB 10.1 Introduction to Pointer Variables

Retrieve program `pointers.cpp` from the Set 10 folder. The code follows.

```
// This program demonstrates the use of pointer variables.
// PLACE YOUR NAME HERE.

#include <iostream>
using namespace std;

int main()
{
   int length;
   int width;
   int area;

   int *lengthPtr;        // int pointer which will be set to point to length
   int *widthPtr;         // int pointer which will be set to point to width

   cout << "Please input the length of the rectangle: ";
   cin  >> length;
   cout << "Please input the width of the rectangle: ";
   cin  >> width;

   // Fill in code to make lengthPtr point to length (i.e. hold its address).
   // Fill in code to make widthPtr point to width (i.e. hold its address).

   area = // Fill in code to find the area by using only the pointer variables.
   cout << "The area is " << area << endl;

   if  (// Fill in code to fill in the condition of length > width by using
        // only the pointer variables.)
      cout <<"The length is greater than the width." <<endl;

   else if (// Fill in code to fill in the condition of width > length by
        // using only the pointer variables.)
      cout <<"The width is greater than the length." <<endl;

   else
      cout << "The width and length are the same" << endl;

   return 0;
}
```

Exercise 1: Complete this program as instructed. Note: use only pointer variables when instructed to do so by the comments in bold. This program is to test your knowledge of pointer variables and the & and * symbols.

Exercise 2: Run the program with the following data: 10 15. Record the output here.

____

____

LAB 10.2 Dynamic Memory

Retrieve program `dynamic.cpp` from the Set 10 folder. The code follows.

```
// This program demonstrates the use of dynamic variables.
// PLACE YOUR NAME HERE.

#include <iostream>
using namespace std;

const MAXNAME = 10;

int main()
{
   int pos,result;

   // This defines pointer variables that will be used to hold addresses
   // of dynamically allocated variables.
   int  *one;
   int  *two;
   int  *three;
   char *name;  // This will be used to point to an array of characters.

   // Fill in code to allocate the integer variable one here.
   // Fill in code to allocate the integer variable two here.
   // Fill in code to allocate the integer variable three here.
   // Fill in code to allocate the 10-character array pointed to by name.

   cout << "Enter your last name with exactly 10 characters." << endl;
   cout << "If your name has < 10 characters, repeat the last letter." << endl
        << "Blanks at the end do not count." << endl;
   for (pos = 0; pos < MAXNAME; pos++)
   {
      cin >>   // Fill in code to read a character into the
               // array WITHOUT USING a bracketed subscript.
   }
   cout << "Hi ";
   for (pos = 0; pos < MAXNAME; pos++)
   {
      cout << // Fill in code to print a character from the
              // name array WITHOUT USING a bracketed subscript.
   }

   cout << endl << "Enter three integer numbers separated by blanks. ";

   // Fill in code to input three numbers and store them in the
   // dynamic variables pointed to by pointers one, two, and three.
   // You are working only with pointer variables.

   // echo print
   cout << "The three numbers are " << endl;
```

continues

```
    // Fill in the code to output those numbers.

    result = // Fill in code to calculate the sum of the three numbers.
    cout << "The sum of the three values is " << result << endl;

    // Fill in code to deallocate one, two, three, and name.

    return 0;
}
```

Exercise 1: Complete the program by filling in the code as instructed. This problem requires that you study very carefully the code already written to prepare you to complete the program.

Sample Run

```
Enter your last name with exactly 10 characters.
If your name has < 10 characters,  repeat the last letter.
Blanks at the end do not count.
DeFinooooo
Hi DeFinooooo
Enter three integer numbers separated by blanks.  5  6  17
The three numbers are 5  6  17
The sum of the three values is 28
```

Exercise 2: In inputting and outputting the name, you were asked *not* to use a bracketed subscript. Why is a bracketed subscript not necessary?

____

____

____

Would using `name[pos]` work for inputting and outputting the name? Why or why not?

____

____

____

Try this and see.

LAB 10.3 Dynamic Arrays

Retrieve program `darray.cpp` from the Set 10 folder. The code follows.

```
// This program demonstrates the use of dynamic arrays.
// PLACE YOUR NAME HERE.

#include <iostream>
#include <iomanip>
using namespace std;
```

continues

```
int main()
{
   float  *monthSales;          // a pointer that will be used to point to
                                // an array holding monthly sales
   float  total = 0;            // total of all sales
   float  average;              // average of monthly sales
   int    numOfSales;           // number of sales to be processed
   int    count;                // loop counter

   cout << fixed << showpoint << setprecision(2);

   cout << "How many monthly sales will be processed? ";
   cin >> numOfSales;

   // Fill in the code to allocate memory for the array pointed to by
   // monthSales.

   if ( // Fill in the condition to determine if memory has been allocated.)
        // Or eliminate this whole if construct if your teacher tells you
        // it is not needed for your compiler.
   {
      cout << "Error allocating memory!\n";
      return 1;
   }

   cout << "Enter the sales below\n";

   for (count = 0; count < numOfSales; count++)
   {
     cout << "Sales for Month number  "
          << // Fill in code to output month number.  << ":";

     // Fill in the code to bring sales into an element of the array.
   }

   for ( count = 0; count < numOfSales; count++)
   {
      total = total + monthSales[count];
   }

   average = // Fill in the code to find the average.

   cout << "Average Monthly sale  is $" << average << endl;
   // Fill in the code to deallocate the memory assigned to the array.

   return 0;
}
```

Exercise 1: Complete the program as instructed.

Sample Run

```
How many monthly sales will be processed? 3
Enter the sales below
Sales for Month number 1: 401.25
Sales for Month number 2: 352.89
Sales for Month number 3: 375.05
Average Monthly sale is $376.40
```

LESSON 10B

LAB 10.4 Pointers to Structures

Retrieve program `structs.cpp` from the Set 10 folder. The code follows.

```
// This program illustrates passing a structure to a function by pointer,
// i.e. by passing the function the address of the structure and having the
// function access it through that address.

// PLACE YOUR NAME HERE.

#include <iostream>
#include string
using namespace std;

struct studentRec
{
   int studentId;
   string firstName;
   string lastName;
   double gpa;
};

// Function prototypes
void getStudentInfo (studentRec *);
void displayStudentInfo(studentRec *);

int main()
{
   // Fill in the code to define student to be a studentRec.
   // Fill in the code to define ptr to be a pointer to a studentRec.
   // Fill in the code to make ptr point to student.

   getStudentInfo(// Fill in the actual argument that sends the function
                  // the address of student. Use the & operator.);
   displayStudentInfo(// Fill in the actual argument that sends the function
                      // the address of student. Use the & operator.);
   return 0;
}
```

continues

```
/*******************************************************************
 *                        getStudentInfo                           *
 * This function inputs student data and places it in student, which *
 * is a studentRec structure.  The structure is passed to the function*
 * by pointer, (i.e. by sending an address) so that the function can *
 * modify its contents.                                             *
 *******************************************************************/

void getStudentInfo(studentRec *s)
{
   cout << "Please enter student ID: ";
   // Fill in the code to input the id.
   cout << "Please input student's first name: ";
   // Fill in the code to input the first name.
   cout << "Please input student's last name: ";
   // Fill in the code to input the last name.
   cout << "Please input student's gpa: ";
   // Fill in the code to input the gpa.
}

/*******************************************************************
 *                    displayStudentInfo                           *
 * This function displays the student information. Even though the  *
 * function is not modifying the contents of the structure, the     *
 * structure is passed to it by pointer (i.e. by address), rather than*
 * by value, to avoid having to make a copy of the entire structure. *
 *******************************************************************/

void displayStudentInfo(studentRec *s)
{
  // Fill in the code to display the 4 pieces of student information.
}
```

Exercise 1: Complete the program as instructed.

Sample Run

```
Please enter student ID: 1234
Please input student's first name: Johnny
Please input student's last name: Appleseed
Please input student's gpa: 3.872

Student Information

ID:   1234
Name: Johnny Appleseed
gpa:  3.872
```

Exercise 2: Could you have used `ptr` as the actual argument to the two functions instead of using the & address operator? ____________________

Modify the call to `getStudentInfo()` to do this and rerun the program. See what happens.

LAB 10.5 Pointers to Objects

Retrieve program `dcube.cpp` from the Set 10 folder. The code follows.

```
// This program defines a class Cube and then dynamically allocates and
// manipulates a Cube object.
// PLACE YOUR NAME HERE.

#include <iostream>
using namespace std;

class Cube
{
  public:
     Cube() {side = 1.0;}                     // default constructor
     Cube (float length){side = length;}  // constructor with 1 parameter
     float calcVolume();
     float calcSurfaceArea();

  private:
     float side;                              // length of each side of the cube
};

// Member function implementation

/******************************************************************
 *                          calcVolume                            *
 * This function will calculate and return the cube's volume.     *
 ******************************************************************/

float Cube::calcVolume()
{
   return side * side * side;
}

/******************************************************************
 *                          calcSurfaceArea                       *
 * This function will calculate and return the cube's surface area.*
 ******************************************************************/

float Cube::calcSurfaceArea()
{
   return side * side * 6;
}

// Client file

int main()
{
   float length;

   cout << "Please input the length of each edge of the cube: ";
   cin  >> length;

   Cube box(length);               // This creates the box object.
```

continues

```
    // Replace the above statement with two statements.
    // The first should define box as a pointer to a Cube object.
    // The second should dynamically allocate a Cube object (with side
    // equal to length). box will point to it.

    cout << "The volume of the box is " << box.calcVolume() << endl;
    cout << "The surface area of the box is " << box.calcSurfaceArea() << endl;

    // Modify the above 2 statements so they correctly invoke the box member
    // functions by using the box pointer variable.

    // Fill in the code to deallocate the dynamic object.

    return 0;
}
```

Exercise 1: Before making any changes to the code, run the program, inputting 2 for `length`. The output should look like the following.

Sample Run

```
Please input the length of each edge of the cube: 2
The volume of the box is 8
The surface area of the box is 24
```

Exercise 2: Now make the changes as instructed in the code so the program will match the documentation, which says that the program uses a dynamically allocated object. Rerun the program, again inputting 2 for the length. You should get the same results.

LAB 10.6 Student-Generated Code Assignments (Homework)

Option 1: Write a program that will create a dynamically allocated array of integer test scores whose size has been input by the user. The program should then perform the following tasks: read the scores into the array, sort the array (bubble sort), print out the sorted array, and calculate and print the average score. The program should be modular with each major task being handled by its own function.

Sample Run

```
Please input the number of scores: 5

Please enter a score: 100
Please enter a score: 90
Please enter a score: 95
Please enter a score: 93
Please enter a score: 90

The scores in ascending order are:
90
90
93
95
100

The average score is: 93.6
```

Option 2: Write a program that will create a dynamically allocated array of integer ID numbers whose size has been input by the user. The program will prompt the user to input the ID numbers and will store them in the array. It will then allow the user to input an ID number to be searched for and will report whether or not the given ID is in the array. The program should loop, allowing additional IDs to be entered and searched for, until the user indicates they want to quit. The program should be modular with each major task being handled by its own function.

Sample Run

```
Please input the number of id numbers to be read: 4

Enter an id number: 96
Enter an id number: 37
Enter an id number: 98
Enter an id number: 74

Input an id number to be searched for: 67
67 is not in the array.

Search for another id (y/n)? y

Input an id number to be searched for: 98
98 is in the array.

Search for another id (y/n)? n
```

Option 3: Write a program that will create a dynamically allocated array of monthly sales figures whose size has been input by the user. After prompting the user to input the sales figures, it will find the highest monthly sales amount and the lowest monthly sales amount. The program should be modular with each major task being handled by its own function.

Sample Run

```
Please input the number of monthly sales figures to be input: 4

Please input the sales for month 1: 1290.89
Please input the sales for month 2: 905.95
Please input the sales for month 3: 1567.98
Please input the sales for month 4: 994.83

The highest monthly sales amount was $ 1567.98
The lowest monthly sales amount was $ 905.95
```

LESSON SET

11 More About Classes

PURPOSE

1. To introduce static member variables and functions
2. To introduce and work with friend functions
3. To introduce and use memberwise assignment and copy constructors
4. To introduce and work with overloaded operators

PROCEDURE

1. Students should read the Pre-lab Reading Assignment before coming to lab.
2. Students should complete the Pre-lab Writing Assignment before coming to lab.
3. In the lab, students should complete labs assigned to them by the instructor.

Contents	Prerequisites	Approximate completion time	Page number	Check when done
Pre-lab Reading Assignment		45 min.	216	
Pre-lab Writing Assignment	Pre-lab reading	10 min.	234	
LESSON 11A				
Lab 11.1 Working with Static Member Variables and Member Functions	Basic understanding of static member variables and member functions	30 min.	234	
Lab 11.2 Using Friend Functions	Basic understanding of friend functions	20 min.	237	
LESSON 11B				
Lab 11.3 Using Copy Constructors	Basic understanding of memberwise assignment and copy constructors	25 min.	239	
Lab 11.4 (Optional) Overloading Operators	Basic understanding of operator overloading	30 min.	241	
Lab 11.5 Inheritance	Basic understanding of inheritance	25 min.	244	
Lab 11.6 Student-Generated Code Assignments	Completion of the above labs	homework	246	

PRE-LAB READING ASSIGNMENT

Static Member Variables

You will recall that each object (instance of a class) has its own copy of the class member variables. Thus two objects of the same class may, and likely do, have different values for a given member variable. For example, two savings accounts may have different account numbers and balances. Consider Sample Program 11.1.

Sample Program 11.1

```
#include <iostream>
using namespace std;

class SavingsAcct
{
   private:
      int acctNum;                         // member variables
      double balance;

   public:
      SavingsAcct();                       // default constructor
      SavingsAcct(int, double);            // constructor
      void newAcctInfo();
      void displayAcctInfo();
      void deposit(double);
      void withdraw(double);
};

// Member Function Implementation Section

SavingsAcct::SavingsAcct()                 // default constructor
{
   acctNum = 0;
   balance = 0;
   newAcctInfo();
}

SavingsAcct::SavingsAcct(int num, double startBal) // constructor
{
   acctNum = num;
   balance = startBal;
   newAcctInfo();
}

void SavingsAcct::newAcctInfo()
{  cout << "New account number: " << acctNum << "   Initial Balance: $"
        << balance << endl;
}

// Implementation of other member functions would be placed here.

// Client code
```

continues

```
int main()
{  SavingsAcct acct1(1001, 500);
   SavingsAcct acct2(1002, 350);

   // Other code

   return 0;
}
```

Running this program would produce the following output.

```
New account number: 1001 Initial Balance: $500
New account number: 1002 Initial Balance: $350
```

There are times, however, when we would like all class objects to share, or have access to, a common copy of a member variable. For example, we might want the program to keep track of the total balance of all accounts. Or, rather than having the initial account number input by the user, we might want to have the program generate an account number, by keeping track of the next available number to be given out. We can do these kinds of things by using **static member variables**.

A static member variable is declared by placing the word `static` in front of it in the class declaration and then placing a separate definition of the variable outside the class. The definition itself does not include the word `static`, but does include the class name and scope resolution operator (`::`), just like class member function implementations do. As with any variable, an initial value can be given to the static member variable at the time of its definition. The variable exists for the entire duration of the program that uses the class and is accessible to all instances of the class.

Sample Program 11.2 modifies Sample Program 11.1 to include two static member variables. Changes to the earlier sample program are noted in bold type.

Sample Program 11.2

```
// This program introduces the use of static member variables.

#include <iostream>
using namespace std;

class SavingsAcct
{
   private:
      int acctNum;                      // member variables
      double balance;
      static int nextNumber;            // static member variables
      static double totalBalances;

   public:
      SavingsAcct();                    // default constructor
      SavingsAcct(double);              // constructor
      void newAcctInfo();
      double getTotalBalances();
      void displayAcctInfo();
      void deposit(double);
      void withdraw(double);
};
```

continues

```
// Static Variable Definitions -- Place these just before the Member Function
// Implementation Section

int    SavingsAcct::nextNumber = 1001;    // first number to be given out
double SavingsAcct::totalBalances = 0;    // start static accumulator at 0

// Member Function Implementation Section

SavingsAcct::SavingsAcct()    // default constructor
{
      acctNum = nextNumber;  // gives out the next available acct number
      nextNumber++;          // increments next available acct number
      balance = 0;           // uses a default value for balance
      newAcctInfo();         // calls function to display info. on the new account
}

SavingsAcct::SavingsAcct(double startBal)  // constructor
{
      acctNum = nextNumber;  // gives out the next available acct number
      nextNumber++;          // increments next available acct number
      balance = startBal;    // sets balance to starting amount passed in
      totalBalances =        // increments totalBalances by new starting balance
         totalBalances + balance;
      newAcctInfo();
}

void SavingsAcct::newAcctInfo()
{   cout << "New account number: " << acctNum << "   Initial Balance: $"
         << balance << endl;
}

double SavingsAcct::getTotalBalances()
{   return totalBalances;
}

// Implementation of other member functions would be placed here.

// Client code

int main()
{
   SavingsAcct acct1(500); // Objects are now created with just
   SavingsAcct acct2(350); // one parameter, starting balance.

   // The next statement invokes acct1's getTotalBalances() member function to
   // return totalBalances.  We could just as easily have invoked it through
   // acct2 since they both have access to this common member variable.

   cout << "Total savings deposits = $" << acct1.getTotalBalances() << endl;

   // Other code

   return 0;
}
```

Static Member Functions

A **static member function** is a special function that is normally used to initialize static member variables or to perform other setup tasks for a class. You will recall that static member variables exist for the entire duration of a program. That means they exist even before any instances of the class are created. Static member functions, likewise, exist separate from individual class objects and can be called even before any instances of the class are created. Because of this, however, they can only access static member variables. Static member variables can either be initialized at the time they are defined, or by static member functions. They should not be initialized by constructors because we only want them to be initialized once, not each time an instance of the class is created. A static member function is declared by placing the word `static` in front of its prototype within the class declaration. If `initGoal` were a static function belonging to a class named `SalesForce`, its prototype within the class declaration might look like the following:

```
static void initGoal(double);     // used to initialize a static
                                  // member variable named salesGoal
                                  // of the SalesForce class
```

The function implementation would be identical to that of any regular member function.

```
void SalesForce::initGoal(double amt)
{   salesGoal = amt;
}
```

There is a difference in the way it would be called, however. Since static member functions exist separate from class objects and can be called before any class objects even exist, they are not called by naming a class object. Instead they are called by preceding the function name with the name of the class and the scope resolution operator. The following line of code would call the static function `initGoal` to initialize `salesGoal` to 15000.

```
SalesForce::initGoal(15000);
```

Sample Program 11.3 uses this static function.

Sample Program 11.3

```
// This program introduces the use of static member functions.
// It also illustrates passing an object by reference to a function.

#include <iostream>
using namespace std;

class SalesForce
{
   private:
      static double salesGoal;         // static variable shared by
                                       // all class objects
      int    snum;                     // sales rep. number
      double monthlySales;
```

continues

```
   public:
      static void initGoal(double);    // static function to set salesGoal

      SalesForce(){snum = monthlySales = 0;}  // default constructor
      SalesForce(int, double);         // constructor
      void displayInfo();              // displays an object's member data
      bool metGoal();                  // indicates if sales goal has been met
};

// Static Member Variable Definitions
double SalesForce::salesGoal;

// Member Function Implementation Section

void SalesForce::initGoal(double amt)
{
   salesGoal = amt;
}

SalesForce::SalesForce(int num, double amt)    // constructor
{  snum = num;
   monthlySales = amt;
}

void SalesForce::displayInfo()
{  cout << "Sales Rep Number: " << snum << "  Total sales $" << monthlySales
        << endl;
}

bool SalesForce::metGoal()
{  if(monthlySales >= salesGoal)
      return true;
   else
      return false;
}

// Client Code
// Function prototypes
void salesReport(SalesForce &);

int main()
{
   double goalAmount;

   cout << "Input monthly sales goal: ";
   cin  >> goalAmount;
   SalesForce::initGoal(goalAmount);        // set the sales goal for the class
   SalesForce repOne(101, 13500);           // create 1st sales rep.
   SalesForce repTwo(202, 16800);           // create 2nd sales rep.

   salesReport(repOne);
   salesReport(repTwo);

   return 0;
}
```

continues

```
void salesReport(SalesForce &rep)
{
   rep.displayInfo();
   if (rep.metGoal())
      cout << "Met sales goal\n\n";
   else
      cout << "Did not meet sales goal\n\n";
}
```

Friend Functions

A **friend function** is a function that is not a member of a class, but which has access to the private members of the class. Normally private member variables and member functions are hidden from all parts of a program outside the class. This safeguards member variables as well as shields outside functions from implementation details they do not need to know about. For a function to access a private member variable, it normally must do so through a call to a public member function which can carefully control how the variable is accessed. Friend functions allow us to make an occasional exception to this protocol. They can be stand-alone functions or members of another class. In fact, even an entire class can be declared to be a friend of another class.

Classes declare their friends. That is, in order to have "friend" status, a function must be granted that status by the class whose private members it will be allowed to access. A friend function is declared by placing its prototype, preceded by the key word `friend`, inside the class declaration of the class granting the friend status. Strictly speaking, friend functions are neither private nor public, so they could be placed in either section of the class declaration. However, it is most common to place them in the public section. For example, in Sample Program 11.3, the `SalesForce` class could declare a stand-alone function named `salesReport` to be a friend function by including the following prototype within its class declaration:

```
friend void salesReport(SalesForce &);
```

If instead the `salesReport function` were a member of another class, let us call it `SalesOffice`, it would be declared a friend function with the following declaration:

```
friend void SalesOffice::salesReport(SalesForce &);
```

Either way, this indicates that the `salesReport` is not a member of the `SalesForce` class, but rather an outside function, declared elsewhere, which can access `SalesForce` private members.

Notice that the `salesReport` function must receive as a parameter a reference to an object of the class whose private members it is being allowed to access. In the program where the `salesReport` function is defined, this parameter must appear in the prototype and the function heading. However, the keyword `friend` will not appear in either since a function cannot declare itself to be a friend. The `salesReport` function heading would look like the following:

```
void salesReport(SalesForce & salesRep)
```

It would be called as follows, with some SalesForce object passed to it:

```
salesReport(repOne);
```

It could then access either static or regular data members of the object passed to it by using the dot operator, as if it were accessing a data member of a simple structure.

```
cout << salesRep.monthlySales << endl;
cout << salesRep.salesGoal << endl;
```

Sample Program 11.4 modifies Sample Program 11.3 to use a friend function. Changes to the earlier sample program are noted in bold type.

Sample Program 11.4

```
// This program introduces the use of friend functions.

#include <iostream>
using namespace std;

class SalesForce
{
   private:
      static double salesGoal;        // static variable shared by
                                      // all class objects
      int    snum;                    // sales rep. number
      double monthlySales;

   public:
      static void initGoal(double);   // static function to set salesGoal

      SalesForce(){snum = monthlySales = 0;}  // default constructor
      SalesForce(int, double);        // constructor
      void displayInfo();             // displays an object's member data
      bool metGoal();                 // indicates if sales goal has been met

      friend void salesReport(SalesForce &); // declares a friend function
};

// Static Member Variable Definitions
double SalesForce::salesGoal;

// Member Function Implementation Section

void SalesForce::initGoal(double amt)
{
   salesGoal = amt;
}

SalesForce::SalesForce(int num, double amt)   // constructor
{  snum = num;
   monthlySales = amt;
}
```

continues

```
void SalesForce::displayInfo()
{  cout << "Sales Rep Number: " << snum << "  Total sales $" << monthlySales
        << endl;
}

bool SalesForce::metGoal()
{  if(monthlySales >= salesGoal)
      return true;
   else
      return false;
}

// Client Code

// Function prototypes
void salesReport(SalesForce &);

int main()
{
   double goalAmount;

   cout << "Input monthly sales goal: ";
   cin  >> goalAmount;
   SalesForce::initGoal(goalAmount);       // set the sales goal for the class
   SalesForce repOne(101, 13500);          // create 1st sales rep.
   SalesForce repTwo(202, 16800);          // create 2nd sales rep.

   salesReport(repOne);
   salesReport(repTwo);

   return 0;
}

/**************************************************************************
 *                            salesReport                                 *
 * Revised salesReport function to produces a sales report.  Now that the *
 * SalesForce class has declared this a friend function, it can access    *
 * private members of SalesForce class objects directly, by using the     *
 * dot operator, instead of through calls to public member functions.     *
 **************************************************************************/

void salesReport(SalesForce & rep)
{
   cout << "Report for Sales Rep. number: " << rep.snum << endl;
   cout << "Monthly sales: $" << rep.monthlySales
        << "   Goal: $" << rep.salesGoal << endl;

   if (rep.metGoal())
      cout << "Met sales goal\n\n";
   else
      cout << "Did not meet sales goal\n\n";
}
```

The risk in using friend functions is that once given friend status they can access any private data of the class object they are passed, including data they do not need in order to complete their tasks. Nothing is really safeguarded from a friend function. For this reason, most programmers greatly limit their use of these functions.

Memberwise Assignment

You know that one variable can be assigned the value of another by using the assignment operator, as in the assignment statement `side1 = side2;` When working with objects, this operator can be used to assign one object the values of all the member variables of another object. For example, if `item1` and `item2` are two objects of class `Inventory`, the following statement would assign all of `item1`'s member variables the values of their counterparts in object `item2`.

```
item1 = item2;          // This copies the data values of one
                        // existing Inventory object to another.
```

This data copy from one object to another is called **memberwise assignment**. Memberwise assignment can also be used to initialize an object when it is created. The following statement would create a new `Inventory` object, `item3`, and initialize its member variables to the values of `item2`'s corresponding member variables.

```
Inventory item3 = item2;     // This creates a new inventory object
                             // and initializes its data values with
                             // another Inventory object's data.
```

Problems with Memberwise Assignment

Memberwise assignment provides a convenient way to set one object's data equal to another's or to initialize an object when it is created. In fact, if we pass an object to a function using pass by value, this is what automatically occurs. A new local object is created and it is initialized, using a memberwise copy, with the data of the object that was passed to the function. However, in certain circumstances, as when a pointer to dynamic memory is involved, memberwise copy causes a problem. This is because we want the new object to have its own memory space for its variable and just be initialized with the data being copied. Instead, memberwise copy would give the new object the address of the old object's data member. The following diagram illustrates this. Assume `item1` and `item2` are two objects of a class with a data member called `description`. `description` is a pointer to dynamic memory where the description information is stored.

The statement

```
item1 = item2;
```

would have the following result.[1]

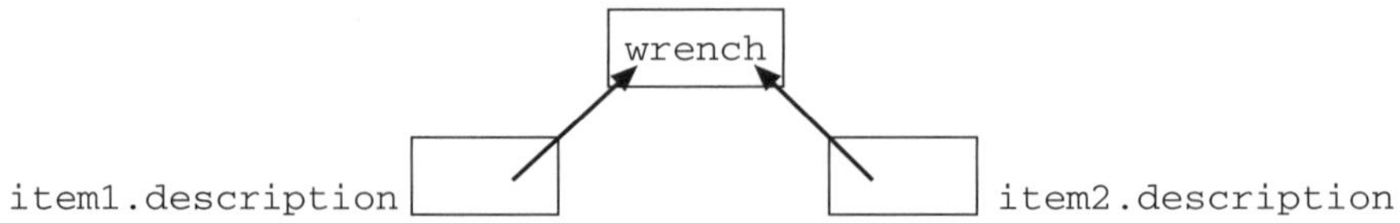

This is not what we want to happen. Any change `item1` or `item2` now makes to its `description` variable would change the `description` of the other object as well.

[1] Some compilers may cause a program to abort when attempting to access memory pointed to by two different variables.

Sample Program 11.5, which uses a dynamic character array to store the description string, will further illustrate this problem. Before looking at the program, however, let us examine two string functions it uses: `strlen()` and `strcpy()`. The first returns the length of a C-string, that is, the number of characters it currently holds, not counting the '\0' string terminator character. The second places a copy of one C-string in another.

Example:

```
char string1[10] = "Merry";
char string2[10] = "Christmas";

cout << string1 << " " << string2 << endl;
cout << "string1 has length " << strlen(string1)
     << " and string2 has length " <<strlen(string2) << endl;

strcpy(string2, string1);    //string2 receives a copy of string1
cout << string1 << " " << string2 << endl;
```

Output

```
Merry Christmas
string1 has length 5 and string2 has length 9
Merry Merry
```

More on string functions will be covered in Lesson Set 12.

Sample Program 11.5

```
// This program illustrates problems with memberwise assignment
// when using pointers.
#include <iostream>
#include <iomanip>
#include <cstring>
using namespace std;

class Inventory  // class declaration with member functions defined in-line
{  private:
      char   *description;    // pointer to the start of an array of
                              // characters that will be dynamically allocated
      double price;
   public:
      Inventory()             // default constructor
      {  price = 0;
         description = new char[6];
          strcpy(description, "empty");
      }

      Inventory(char* d, double p)              // constructor
      {  description = new char[strlen(d) + 1]; // gets the right amount
                                 // of memory to hold the string passed in.
         strcpy(description, d);
         price = p;
      }
```

continues

```
       ~Inventory()                      // destructor
       {  delete[] description;          // used to free the memory previously
       }                                 // allocated for the dynamic variable

       const char* getDescription()
       {  return description;  }

       double getPrice()
       {  return price;  }

       void setDescription(char* d)      // "Assumes" dynamic description
       {  strcpy(description, d);        // variable has enough memory to hold
       }                                 // the new string.

       void setPrice(double p)
       {   price = p;   }
};

int main()
{
   Inventory item1("hammer", 12.49);
   Inventory item2 = item1;              // Create item2 and initialize
                                         // it with item1's data.

   cout << fixed << setprecision(2) << showpoint;
   cout << "item1: " << item1.getDescription() << "  $"
        << item1.getPrice()  << endl;
   cout << "item2: " << item2.getDescription() << "  $"
        << item2.getPrice()  << endl << endl;

   item1.setDescription("wrench"); // Change item1's description.
                                   // This changes item2's description!
   cout << "item1: " << item1.getDescription() << "  $"
        << item1.getPrice()  << endl;
   cout << "item2: " << item2.getDescription() << "  $"
        << item2.getPrice()  << endl << endl;

   return 0;
}
```

Output

```
item1: hammer $12.49    // item1 was created with this data
item2: hammer $12.49    // item2 was created and set = to item1

item1: wrench $12.49    // item1's description was changed
item2: wrench $12.49    // item2's description changed too!
```

This output illustrates the problem with using memberwise assignment when pointers are involved. Since `item2` was initialized with `item1`'s data, its constructor did not run and so it was never allocated memory to hold its own description. Instead, the address of where `item1`'s description was located was copied into `item2`'s description pointer, causing both objects to point to the *same* memory location. Clearly this is not the result we want. In fact, the problem is considered so severe that some systems report a fatal runtime error when one object attempts to access another object's memory like this.

Copy Constructors

Luckily, the use of a **copy constructor** will solve the above problem in most cases. A copy constructor is a special constructor that is automatically called whenever a new object is created and initialized with another object's data.

A copy constructor looks like a regular constructor except that it must have a reference parameter of the same class type as the object itself. It is through this parameter that it receives the object whose data members are to be copied. The purpose of the copy constructor is to ensure that everything, including pointer values, are transferred to the newly created object in such a way that it has its own copy of everything. Here is a copy constructor for the `Inventory` class:

```
Inventory(Inventory &object)           // copy constructor
{
   description = new char[strlen(object.description) + 1];
   strcpy(description, object.description);
   price = object.price;
}
```

Notice how this constructor works. It allocates enough memory for the new object to hold the description. Then it copies the description from the object being passed in to the space set up to hold the new object's description. Finally the price, which is a simple variable, not a pointer, is copied from the passed in object to the new object. When this copy constructor is added to the class declaration of Sample Program 11.5, it will behave properly.

Operator Overloading

Copy constructors solve the problem of memberwise assignment when an object containing pointers is assigned the data values of another object *at the time of its creation.* However, they don't solve the problem of assigning one object to another at some later time, once the object has already been created. This, you will recall, is because constructors, even copy constructors, only run when an object is first created. To solve this second problem, we can use a technique called **operator overloading**.

Operator overloading allows the programmer to redefine how an existing operator behaves when it is used with a class object. Most C++ operators can be overloaded. To overload an operator in C++ the programmer writes an **operator function**. This is a special public member function that defines how the overloaded operator is to behave. Once this function is included in a class declaration, whenever the operator is used with an object of that class, the operator function is executed to carry out the desired series of operations. To cause the assignment statement to do a correct memberwise copy when one object is "assigned" to another we can *overload the assignment operator* and write an operator function that looks very much like the copy constructor we wrote above.

An operator function is like most other member functions but it has a special name. Its name must be `operator`**x**, where **x** is the symbol for the operator to be overloaded. So, for example we would use

```
operator=        // name of the function to overload the = operator
operator+        // name of the function to overload the + operator
```

and so forth. If the operator being overloaded is a binary operator (i.e., has two operands as = and + do) the operator function must, like a copy constructor, have a reference parameter whose type is the type of the class.

Overloading the Assignment Operator

The following is an operator function to overload the assignment operator for use with objects of the `Inventory` class.

```
void  operator=(const Inventory &right)
{   delete [] description;
    description = new char[strlen(right.description) + 1];
    strcpy(description, right.description);
    price = right.price;
}
```

Note how similar it is to the copy constructor we previously wrote. It does just one thing that the copy constructor did not do. It includes code to delete dynamic memory previously acquired for the description before it allocates new memory. The copy constructor did not have to do this because it only operates when a new object is created that has no previously acquired dynamic memory. Otherwise the two functions are really the same. The copy constructor called its formal parameter `object` whereas the operator function calls its parameter `right`. This is just a difference of choice. We could have called either formal parameter anything we wanted. When overloading a binary operator, however, it is customary to call the parameter `right` since we think of the function as operating on the left-hand object and accepting information about the right-hand object through the parameter. In the statement

```
item3 = item1;
```

for example, you can think of `item3` as the left operand and `item1` as the right operand of the `=` operator. Since the assignment operator has been overloaded, this statement invokes `item3`'s `operator=` function, passing it `item1` as a reference parameter. Although it would be unlikely to see it written this way, the same function could be invoked with the following statement.

```
item3.operator=(item1);
```

Operator functions do not have to be void functions. If, for example, we wanted the `operator=` function to return a copy of `item3`, the object for whom the function is being invoked, we could make the function return type `Inventory` instead of `void`. We would then need to add the following line of code as the last statement in the `operator=` function.

```
return *this;
```

`this` is a special variable in C++. It is a pointer to the object whose member function is being invoked. In our example, `this` is a pointer to the `item3` object. `*this` dereferences the pointer and allows the actual `item3` object to be returned.

The final version of the `operator=` function, with the `Inventory` return type, would look like the following:

```
Inventory operator=(const Inventory &right)
{  delete [] description;
   description = new char[strlen(right.description) + 1];
   strcpy(description, right.description);
   price = right.price;
   return *this;
}
```

Overloading the Addition Operator

Suppose, in the `Inventory` example, we wanted to keep track of the quantity in stock for each item. We could add the following member variable to the class.

```
int quantity;
```

Say we did this and `item1` had the `description` "7 inch screwdriver" and the `quantity` 22 while `item2` had the `description` "9 inch screwdriver" and the `quantity` 14. We might then want to define an overloaded addition operator for the class that would add the `quantity` values of two objects and return the sum. The `operator+` function for this class would look like the following:

```
int operator+(const Inventory &right)
{   return quantity + right.quantity;
}
```

It could be invoked as follows:

```
cout << "Total number of screwdrivers on hand: " << (item1 + item2);
```

General Operator Overloading Principles

C++ allows most of its operators to be overloaded and, although programmers can overload operators to make them do pretty much anything they want, there are several general principles to keep in mind.

1. It is generally not a good idea to completely change an operator's meaning in a way that is not obvious and reasonable. For example, it would be a bad idea to make the * operator add quantities, rather than multiply them.
2. You cannot change the number of operands taken by an operator. A unary operator, like ++, can have only one operand, the object for which it is called, and thus has no arguments. Binary operators, like + or –, must have two operands. The left operand is the object for which the operator function is invoked. The right operand should be passed in as a reference parameter.
3. The return type of most operator functions depends on what the overloaded operator is being defined to do rather than which operator is being overloaded. For example, an overloaded addition operator that adds an integer data member from one object to an integer data member from a second object and wants to return their sum would likely have a return type of `int`. On the other hand, an overloaded addition operator that adds values in a whole set of corresponding data members of two objects might create a temporary object to hold all the sums and then return that entire object.
4. There is one exception to the above general principle. Although an overloaded relational operator (such as == or >) that compares two objects may define in any way it wishes what constitutes being equal or greater than, etc., such a function should always return *true* or *false*.

Inheritance

A sub-class can be described as a specialized version of a larger class. For example: beagle is a sub-class of dog. Everything that describes a dog can be used to describe a beagle; however a beagle has certain characteristics that may not be true of other types of dogs. This describes what is called an "is a" relationship. A beagle *is a* dog. The following is a list of common "is a" relationships:

A woman *is a* person

A bus *is a* vehicle

A salmon *is a* fish

A rose *is a* flower

Notice that the noun to the left of the "is a" statement is a component of the noun to the right of that statement. All busses are vehicles. The inverse is not true. Not all vehicles are busses. The specialized object (the noun to the left of the "is a" statement) has all of the characteristics of the general object (the noun to the right of the "is a" statement), plus additional characteristics that make it special.

Inheritance is used in object-oriented programming to create an "is a" relationship between classes. Inheritance describes a base class (the general class or noun to the right of the "is a" statement) and a derived class which is the specialized class.

The derived class "inherits" the members (both member variables and member functions) of the base class without any of them rewritten. The derived class

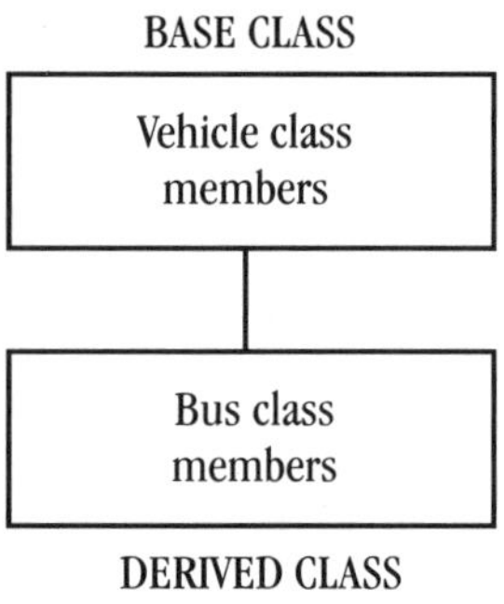

can then have extra "specialized" members that are not part of the base class.

Example:

Suppose we want to make a distinction between show dogs and other types of dogs. A show dog "is a" dog. Thus dog is our base class and show dog is our derived class. For our purpose, let us assume that all dogs have a color, weight and name. These are the private member variables of our base class. In addition to these characteristics, let us assume that show dogs have the following characteristics:

number of contests entered: `numOfContests`

number of first place finishes: `numOfWins`

The private member variables of a show dog will also include these items.

The base class can be declared as follows:

```
class DogType           // name of the base class
{
   private:
      string name;     // name of dog
      float weight;    // weight of dog
      string color;    // color of dog
   public:
      DogType();       // default constructor
      DogType(string n, float w, string c);  // constructor
      void printDogInfo() const;    // prints dog information
};
```

The following is the implementation of the member functions:

```
DogType::DogType()
{
   name = "Unknown";
   weight = 0;
   color = "unknown";
} // default constructor


DogType::DogType(string n, float w, string c)
{
   name = n;
   weight = w;
   color = c;
}

void DogType::printDogInfo() const
{
   cout << "The dog's name is " << name << endl;
   cout << "The dog's weight is " << weight << endl;
   cout << "The dog's color is " << color << endl << endl;
}
```

The derived class `ShowDogType` will inherit the members of `DogType`. It could be declared as follows:

```
class ShowDogType: public DogType
   // name of the derived class followed by colon, the word
   // public to indicate that it is inheriting members, and the
   // name of the base class from which it inherits those members
{
   private:
      int numOfContests;  // number of contests entered
      int numOfWins;      // number of contests won
   public:
      ShowDogType(string n, float w, string c, int con,
                               int win);
   // This is a constructor that will give values to all the
   // member variables of this class including the ones it
   // inherites. See the implementation of this constructor
   // below.
      ShowDogType();                   // default constructor
      void printShowDogInfo() const; // prints contests & wins
};
```

Although this derived class (`ShowDogType`) inherits the members of its base class both private and public, it can access only the public members of the base class. To change the private members of `DogType`, `ShowDogType` must access the public members just as other users would have to do.

The following is the implementation of ShowDogType member functions.

```
ShowDogType::ShowDogType(string n, float w, string c, int con, int win): DogType(n, w, c)
{
   numOfContests = con; // assigns con to private variable numOfContests
   numOfWins = win;     // assigns win to private variable numOfWins
}
```

Notice that this constructor calls the DogType constructor to initialize the private member variables defined in DogType. Since name, weight and color are defined in the base class, the derived class cannot access them and thus must call the base class constructor. It does this by inserting a colon just before the call.

```
ShowDogType::ShowDogType(): DogType()
{
   numOfContests = 0;  // set default contests to 0;
   numOfWins = 0;      // set default wins to 0;
}
// The other member variables (name, weight, color) are given
// default values by the call to the default constructor DogType()

void ShowDogType::printShowDogInfo() const
{
   printDogInfo();
   cout << "The dog has been entered in " << numOfContests
        << " contests" << endl;
   cout << "The dog has won " << numOfWins << " contests"
        << endl << endl;
}
```

The following is a complete program that uses inheritance. Notice that the member functions are written inline (inside the class declaration).

Sample Program 11.6

```
#include <iostream>
#include <string>
using namespace std;

class DogType          // name of the base class
{
   private:
      string name;     // name of dog
      float weight;    // weight of dog
      string color;    // color of dog
   public:
      DogType()
      {
         name = "Unknown";
         weight = 0;
         color = "unknown";
      } // default constructor
```

continues

```
        DogType(string n, float w, string c)
        {
           name = n;
           weight = w;
           color = c;
        }  // constructor

        void printDogInfo() const   // prints dog information
        {
           cout << "The dog's name is " << name << endl;
           cout << "The dog's weight is " << weight << endl;
           cout << "The dog's color is " << color << endl << endl;
        }
};

class ShowDogType: public DogType
   // The name of the derived class followed by a colon, then the word
   // public to indicate that it is inheriting members, and finally the
   // name of the base class from which it inherits those members
{
   private:
      int numOfContests;          // number of contests entered
      int numOfWins;              // number of contests won
   public:
      ShowDogType::ShowDogType(string n, float w, string c,
                               int con, int win): DogType(n,w,c)
      {
         numOfContests = con;     // assigns con to private
                                  // variable numOfContests
         numOfWins = win;         // assigns win to private
                                  // variable numOfWins
      }

      ShowDogType::ShowDogType(): DogType()
      {

         numOfContests = 0;       // set default contests to 0;
         numOfWins = 0;           // set default wins to 0;
      }

         // The other member variables (name, weight, color) are
         // given default values by the call to the default
         // constructor DogType()

      void ShowDogType::printShowDogInfo() const
      {
         printDogInfo();
         cout << "The dog has been entered in "
              << numOfContests << " contests" << endl;
         cout << "The dog has won " << numOfWins
              << " contests" << endl <<endl;
      }
};
```

continues

```
int main()
{
   ShowDogType  dog1("Fido", 12, "Black", 12, 2);
   ShowDogType  dog2;

   dog1.printShowDogInfo();
   dog2.printShowDogInfo();

   return 0;
}
```

PRE-LAB WRITING ASSIGNMENT

Fill-in-the-Blank Questions

1. A _______________ member variable is shared by all instances of a class.
2. A _______________ function is a special function that is allowed to be executed before any objects of a class are created.
3. A _______________ function is a function outside of a class that is allowed to access even private member data and member functions of class objects.
4. A class object _______________ (can/cannot) be assigned to another object of the same class.
5. In order for a function to be a friend of a class, it must be granted this status by _______________________.
6. When memberwise assignment occurs _______________ (all/just the public/just the private) data values are copied from one object to the other object.
7. A _______________________ is used to ensure that memberwise assignment handles pointers correctly when a new object is created and initialized with another object's data.
8. Redefining the way an operator works when applied to objects is called _______________________.
9. The operator function to redefine the way the subtraction operator works would have to be named _______________________.
10. A copy constructor should be passed the object whose values are being copied by _______________ (value/reference/pointer) .

LESSON 11A

LAB 11.1 Working with Static Member Variables and Member Functions

Retrieve program `savings.cpp` from the Set 11 folder. This is similar to Sample Program 11.2. The code follows.

```
// This program introduces the use of static member variables.
// PLACE YOUR NAME HERE.

#include <iostream>
using namespace std;

class SavingsAcct
{
    private:
       int acctNum;                          // "regular" member variables
       double balance;

       // Fill in the code to declare a static int variable named
       // nextAcctNumber.

       // Fill in the code to declare a static double variable named
       // totalDeposits.
   public:
      SavingsAcct();                         // default constructor
      SavingsAcct(double);                   // constructor
      void newAcctInfo();
      double getTotalDeposits();
      void displayAcctInfo();
      void deposit(double);
      void withdraw(double);
};

// Static Variable Definitions

// Fill in the code to define the static variable nextAcctNumber and
// initialize it to 5000.

// Fill in the code to define the static variable totalDeposits and initialize
// it to 0.

// Member Function Implementation Section

void SavingsAcct::newAcctInfo()
{   cout << "New account number: " << acctNum << "   Initial Balance: $"
         << balance << endl;
}

SavingsAcct::SavingsAcct()                   // default constructor
{   // Fill in the code to assign acctNum the next available account number.
    // Fill in the code to increment the next available account number.

    balance = 0;
    newAcctInfo();
}

SavingsAcct::SavingsAcct(double startBal)  // constructor
{   // Fill in the code to assign acctNum the next available account number.
    // Fill in the code to increment the next available account number.
```

continues

```
        // Fill in the code to set balance to the starting balance passed in.

        // Fill in the code to add this account's starting balance to the static
        // variable named totalDeposits.

        newAcctInfo();
}

double SavingsAcct::getTotalDeposits()
{   return totalDeposits;
}

void displayAcctInfo()
{
    // Fill in the code to display the account's account number and balance.
}
void deposit(double)
{
    // Fill in the code to implement this function. The amount passed in
must
    // be added to the account's balance. Remember that any change to an
    // account's balance also affects totalDeposits.
}

void withdraw(double)
{   // This function is not being implemented at this time.
}

// Client code

int main()
{
    // Fill in the code to create acct1 with a starting balance of $100.
    // Fill in the code to create acct2 with a starting balance of $250.

    // Fill in the code to deposit $50 in acct2.

    // Fill in the code to display the account information for acct1.
    // Fill in the code to display the account information for acct2.

    // Fill in the code to display totalDeposits.

    return 0;
}
```

Exercise 1: Complete this program as directed. When you run it you should get the following output.

```
New account number: 5000   Initial Balance: $100
New account number: 5001   Initial Balance: $250
Account number 5000 has a balance of $100
Account number 5001 has a balance of $300
Total savings deposits = $400
```

Exercise 2: Notice that the `newAcctInfo()` function is never called by any user function outside the class. It is called only by other class functions. This means it can be a `private` member function. Modify the program you completed in Exercise 1 to move the declaration of this member function from the `public` section to the `private` section and then rerun this program. You should get the same results.

Exercise 3: Modify the program you created in Exercise 2 to add a `static void public` function named `firstAcctNumber` which allows the starting account number to be input to the program, rather than hard coded within it. Write the function prototype and implementation for this function. The static variable `nextAcctNumber` will still need to be defined, as it was before, but it will not be initialized when it is defined. Instead, before creating any accounts, the `main` function should have the user input the starting account number and then call your `firstAcctNumber` function to initialize it with the input number. After making these modifications run your program again, inputting 5000 as the starting account number. The results should be the same as those shown in Exercise 1.

LAB 11.2 Using Friend Functions

Retrieve `salesrep.cpp` from the Set 11 folder. It is very similar to Sample Program 11.4. The code follows.

```
// This program introduces the use of friend functions. It also reviews the
// use of static member variables and functions.
// PLACE YOUR NAME HERE.

#include <iostream>
using namespace std;

class SalesForce
{
   private:
      static double salesGoal;         // static variable shared by
                                       // all class objects
      int    snum;                     // sales rep. number
      double monthlySales;

   public:
      static void initGoal(double);    // static function to set salesGoal

      SalesForce(){snum = monthlySales = 0;}  // default constructor
      SalesForce(int, double);         // constructor
      void displayInfo();              // displays an object's member data
      bool metGoal();                  // indicates if sales goal has been met

      friend void salesReport(SalesForce &); // declares a friend function
};

// Static Member Variable Definitions
double SalesForce::salesGoal;

// Member Function Implementation Section
```

continues

```
void SalesForce::initGoal(double amt)
{
   salesGoal = amt;
}

SalesForce::SalesForce(int num, double amt)    // constructor
{  snum = num;
   monthlySales = amt;
}

void SalesForce::displayInfo()
{  cout << "Sales Rep Number: " << snum << "  Total sales $" << monthlySales
        << endl;
}

bool SalesForce::metGoal()
{  if(monthlySales >= salesGoal)
      return true;
   else
      return false;
}

// Client Code

// Function prototypes
void salesReport(SalesForce &);

int main()
{
   double goalAmount;

   cout << "Input monthly sales goal: ";
   cin  >> goalAmount;
   SalesForce::initGoal(goalAmount);        // set the sales goal for the class
   SalesForce repOne(101, 13500);           // create 1st sales rep.
   SalesForce repTwo(202, 16800);           // create 2nd sales rep.

   salesReport(repOne);
   salesReport(repTwo);

   return 0;
}

/************************************************************************
 *                              salesReport                             *
 * This function produces a sales report using data in a SalesForce     *
 * object. Since the SalesForce class has declared this a friend function,*
 * it can access private members of SalesForce class objects directly,  *
 * by using the dot operator, instead of through calls to public member *
 * functions.                                                           *
 ************************************************************************/

void salesReport(SalesForce & rep)
{
   cout << "Report for Sales Rep. number: " << rep.snum << endl;
   cout << "Monthly sales: $" << rep.monthlySales
        << "   Goal: $" << rep.salesGoal << endl;
```

continues

```
    if (rep.metGoal())
       cout << "Met sales goal\n\n";
    else
       cout << "Did not meet sales goal\n\n";
}
```

Exercise 1: Run the program, inputting 15000 when prompted to enter the monthly sales goal amount. Observe the output. Compare the code to the output to see which statements are creating which outputs.

Exercise 2: Make the following modifications to the program. Add a second `void friend` function to the `SalesForce` class named `modifyGoal` which has two parameters, a type `double` parameter which receives the amount to raise the goal and a reference parameter that receives the `SalesForce` object being modified. Write a prototype for this function and the code for this function and place them in the appropriate locations of the `Client Code` section. The function is supposed to raise the object's `salesGoal` by the amount passed in. Add a line of code in the `main` function, just before the calls to the `salesReport` function, to call this function to raise `repOne`'s `salesGoal` by 1000.

Exercise 3: Rerun the modified program, again inputting 15000 for the monthly goal amount, and observe the output. Did `repOne`'s `salesGoal` rise to 16000? What happened to `repTwo`'s `salesGoal`?
Explain.

____

____

Exercise 4: Do you feel it is a good idea to allow friend functions to modify member data?

LESSON 11B

LAB 11.3 Using Copy Constructors

Bring in program `copycon.cpp` from the Set 11 folder. This is similar to Sample Program 11.5. The code follows.

```
// This program illustrates the use of copy constructors
// PLACE YOUR NAME HERE.

#include <iostream>
#include <iomanip>
using namespace std;

class Inventory  // class declaration with member functions defined in-line
{
   private:
      char   *description;
      double price;
   public:
      Inventory()                                   // default constructor
      {  price = 0;
```

continues

```
            description = new char[6];
            strcpy(description, "empty");
        }
        Inventory(char* d, double p)               // constructor
        {  description = new char[strlen(d) + 1]; // Get needed amount of memory
                                                   // to hold the description.
            strcpy(description, d);
            price = p;
        }
        ~Inventory()
        {  delete[] description; }        // Use destructor to free the memory
                                          // allocated for the dynamic variable.
        const char* getDescription()
        {  return description;  }
        double getPrice()
        {  return price;  }

        void setDescription(char* d)     // "Assumes" dynamic description
        {  strcpy(description, d);       // variable has enough memory to hold
        }                                // the new string.

        void setPrice(double p)
        {   price = p;    }
};

int main()
{
    Inventory toolOne("screwdriver", 2.99);

    // Fill in the code to create a new Inventory object named
    // toolTwo that is initialized with the values of toolOne.

    cout << fixed << setprecision(2) << showpoint;
    cout << "toolOne: " << toolOne.getDescription() << "  $"
         << toolOne.getPrice()  << endl;
    cout << "toolTwo: " << toolTwo.getDescription() << "  $"
         << toolTwo.getPrice()  << endl << endl;

    // Fill in the code to change toolTwo's description to "electric screwdriver".

    cout << "toolOne: " << toolOne.getDescription() << "  $"
         << toolOne.getPrice()  << endl;
    cout << "toolTwo: " << toolTwo.getDescription() << "  $"
         << toolTwo.getPrice()  << endl << endl;

    return 0;
}
```

Exercise 1: Fill in the code where indicated to complete the program. Run it and observe the output.

Exercise 2: This may cause your program to abort on some systems. If it ran and produced output, rather than aborting, explain why `toolOne`'s description changed.

____

____

Exercise 3: Write a copy constructor, as illustrated in the pre-lab reading, and place it in the `Inventory` declaration with the other constructors. Rerun the program. Now, when `toolTwo`'s description is changed, `toolOne` should not be affected.

Exercise 4: The `setDescription` member function, assumes there has been enough memory has already been allocated for the `description` to hold any new string being passed to it. This is not a safe assumption. Rewrite the code in this function to free the current memory pointed to by the `description` pointer and allocate the right amount of memory for the new string being passed to the function. Rerun your program with the new function to make sure it still works correctly.

LAB 11.4 Overloading Operators (Optional)

Retrieve program `overload.cpp` from the Set 11 folder. The code follows.

```
// This program contains a revised version of the Inventory class
// and uses it to illustrate operator overloading.
// PLACE YOUR NAME HERE.

#include <iostream>
#include <iomanip>
using namespace std;

class Inventory  // class declaration with member functions defined in-line
                 // a quantity member variable has replaced the price variable
{  private:
      char *description;
      int  quantity;
   public:
      Inventory()                              // default constructor
      {  description = new char[6];
         strcpy(description, "empty");
         quantity = 0;
      }

      Inventory(char* d, int q    )            // constructor
      {  description = new char[strlen(d) + 1]; // Get needed amount of memory
                                               // to hold the description.
         strcpy(description, d);
         quantity = q;
      }

      Inventory(Inventory &object)             // copy constructor
      {  description = new char[strlen(object.description) + 1];
         strcpy(description, object.description);
         quantity = object.quantity;
      }
```

continues

```
        ~Inventory()
        {  delete[] description; }        // Use destructor to free the memory
                                          // allocated for the dynamic variable.
        const char* getDescription()
        {  return description;  }

        double getQuantity()
        {  return quantity;  }

        void setDescription(char* d)
        {  delete [] description;
           description = new char[strlen(d) + 1];
           strcpy(description, d);
        }

        void setQuantity(int q)
        {   quantity = q;   }

        Inventory operator=(const Inventory &right) // Overload the = operator
        {
           // Fill in the code to deallocate the memory previously acquired to
           // hold the description.

           // Fill in the code to allocate the right amount of memory to hold the
           // new description.  Place the address of this new memory in the
           // description pointer variable.

           // Fill in the code to set the description of this object to right's
           // description. Remember you need to use strcpy to copy a string.
           // Fill in the code set this object's quantity to right's quantity.

           return *this;
        }

        int operator+(const Inventory &right)       // Overload the + operator
        {
           // Fill in the code to return the sum of this object's quantity and
           // right's quantity.
        }
};

int main()
{
   // Fill in the code to create an Inventory object named item1 which is a
   // "7 inch screwdriver" with a quantity of 22.

   // Fill in the code to create an Inventory object named item2 which is a
   // "9 inch screwdriver" with a quantity of 14.

   // Fill in the code to create an Inventory object named item3 which is a
   // "wrench" with a quantity of 10.

   cout << "item1: " << item1.getDescription() << "  "
        << item1.getQuantity()  << endl;
   cout << "item2: " << item2.getDescription() << "  "
        << item2.getQuantity()  << endl;
   cout << "item3: " << item3.getDescription() << "  "
        << item3.getQuantity()  << endl << endl;
```

continues

```
    // Fill in the one statement that will assign item3
    // all of the values stored in item2.

    cout << "The following two items should now be identical." << endl;
    cout << "item2: " << item2.getDescription() << "   "
         << item2.getQuantity()  << endl;
    cout << "item3: " << item3.getDescription() << "   "
         << item3.getQuantity()  << endl << endl;

    // Fill in the code to change item3's description back to "wrench".

    cout << "The change to item3 should not affect item2." << endl
         << "item2 should still be a screwdriver." << endl;
    cout << "item2: " << item2.getDescription() << "   "
         << item2.getQuantity()  << endl;
    cout << "item3: " << item3.getDescription() << "   "
         << item3.getQuantity()  << endl << endl;

    cout << "Total number of screwdrivers on hand: "
         << (// Fill in the code to add the quantities of item1 and item2 by
             // using your overloaded + operator, NOT by using getQuantity.)
         << endl;

    return 0;
}
```

Exercise 1: Fill in the code to complete the program as instructed. Run the program. The output should be as follows.

```
item1: 7 inch screwdriver   22
item2: 9 inch screwdriver   14
item3: wrench   10

The following two items should now be identical.
item2: 9 inch screwdriver   14
item3: 9 inch screwdriver   14

The change to item3 should not affect item2.
item2 should still be a screwdriver.
item2: 9 inch screwdriver   14
item3: wrench   14

Total number of screwdrivers on hand: 36
```

Exercise 2: When you changed `item3`'s description it, correctly, did not affect `item2`'s description. Why was this?

____

____

Exercise 3: Write a function to overload the subtraction operator and add it to the class. It should find the difference between two quantities. Test out your overloaded subtraction operator by adding a line of code just before the `return` statement to print out how many more 7 inch screwdrivers (`item1`) there are than 9 inch screwdrivers (`item2`).

Lab 11.5 Inheritance

Retrieve program `inherit.cpp` from the Set 11 folder. This is the same program as Sample Program 11.6.

```
// This program demonstrates the use of inheritance
// PLACE YOUR NAME HERE.

#include <iostream>
#include <string>
using namespace std;

class DogType                    // name of the base class
{
   private:
      string name;     // name of dog
      loat weight;     // weight of dog
      string color;    // color of dog
   public:
      DogType()
      {
         name = "Unknown";
         weight = 0;
         color = "unknown";
      } // default constructor

      DogType(string n, float w, string c)
      {
         name = n;
         weight = w;
         color = c;
      }  // constructor

      void printDogInfo() const   // prints dog information
      {
         cout << "The dog's name is " << name << endl;
         cout << "The dog's weight is " << weight << endl;
         cout << "The dog's color is " << color << endl
              << endl;
};

class ShowDogType: public DogType
   // The name of the derived class followed by a colon, then the word
   // public to indicate that it is inheriting members, and finally the
   // name of the base class from which it inherits those members
{
   private:
      int numOfContests;  // number of contests entered
      int numOfWins;      // number of contests won
   public:
      ShowDogType::ShowDogType(string n, float w, string c, int con, int win): DogType(n,w,c)
      {
         numOfContests = con; // assigns con to private
                              // variable numOfContests
```

continues

```
        numOfWins = win;        // assigns win to private
                                // variable numOfWins
    }

    ShowDogType::ShowDogType(): DogType()
    {

        numOfContests = 0;  // set default contests to 0;
        numOfWins = 0;      // set default wins to 0;
    }

        // The other member variables (name, weight, color) are
        // given default values by the call to the default
        // constructor DogType()

    void ShowDogType::printShowDogInfo() const
    {
        printDogInfo();
        cout << "The dog has been entered in "
             << numOfContests << " contests" << endl;
        cout << "The dog has won " << numOfWins
             << " contests" << endl <<endl;
    }
};

// Fill in the code to create the class RaceDogType. See Exercise 1 below

int main()
{
    ShowDogType  dog1("Fido", 12, "Black", 12, 2);
    ShowDogType  dog2;

  //  Fill in the code to define an object called dog3 that has the
  //  following information:
  //  name --->  Anchovi
  //  weight --> 14
  //  color ---> Black
  //  number of races -----> 28
  //  number of wins  -----> 27

  //  Fill in the code to define an object called dog4 that has all
  //  default values

    dog1.printShowDogInfo();
    dog2.printShowDogInfo();

    // Fill in the code to print out all the information about dog3
    // Fill in the code to print out all the information about dog4

    return 0;
}
```

Exercise 1: Create another class called `RaceDogType` that is derived from the `DogType` class. It will inherit all the members from `DogType`. It will also have the additional following members:

Private member variables:

1) `numOfRaces` // an integer value that keeps track of the number of races // the dog entered

2) `numOfRacesWon` // an integer value that keeps track of the number of races // the dog won

Public member functions and constructors:

1) Default constructor that sets `numOfRaces` and `numOfRacesWon` to 0. It should call the default constructor of `DogType` to make sure the inherited variables are also initialized.
2) Constructor that will take values for ALL private member variables (those inherited as well as those listed is the derived class). Make sure you correctly call the appropriate constructor in the base class.
3) A member function (`void printRaceDogInfo() const`) that will print ALL the information about a race dog.

Fill in all the code (places in bold) so that the following output is produced when the program is run.

```
The dog's name is Fido
The dog's weight is 12
The dog's color is Black

The dog has been entered in 12 contests
The dog has won 2 contests

The dog's name is Unknown
The dog's weight is 0
The dog's color is unknown

The dog has been entered in 0 contests
The dog has won 0 contests

The dog's name is Anchovi
The dog's weight is 14
The dog's color is Black

The dog has been entered in 28 races
The dog has won 27 races

The dog's name is Unknown
The dog's weight is 0
The dog's color is unKnown

The dog has been entered in 0 races
The dog has won 0 races
```

LAB 11.6 Student-Generated Code Assignments (Homework)

Option 1: Write a program that creates a `Circle` class and uses it to find out how far apart the centers of `Circle` objects are. Recall that at the very least `Circle` objects will need to have `radius`, `center_x`, and `center_y` as data members. The class should have a default constructor to set `radius` = 1 and to place the center at (0,0). It should also have a constructor to allow all three values to be initialized with user-supplied data when a `Circle` object is created. It should also have functions to `set` and to `get` (i.e., retrieve) each of the data members. Include an overloaded subtraction operator that returns how far apart two `Circle` object centers are. It must not return any negative numbers. For example if `circle1` is centered at (3,2) and `circle2` is centered at (4,4), the operation `circle1 - circle2` should return 2.236, not –2.236. Have the program create a pair of `Circle` objects and then output where their centers are and how far apart they are. Display the result to 3 decimal places.

Sample output (once two circles have been created)

```
circle1 center:  (3,2)
circle2 center:  (4,4)
The two circles are 2.236 units apart.
```

Option 2: Write a program that will keep track of package characteristics for a shipping company. It should declare a `Shipping` class that includes 5 integer member variables: `packageNum`, `length`, `width`, `height`, and `weight`. Dimensions are in inches and weight is in ounces. Include a default constructor that sets `packageNum` to –99 and other member variables to 1. Include a regular constructor to initialize all the values with user-supplied data. The class should have functions to `set` and `get` (i.e., retrieve) each of the data members. Include a function to calculate package volume and include overloaded operators ==, >, and < to compare two packages. Two packages are "equal" if they have the same volume *and* the same weight. A package is "greater than" another if it has a greater volume *or* has the same volume but a greater weight. Have the program create a pair of `Shipping` objects, output their characteristics, and then indicate if they are equal or which is greater.

Sample output (once the two packages have been created)

```
package number: 101   dimensions: 12 x 8 x 4  weight:  7 oz.
package number: 102   dimensions:  8 x 8 x 6  weight:  7 oz.
The packages are equal.
```

LESSON SET

12 Characters and Strings

PURPOSE

1. To work with character data
2. To work with C-strings and string functions
3. To work with C++ string objects

PROCEDURE

1. Students should read the Pre-lab Reading Assignment before coming to the lab.
2. Students should complete the Pre-lab Writing Assignment before coming to lab.
3. In the lab, students should complete labs assigned to them by the instructor.

Contents	Prerequisites	Approximate completion time	Page number	Check when done
Pre-lab Reading Assignment		20 min.	250	
Pre-lab Writing Assignment	Pre-lab reading	10 min.	259	
LESSON 12A				
Lab 12.1 Character Testing and String Validation	Minimal knowledge of arrays and pointers	20 min.	260	
Lab 12.2 Case Conversion	Basic knowledge of character functions	10 min.	262	
Lab 12.3 Sorting Strings	Basic knowledge of C-strings and string objects	25 min.	264	
LESSON 12B				
Lab 12.4 Programmer-Defined String functions	Basic knowledge of string objects	20 min.	268	
Lab 12.5 Student-Generated Code Assignments	Completion of Labs 12.1–12.4	40 min.	270	

PRE-LAB READING ASSIGNMENT

Characters and Character Functions

You recall that the character data type can hold only a single character. This data type includes letters, digits, and special symbols such as $ and @. For example,

```
char letter = 'B';
```

defines a character variable and assigns it the character `'B'`. `'B'` is an example of a **character constant**, or **character literal**. Character constants must be enclosed in single quotation marks.

You have already encountered some functions for working with characters, such as `toupper()`, which was used in Lesson Set 7.1 to convert a character to uppercase. The C++ library also provides numerous functions for testing characters. These functions test a single character and return either a non-zero `int` value (`true`) or zero (`false`). For example, the `isdigit()` function tests a character to see if it is between `'0'` and `'9'`. So `isdigit('7')` returns a non-zero value (`true`) whereas `isdigit('y')` and `isdigit('$')` both return 0 (`false`). We will not list all the character-testing functions here, but the following program demonstrates a number of them. Additional character-testing functions are listed in your textbook. Note that programs must `#include <cctype>` to use them.

Sample Program 12.1

```
// This program utilizes several functions for character testing.

#include <iostream>
#include <cctype>
using namespace std;

int main()
{
   char ch;

   cout << "Please Enter Any Character: ";
   cin  >> ch;
   cout << "The character entered is " << ch << endl;
   cout << "Its ASCII code is " << int(ch)   << endl;

   if ( isalpha(ch) )                                 // tests if ch is a letter
   {  cout << "The character is a letter." << endl;
      if ( islower(ch) )                              // tests if the letter
          cout << "The letter is lowercase." << endl; // is lowercase
      if ( isupper(ch) )                              // tests if the letter
         cout << "The letter is uppercase." << endl;  // is uppercase
   }
   else if ( isdigit(ch) )                            // tests if ch is a digit
      cout << "The character is a digit." << endl;
   else
      cout << "The character is neither a letter nor a digit." << endl;

   return 0;
}
```

In Lab 12.1 you will see a more practical application of character-testing functions.

Character Case Conversion

The C++ library provides the `toupper` and `tolower` functions for converting the case of a character. `toupper()`, which you have worked with before, returns the uppercase equivalent of a letter and `tolower()` returns the lowercase equivalent. For example, `cout << tolower('F');` causes an `f` to be displayed on the screen. If `tolower()` is passed a letter that is already lower case, or is passed a character that is not a letter at all, it returns the value unchanged. The `toupper` function behaves in a similar manner, returning the uppercase equivalent if a lowercase letter is passed to it, and otherwise returning the value it was passed unchanged. These functions are useful when an application needs to compare characters without considering case differences. The following program does this, using `toupper` to convert a character to uppercase before it is compared to another uppercase character.

Sample Program 12.2

```
// This program shows how the toupper function can be used in a C++ program.

#include <iostream>
#include <cctype>
#include <iomanip>
using namespace std;

int main()
{
   int week, total, dollars;
   float average;
   char choice;

   cout << showpoint << fixed << setprecision(2);
   do
   {
      total = 0;
      for(week = 1; week <= 4; week++)
      {
         cout << "How much (to the nearest dollar) did you"
              << " spend on food during week " << week << "? : " ;
         cin  >> dollars;

         total = total + dollars;
      }
      average = total / 4.0;

      cout << "Your average weekly food bill over the chosen month is $"
           << average << endl << endl;
      do
      {
         cout <<"Would you like to find the average for another month (Y/N)? ";
         cin  >> choice;
         choice = toupper(choice);
      } while (choice != 'Y' && choice != 'N');

   } while (choice == 'Y');

   return 0;
}
```

This program prompts the user to input weekly food costs, to the nearest dollar (an integer), for a four-week period. The average weekly total for that month is output. Then the user is asked whether to repeat the calculation for a different month. The flow of this program is controlled by a `do-while` loop which determines whether to loop again based on the user's answer. The line `choice = toupper(choice);` allows the user to enter the answer using either an uppercase or lowercase letter. Note the second, inner, `do-while` loop near the end of the program. Can you determine the purpose of this second loop? How would the execution of the program be affected if we removed this loop (but left in the lines between the curly brackets)?

String Constants

Often we need to put characters together to form strings. For example, the price "`$1.99`" and the phrase "`one for the road!`" are both string constants. The phrase contains blank space characters in addition to letters and an exclamation mark. In C++ a string constant is treated as a sequence of characters stored in consecutive memory locations. The end of the string in memory is marked by the null character `'\0'`. Do not confuse the null character with a sequence of two characters. `'\0'` designates a single special character whose ASCII code is 0. For example, the phrase above is stored in computer memory as

o	n	e		f	o	r		t	h	e		r	o	a	d	!	\0

Unlike a character constant that is enclosed in single quotation marks, a **string constant** is a string enclosed in double quotation marks. For example,

"Learn C++"

"What time is it?"

"Code Word 7dF#c&Q"

are all string constants. When they are stored in the computer's memory, the null character is automatically appended. When a string constant is used in C++, it is the memory address that is actually accessed. In the statement

```
cout << "Please enter a digit. ";
```

the memory address of the string constant is passed to the `cout` object which then displays the consecutive characters until the null character is reached.

C-Strings

Throughout most of your text and this lab manual you have used string objects to store strings. However, you were introduced to C-strings in Lesson Set 3 and have used them occasionally throughout this manual, for example in Lesson Set 11. Here we will examine them in more detail.

Often we need to access parts of a string rather than the whole string. For instance, we may want to alter characters in a string or compare two strings. If this is the case, a string constant is not what we need. Instead we need to store the string in such a way that we can access and manipulate it, either in pieces or as a whole. In C++ this is sometimes done using an array of characters, or C-string. The following line of code defines an array large enough to hold up to 11 characters plus the null character that marks the end of the string.

```
char name[12] = "simon";
```

The string would be stored as shown in the following:

s	i	m	o	n	\0						

This string can now be manipulated a character at a time or treated as a single entity.

```
name[0] = toupper name[0];     // This accesses a single character
                               // of the string.
cout << name;                  // This treats the entire string as a
                               // single entity.
```

Executing the above two lines of code would cause the following output.

```
Simon
```

Although C-strings can have their values input using `cin >>` as in the statement

```
cin >> name;
```

you will recall from Lesson Set 3 that this can cause problems. If the user enters `Santa Claus`, only `Santa` will be input because `cin >>` stops reading when it encounters a space. If the user enters `Newmanouskous` there will be another problem because the array is not large enough to hold this string. Since C++ does not do array bounds checking, if too long a string is entered it will write past the end of the array, changing the contents of other memory it should not touch.

The solution to both these problems, when reading in C-strings, is to use `cin.getline()` instead of `cin >>`.

```
cin.getline(name, 12);
```

This will allow characters to be read in, including blanks spaces, until the user hits ENTER or until 11 characters have been read, whichever occurs first.

Library Functions for C-Strings

The C++ library provides many functions for testing and manipulating C-strings. Two of these were introduced in Lesson Set 11, `strcpy()` to copy the contents of one string to another and `strlen()` to find the length of a string. The length of a string you will recall is not the size of the array holding it, but rather the number of characters in it, not including the null character. For example, `strlen("A New Day")` would be 9.

Sample Program 12.3 illustrates how useful the `strlen` function can be. This program reads in a string and then writes it out backward. If we allowed only strings of a fixed size, say length 30, the task would be easy. We would simply read the string into an array of size 31 or more. Then we would write the 29th entry followed by the 28th entry and so on, until we reached entry 0. However, if we wish to allow the user to input strings of different lengths, it is unclear where the end of the string is. Without the `strlen` function we would have to search the array until we found the null character and then figure out what position it was in. But the `strlen` function does this for us.

Sample Program 12.3

```
#include <iostream>
#include <cstring>          // for C-string functions

using namespace std;

int main()
{
   char line[50];
   int length, count = 0;

   cout << "Enter a sentence of no more than 49 characters:\n";
   cin.getline(line,50);

   length = strlen(line);  // strlen returns the length of the string
                           // currently stored in line.

   cout << "The sentence you entered printed backwards is:\n";

   for(count = length-1; count >= 0; count--)
   {
      cout << line[count];
   }
   cout << endl;

   return 0;
}
```

Sample Run 1

```
Enter a sentence of no more than 49 characters:
luaP deiruB I
The sentence you entered printed backwards is:
I Buried Paul
```

Sample Run 2

```
Enter a sentence of no more than 49 characters:
This sentence is too long to hold a mere 49 characters!
The sentence you entered printed backwards is:
arahc 94 erem a dloh ot gnol oot si ecnetnes sihT
```

Another useful string function, which you will use in Lab 12.3, is `strcat`. This function, which has the form `strcat(string1, string2)`, appends `string2` onto the end of `string1`. The programmer must make sure that the array containing `string1` is large enough to hold the concatenation of the two strings plus the null character.

Consider the following code:

```
char string1[25] = "Total Eclipse ";     // Note the space after the last word.
                                         // strcat does not insert a space.
                                         // The programmer must do this.

char string2[11] = "of the Sun";

cout << string1 << endl;
cout << string2 << endl;

strcat(string1, string2);

cout << string1 << endl;
```

These statements produce the following output:

```
Total Eclipse
of the Sun
Total Eclipse of the Sun
```

What would have happened if we had defined `string1` to be a character array of size 20?

Still another useful string function, which you will also use in Lab 12.3, is `strcmp`. This function compares two strings to see if they are the same or, if not, which string is alphabetically greater than the other. As you can imagine, this function is very useful for sorting strings alphabetically. `strcmp` is passed two strings. If they are identical, it returns a 0. If the first is "alphabetically less than" the second (based on the ASCII values for each character), it returns a negative number. If the first is "alphabetically greater than" the second, it returns a positive number. For two strings to be identical, the arrays that hold them do not have to be the same size. The strings just have to be the same length and contain exactly the same set of characters. Remember that `'a'` and `'A'` are considered different characters since they have different ASCII codes. So the strings `"hello"` and `"HELLO"` would not be reported as identical. Consider the following code.

```
int same;
char name1[10] = "Ann";
char name2[10] = "Adam";

same =  strcmp(name1, name2);

if (same == 0)
   cout << "The two strings are the same." << endl;
else if (same < 0)
   cout << name1 << " is alphabetically less than " << name2 << endl;
else
   cout << name2 << " is alphabetically less than " << name1 << endl;
```

These statements produce the following output:

```
Adam is alphabetically less than Ann
```

String/Numeric Conversions

Sometimes it is useful to store numeric data as a string. For example, you might want to read a numeric input into a string to ensure that a program does not "bomb" if the user enters a character when they are supposed to enter a number. The string can then be checked to make sure it is the character representation of a legal number. If so, it can then be converted to numeric form and used as a number or stored in an integer or floating-point variable. C++ provides several functions for converting between C-strings and numbers. Here are some useful functions that convert C-strings to numeric values.

Function	Conversion	Example
atoi	C-string to integer	number = atoi("415");
atol	C-string to long integer	maxValue = atol("500000");
atof	C-string to double	measure = atof("12.678");

Sample Program 12.4 illustrates the `atoi` function. It also uses the `strlen` and `isdigit` functions discussed earlier in this lesson. These functions are highlighted in bold.

Sample Program 12.4

```
// Program to total raffle tickets sold by members of an
// organization.

#include <iostream>
#include <cstring>
using namespace std;

// Function prototype
bool legalNumber(char*);

const int numPeople = 5;

int main()
{   int totalTickets = 0;
    char sold[6];

    for (int person = 0; person < numPeople; person++)
    {  cout << "Enter number of tickets sold: ";
       cin >> sold;

       if (legalNumber(sold))
          totalTickets += atoi(sold);
       else
          cout << "Illegal number entered.\n";
    }
    cout << "Total tickets sold = " << totalTickets << endl;
    return 0;
}
```

continues

```
/*********************************************************
 *                   legalNumber                         *
 * Function that checks if the string passed to it is the  *
 * character representation of a non-negative integer.     *
 *********************************************************/

bool legalNumber (char *numString)
{   bool legal = true;

    for (int pos = 0; pos < strlen(numString); pos++)
    {   if(!isdigit(numString[pos]))
        {   legal = false;
            break;
        }
    }
    return legal;
}
```

Pointers and Strings

Pointers can be very useful for writing string processing functions. If one needs to process a certain string, the beginning address can be passed to the function, which stores it in a pointer variable. The length of the string does not even need to be known since the function can start processing by using the address and can continue through the string until the null character is encountered.

Sample Program 12.5, which follows, reads in a string of no more than 50 characters and then counts the number of letters, digits, and whitespace characters in the string. Notice the use of the pointer `strPtr`, which points to the string being processed. The three functions `countLetters`, `countDigits`, and `countWhiteSpace` all perform basically the same task. The `while` loop is executed until `strPtr` points to the null character marking the end of the string. In the `countLetters` function, characters are tested to see if they are letters. The `if(isalpha(*strPtr))` statement determines if the character pointed at by `strPtr` is a letter. If so, the counter `occurs` is incremented by one. After the character has been tested, `strPtr` is incremented by one to test the next character. The other two functions are analogous.

Sample Program 12.5

```
#include <iostream>
#include <cctype>
using namespace std;

// Function prototypes
int countLetters(char*);
int countDigits(char*);
int countWhiteSpace(char*);

int main()
{
   int numLetters, numDigits, numWhiteSpace;
   char inputString[51];
```

continues

```
    cout << "Enter a string of no more than 50 characters: " << endl << endl;
    cin.getline(inputString,51);

    numLetters = countLetters(inputString);
    numDigits = countDigits(inputString);
    numWhiteSpace = countWhiteSpace(inputString);

    cout << "The number of letters in the entered string is "
         << numLetters << endl;
    cout << "The number of digits in the entered string is "
         << numDigits << endl;
    cout << "The number of white spaces in the entered string is "
         << numWhiteSpace << endl;

    return 0;
}

int countLetters(char *strPtr)      // This function counts the number of letters
{                                   // (both capital and lowercase) in the string.
    int occurs = 0;

    while(*strPtr != '\0')          // The loop is executed as long as strPtr
    {                               // does not point to the null character
                                    // which marks the end of the string.

        if (isalpha(*strPtr))       // Is the character that strPtr points to a letter?
            occurs++;               // If so, add one to the count.

        strPtr++;                   // Move the pointer to point to the next char.
    }
    return occurs;
}

int countDigits(char *strPtr)       // This function counts the number of digits.
{
    // The code to count the digits using the isdigit() function would go here.
}

int countWhiteSpace(char *strPtr) // This function counts the number of
{                                   // whitespace characters (space, newline,
                                    // and tab characters).
    // The code to count whitespace characters using the isspace() function
    // would go here.
}
```

More About the C++ String Class

You should be very familiar by now with the C++ `string` class that programmers can use to create `string` objects. You know that to treat strings this way programs must have `#include <string>`. This section introduces a few new features of string objects. Most older, pre-ANSI C++ compilers, however, cannot use these features as they do not have an analogous library and do not support `string` objects. To use them, a programmer would have to create a `string` class and `string` member functions. How to do this is discussed in your text.

So far to create a string object you have just defined it with the data type `string`.

```
string name1;           // This creates an empty string object.
```

You may have even initialized it at the time you created it, as shown here.

```
string name1 = "Sam";  // This creates a string object holding "Sam".
```

The string class, however, provides many different constructors to initialize string objects. So it is also possible to create and initialize a new string object by passing a string constant or string variable as an argument to the constructor like this:

```
string name2("John");  // This creates a string object holding "John".
string name3(name2);   // This creates a string object which is a copy
                       // of name2, (i.e., "John"). name2 can be either
                       // a string object or a C-string.
```

These are just a few of the constructors the `string` class provides.

Once a string object has been created, the `string` class provides many functions and overloaded operators to facilitate working with it. For example, whereas we must use `strcpy()` to copy one C-string to another, when using `string` objects we can just say `name1 = name2;` Whereas a function like `strcmp` must be used to compare two C-strings, two string objects can be compared using any of the relational operators since they have all been overloaded in the string class. Other useful overloaded operators for string objects include + which concatenates two strings and += which appends a copy of the string on the right onto the string on the left.

```
string s1 = "Hello ";
string s2 = "Sam";
string s3;
s3 = s1 + s2;             // This sets s3 to "Hello Sam".
s1 += "Mary";             // This sets s1 to "Hello Mary".
s3 = s1;                  // Now s3 also holds "Hello Mary".
```

Your text covers many other functions and overloaded operators for use with string objects.

PRE-LAB WRITING ASSIGNMENT

Fill-in-the-Blank Questions

1. The code `cout << toupper('b');` causes a _______________ to be displayed on the screen.
2. The data type of the `isalpha()` function is _______________.
3. After the assignment statement `result = isdigit('$')`, `result` has the value _______________.
4. The code `cout << tolower('#');` causes a _______________ to be displayed on the screen.
5. The end of a string constant or C-string is marked in computer memory by the _______________ character.
6. In `cin.getline(name, 25)`, the 25 indicates that the user can input at most _______________ characters into `name`.

7. Consider the following:

```
char message[35] = "Like tears in the rain";
int length;
length = strlen(message);
```

The value of `length` is _______________.

8. Consider the code

```
char string1[30] = "In the Garden";
char string2[15] = "of Eden";
strcat(string1, string2);
cout << string1;
```

The output for this is ____.

9. The _______________ header file must be included to access the `islower()` and `isdigit()` functions.
10. In C++, a string constant must be enclosed in _______________ whereas a character constant must be enclosed in _______________.
11. To use C++ `string` objects the _______________ header file must be included.
12. One C-string is copied to another by using _______________ whereas one C++ object is copied to another by using _______________ .

LESSON 12A

LAB 12.1 Character Testing and String Validation

The American Equities investment company offers a wide range of investment opportunities ranging from mutual funds to bonds. Investors can check the value of their portfolio from the American Equities web page. Information about personal portfolios is protected via encryption and can only be accessed using a password. The American Equities company requires that a password consist of 8 characters, 5 of which must be letters and the other 3 digits. The letters and digits can be arranged in any order. For example,

rt56AA7q
123actyN
1LoODwa9
myNUM741

are all valid passwords. However, the following are all invalid:

the476NEw // It contains more than 8 characters (also more than 5 letters).
be68moon // It contains more than 5 letters (also fewer than 3 digits).
$retrn99 // It contains an invalid character ('$') (also fewer than 3 digits).

American Equities needs a program for their web page that determines whether or not an entered password is valid. The program `american_equities.cpp` from the Set 12 folder performs this task. The code follows. Some of the functions for this program come from Sample Program 12.5.

```
// This program tests a password for the American Equities web page
// to see if the format is correct.

// PLACE YOUR NAME HERE.

#include <iostream>
#include <cctype>
```

continues

```
#include <cstring>
using namespace std;

// Function prototypes
bool validPassword(char[]);
int countLetters(char*);
int countDigits(char*);

int main()
{
   char password[20];

   cout << "Enter a password consisting of exactly 5 "
        << "letters and 3 digits:" << endl;
   cin.getline(password, 20);

   if( validPassword(password) )   // This calls the validPassword function
                                   // and passes it the password array that
                                   // holds the string to be tested.
                                   // The if statement tests the true/false
                                   // value returned by the function.

      cout << "Please wait - your password is being verified." << endl;
   else
   {
      cout << "Invalid password." << endl
           << "Please enter a password with exactly 5 letters and 3 digits."
           << endl;
      cout << "For example, my37RuN9 is valid." << endl;
   }

   return 0;
}

/*******************************************************************
 *                         validPassword                           *
 *******************************************************************/

bool validPassword(char custPass[])
{
   int numLetters, numDigits, length;

   length = // Fill in the function call to get the length of the
            // custPass string.

   numLetters = // Fill in the call to the countLetters function to
                // get the number of letters in the custPass string.

   numDigits =  // Fill in the call to the countDigits function to
                // get the number of digits in the custPass string.

   if ( length == 8 && numLetters == 5 && numDigits == 3 )
      return true;
   else
      return false;
}
```

continues

```
// The next 2 functions are from Sample Program 12.5

/*****************************************************************
 *                        countLetters                           *
 * This function counts the number of letters (both capital and *
 * lowercase) in the string.                                     *
 *****************************************************************/

int countLetters(char *strPtr)
{
   int occurs = 0;

   while(*strPtr != '\0')
   {
      if ( isalpha(*strPtr) )
         occurs++;

      strPtr++;
   }
   return occurs;
}

/*****************************************************************
 *                        countDigits                            *
 * This function counts the number of digits in the string.      *
 *****************************************************************/

int countDigits(char *strPtr)
{
   // Fill in the code to complete this function.
   // It must use the isdigit() function to count the number of digits
   // in the string pointed to by strPtr.
}
```

Exercise 1: Fill in the code to complete the program as instructed. Then run it several times with both valid and invalid passwords. Does it work correctly? If not, find and fix the errors. Read through the program and make sure you understand the logic of the code.

Exercise 2: Alter the program so that a valid password must have 9 characters and consist of 7 letters and 2 digits. Be sure to modify the prompts as well as the code.

Exercise 3: Modify your program from Exercise 2 so that only lowercase letters are allowed. That is, a valid password must have 9 characters and consist of 7 *lowercase* letters and 2 digits. Again, be sure to modify the prompts as well as the code.

LAB 12.2 Case Conversion

Bring in `foodbill.cpp` from the Set 12 folder. Note that this is Sample Program 12.2. The code follows.

```
// This program shows how the toupper function can be used in a C++ program.
// PLACE YOUR NAME HERE.

#include <iostream>
#include <cctype>
#include <iomanip>
using namespace std;

int main()
{
   int week, total, dollars;
   float average;
   char choice;

   cout << showpoint << fixed << setprecision(2);
   do
   {
      total = 0;
      for(week = 1; week <= 4; week++)
      {
         cout << "How much (to the nearest dollar) did you"
              << " spend on food during week " << week << "? : " ;
         cin  >> dollars;

         total = total + dollars;
      }
      average = total / 4.0;

      cout << "Your average weekly food bill over the chosen month is $"
           << average << endl << endl;
      do
      {
         cout <<"Would you like to find the average for another month (Y/N)? ";
         cin  >> choice;
         choice = toupper(choice);
      } while (choice != 'Y' && choice != 'N');

   } while (choice == 'Y');

   return 0;
}
```

Exercise 1: Run the program and observe its behavior.

Exercise 2: Notice the following `do-while` loop which appears near the end of the program:

```
do
{
    cout <<"Would you like to find the average for another month (Y/N)? ";
    cin  >> choice;
    choice = toupper(choice);
} while (choice != 'Y' && choice != 'N');
```

How would the execution of the program be different if we removed this loop? Remove the loop but leave the three lines inside the curly braces in the program. Rerun the program. What happens if you enter `'y'` for the choice?

What happens if you enter something other than `'y'` or `'n'`, such as `'q'`?

How would the execution of the program be different if we additionally removed the line `choice = toupper(choice);`? Remove it and rerun the program. Now what happens if you enter `'y'` for the choice?

Exercise 3: Reload the original, unmodified `foodbill.cpp` program (or put the `toupper` line and the loop back into the program to restore it to its original form). Now alter the program so it behaves as it originally did, but by using `tolower` rather than `toupper`.

LAB 12.3 Sorting Strings

Program `stringsort.cpp`, found in the Set 12 folder, is a partially completed program that uses the `strcmp` function to sort an array of C-strings. Program `stringsort2.cpp`, also found in the Set 12 folder, is a partially completed program that uses overloaded operators in the C++ `string` class to sort an array of string objects. Both use the selection sort, introduced in Lesson Set 9, modified to order strings alphabetically (i.e., to sort them in ascending order). Your teacher will tell you which of the two programs to use, or whether to use both of them. The code for both is shown here.

`stringsort.cpp`

```
// This program illustrates how the C-string strcmp function is used to sort
// strings in alphabetic (i.e. ascending) order.  It uses selection sort.
// However, any of the sorts we have learned could be modified to sort strings.
// The program also uses the strcpy and strcat functions.

// PLACE YOUR NAME HERE.

#include <iostream>
#include <cstring>
using namespace std;

typedef char NameString[30];        // This creates a data type called NameString
                                    // which is an array of 30 characters.
// Function prototypes
void getArrayData(NameString [], int);        // These functions get passed an
void sortArray(NameString [], int);           // array of elements of type
void displayArray(NameString [], int);        // NameString and an int size.

const int SIZE = 5;

int main()
{
   NameString name[SIZE];                     // This defines the array.

   getArrayData(name, SIZE);
   sortArray(name, SIZE);
   displayArray(name, SIZE);

   return 0;
}
```

continues

```
/*******************************************************************
 *                          getArrayData                          *
 *******************************************************************/

void getArrayData(NameString name[], int numElems)
{
   char firstName[13],
        lastName[16];

   for (int count = 0; count < numElems; count++)
   {  cout << "Enter first name: ";
      cin.getline(firstName, 13);
      cout << "Enter last name:  ";
      cin.getline(lastName,16);
      cout << endl;

      // Fill in the code to place a copy of lastName in name[count].
      // Fill in the code to append the string ", " onto name[count].
      // Fill in the code to append firstName onto name[count].
   }
}

/*******************************************************************
 *                          displayArray                          *
 *******************************************************************/

void displayArray(NameString name[], int numElems)
{
   cout << endl << "The sorted names are: " << endl;
   for (int count = 0; count < numElems; count++)
      cout << name[count] << endl;
   cout << endl;
}

/*******************************************************************
 *                           sortArray                            *
 *******************************************************************/

void sortArray(NameString name[], int numElems)
{
   int seek;                      // array position currently being put in order
   int minPosition;               // array location of "smallest" string found
   NameString minString;          // holds the "smallest" string found

   for (seek=0; seek < (numElems-1); seek++)
   {
      minPosition = seek;
      // Fill in the code to place a copy of name[seek] in minString.

      for(int index = seek + 1; index < numElems; index++)
      {
        if(// Fill in the code to test if name[index] "is less than" minString.)
        {  // Fill in the code to place a copy of name[index] in minString.
           minPosition = index;
        }
      }
```

continues

```
        // Fill in the code to place a copy of name[seek] in name[minPosition].
        // Fill in the code to place a copy of minString in name[seek].
    }
}
```

stringsort2.cpp

```
// This program uses the C++ string class to create and sort an array of
// string objects in alphabetic (i.e. ascending) order using selection sort.
// It uses the overloaded string class operators =, <, and +=.

// PLACE YOUR NAME HERE.

#include <iostream>
#include <string>
using namespace std;

// Function prototypes
void getArrayData(string [], int);          // These functions get passed
void sortArray(string [], int);             // an array of string objects
void displayArray(string [], int);          // and an int size.

const int SIZE = 5;

int main()
{
   // Fill in the code to create an array of string objects named
   // name. The array should have SIZE elements.

   getArrayData(name, SIZE);
   sortArray(name, SIZE);
   displayArray(name, SIZE);

   return 0;
}

/*****************************************************************
 *                         getArrayData                          *
 *****************************************************************/

void getArrayData(string name[], int numElems)
{
   string firstName;
   string lastName;

   for (int count = 0; count < numElems; count++)
   {  cout << "Enter first name: ";
      cin  >> firstName;
      cout << "Enter last name:  ";
      cin  >> lastName;
      cout << endl;

      // Fill in the code to place a copy of lastName in name[count]
      // by using the overloaded = operator.
```

continues

```
      // Fill in the code to append the string ", " onto name[count]
      // by using the overloaded += operator.

      // Fill in the code to append firstName onto name[count]
      // by using the overloaded += operator.
   }
}

/******************************************************************
 *                          displayArray                          *
 ******************************************************************/

void displayArray(string name[], int numElems)
{
   cout << endl << "The sorted names are: " << endl;

   for (int count = 0; count < numElems; count++)
      cout << name[count] << endl;

   cout << endl;
}

/******************************************************************
 *                           sortArray                            *
 ******************************************************************/

void sortArray(string name[], int numElems)
{
   int seek;                      // array position currently being put in order
   int minPosition;               // array location of "smallest" string found
   string minString;              // holds the "smallest" string found

   for (seek=0; seek < (numElems-1); seek++)
   {
      minPosition = seek;
      // Fill in the code to place a copy of name[seek] in minString
      // by using the overloaded = operator.

      for(int index = seek + 1; index < numElems; index++)
      {
        if(// Fill in the code to test if name[index] "is less than" minString
           // by using the overloaded < operator.)
        {
           // Fill in the code to place a copy of name[index] in minString
           // by using the overloaded = operator.
           minPosition = index;
        }
      }

      // Fill in the code to place a copy of name[seek] in name[minPosition]
      // by using the overloaded = operator.

      // Fill in the code to place a copy of minString in name[seek]
      // by using the overloaded = operator.
   }
}
```

Exercise 1: Fill in the code as instructed to complete whichever version(s) of the program your instructor assigned. Run the program using the following data and record the result.

Names Input	Sorted Names Output
George Washington	______________________
Thomas Jefferson	______________________
Abraham Lincoln	______________________
Theodore Roosevelt	______________________
Franklin Roosevelt	______________________

LESSON 12B

LAB 12.4 Programmer-Defined String Functions

Programmers can write their own functions to manipulate strings. In this lab you will create a function to reverse a string. The lab uses a string object, but the same approach would work to reverse a C-string. Bring in `reverse.cpp` from the Set 12 folder. The code follows.

```
// This program includes a programmer-defined string function to
// reverse the characters in a string. It uses string objects whose
// characters are read in with the getline() function.

// PLACE YOUR NAME HERE.

#include <iostream>
#include <string>
using namespace std;

// Write the prototype for a void function named reverseIt that
// receives a string object by reference.

int main()
{
   // Fill in the line to define a string object named aString.

   cout << "Please enter a string: ";
   cin  >> aString;

   cout << "You entered:            " << aString << endl;
   reverseIt(aString);
   cout << "The reversed string is: " << aString << endl;

   return 0;
}

/******************************************************************
 *                          reverseIt                             *
 * This function reverses the characters in a string object.      *
 ******************************************************************/
```

continues

```
void reverseIt(string &s)    // s is the formal parameter name
{                            // of the string to be reversed.
   char temp;
   int length = // Fill in the call to the member function that
                // returns the length of a string object.
   // Left and right are indexes
   int left = 0;
   int right =  // Fill in the code to initialize right to the position
                // of the last character in the string.  Hint: Figure
                // out what this will be relative to length.

   // Fill in the code to loop as long as left < right.
   {   // Fill in the code to swap the characters
       // in the left and right positions of s.
       // Fill in the code to move the left index one position to the right.
       // Fill in the code to move the right index one position to the left.
   }
}
```

Exercise 1: Fill in the code to complete the program as instructed. Run the program inputting the string `"hello"`. The reversed string `olleh` should be output. Does your program work correctly? If not, find and fix the error.

Exercise 2: Now try running the program inputting the string `"snap & stop"`. The result is not what we expect because `cin >>` stops reading when it gets to a blank. Replace the `cin >>` statement with `getline (cin, aString);` and rerun the program, again inputting the string `"snap & stop"`. This time you should get the correct result:

`pots & pans`

Exercise 3 (optional): If your teacher asks you to do so, modify the above program to use C-strings instead of string objects. Define `aString` to be a character array capable of holding 11 characters in addition to the `'\0'` null terminator. In order for your revised program to work for C-strings, you will have to replace the `getline()` and `length()` functions, which work only with string objects, with the functions that perform similar operations on C-strings. You will also no longer need to pass `aString` to the `reverseIt` function by reference. Why not?

____

____

Run the revised program, inputting `"Jack and the Beanstalk"`. Record the results. ______________________ What went wrong?

____

____

Now run the program, inputting `"snap & stop"`. You should get the same correct result you got in Exercise 2.

LAB 12.5 Student-Generated Code Assignments

The following programs all work with strings. In each case your program should prompt the user to input a string, or pair of strings if required, of 50 characters or less with no embedded spaces. The program should then perform the indicated task and produce the specified output. The program should loop so that users can enter and test additional strings until they choose to quit. Your instructor will tell you whether to use C-strings or C++ string objects.

Option 1: A **palindrome** is a string of characters that reads the same forward as backward. For example, the following are both palindromes:

```
1457887541      madam
```

Write a program that determines whether or not the entered string is a palindrome. Output the string and a message indicating whether or not it is a palindrome.

Option 2: Write a program that determines whether or not two entered strings are the same or not, ignoring case. That is, the strings "`Hello_World`" and "`HELLO_WORLD`" would be considered the same. One approach to doing this is to make an lowercase copy of each string before testing them. (Do not change the original strings.) Recall that the `toupper()` function only makes a single character upper case, so if you want to use this approach you will need to write and use your own `stringUpper()` function. Output the entered pair of strings and a message indicating whether or not they are the same.

Option 3: Write a program that determines how many vowels are in the entered string. A vowel is defined as upper or lowercase a, e, i, o, u. Output the entered string and a message telling the total number of vowels in the string.

LESSON SET

13 Advanced File Operations

PURPOSE

1. To review the basic concept of files
2. To understand the use of random access files
3. To understand and use various types of files (binary and text)

PROCEDURE

1. Students should read the Pre-lab Reading Assignment before coming to lab.
2. Students should complete the Pre-lab Writing Assignment before coming to lab.
3. In the lab, students should complete labs assigned to them by the instructor.

Contents	Pre-requisites	Approximate completion time	Page number	Check when done
Pre-lab Reading Assignment		20 min.	272	
Pre-lab Writing Assignment	Pre-lab reading	10 min.	287	
LESSON 13A				
Lab 13.1 Introduction to Files (Optional)	General understanding of basic I/O	15 min.	288	
Lab 13.2 Files as Parameters and Character Data	Understanding of `get` function and parameters	20 min.	289	
Lab 13.3 Binary Files and the `write` Function	Completion of all previous labs	30 min.	291	
LESSON 13B				
Lab 13.4 Random Access Files	Completion of all previous labs	20 min.	294	
Lab 13.5 Student Generated Code Assignments	Completion of all previous labs	30 min.	296	

PRE-LAB READING ASSIGNMENT

Review of Text Files

Chapter three introduced the basic use of files for input and output. We briefly review those concepts in this section.

A file is a collection of information stored (usually) on a disk. Files, just like variables, have to be defined in the program. The data type of a file depends on whether it is used as an input file, output file, or both. Output files have a data type called `ofstream`, input files have a data type of `ifstream`, and files used as both have the data type `fstream`. We must add the `#include <fstream>` directive when using files.

Examples:

```
ofstream outfile;      // defining outfile as an output file
ifstream infile;       // defining infile as an input file
fstream datafile;      // defining datafile to be both an input and
                       // output file
```

After their definition, files must still be opened, used (information stored to or data read from the file), and then closed.

Opening Files

A file is opened with the `open` function. This ties the logical name of the file that is used in the definition to the physical name of the file used in the secondary storage device (disk). The statement `infile.open("payroll.dat");` opens the file `payroll.dat` and lets the program know that `infile` is the name by which this file will be referenced within the program. If the file is not located in the same directory as the C++ program, the full path (drive, etc.) MUST be indicated: `infile.open("a:\\payroll.dat");` This tying of the **logical name** `infile` with the **physical name** `payroll.dat` means that wherever `infile` is used in the program, data will be read from the physical file `payroll.dat`. A program should check to make sure that the physical file exists. This can be done by a conditional statement.

Example:

```
ifstream infile;
infile.open("payroll.dat");
if (!infile)
{
   cout << Error opening file.  It may not exist were indicated.\n;
   return 1;
}
```

In the previous example, `return 1` is used as an indicator of an abnormal occurrence. In this case the file in question can not be found.

Reading from a File

Files have an "invisible" end of line marker at the end of each line of the file. Files also have an invisible end of file marker at the end of the file. When reading from an input file within a loop, the program must be able to detect that marker as the sentinel data (data that meets the condition to end the loop). There are several ways to do this.

Sample Program 13.1

```
#include <fstream>
#include <iostream>
#include <iomanip>
using namespace std;

int main()
{
    ifstream infile;          // defining an input file
    ofstream outfile;         // defining an output file

    infile.open("payroll.dat");
    // This statement opens infile as an input file.
    // Whenever infile is used, data from the file payroll.dat
    // will be read.

    outfile.open("payment.out");
    // This statement opens outfile as an output file.
    // Whenever outfile is used, information will be sent
    // to the file payment.out

    int hours;                // The number of hours worked
    float payRate;            // The rate per hour paid
    float net;                // The net pay

    if (!infile)
    {
        cout << "Error opening file.\n";
        cout << "Perhaps the file is not where indicated.\n";
        return 1;
    }

    outfile << fixed << setprecision(2);
    outfile << "Hours     Pay Rate   Net Pay"  << endl;

    infile >> hours;          // priming the read

    while (!infile.fail())
    {
        infile >> payRate;
        net = hours * payRate;

        outfile    << hours << setw(10) << "$ " << setw(6)
                   << payRate << setw(5) << "$ " << setw(7)
                   << net << endl;

        infile >> hours;
    }

    infile.close();
```

continues

```
    outfile.close();

    return 0;
}
```

Notice the statement `outfile << fixed << setprecision(2);` in the program. This shows that the format procedures learned for `cout` can be used for output files as well. Remember that `setw(x)` can be used as long as the `iomanip` header file is included.

This program assumes that a data file exists and contains an undetermined number of records with each record consisting of two data values, `hours` and `payRate`. Suppose the input data file (`payroll.dat`) contains the following:

```
40  10.00
30   6.70
50  20.00
```

The program will produce the following output file (`payment.out`).

```
Hours     Pay Rate     Net Pay
40         $ 10.00    $ 400.00
30         $  6.70    $ 201.00
50         $ 20.00    $1000.00
```

The input file contains data for one employee on each line. Each time through the `while` loop, information is processed for one employee. The loop executes the same number of times as there are lines (employee records in this case) in the data file. Since there are two items of data for each line (`hours` and `payRate`), these items are read in each time through the loop. Notice that one of the input variables was input before the `while` loop. This is called "priming the read." Input can be thought of as a stream of values taken one at a time. Before the `while` loop condition can be tested, there has to be something in that stream. We **prime** the read by reading in at least one variable before the loop. Observe that the statement `infile >> hours;` is given twice in the program: once before the input loop and as the last statement in the loop. The other item, `payRate`, is read in at the very beginning of the loop. This way each variable is read every time through the loop. Also notice that the heading of the output file is printed outside the loop before it is executed. In addition to checking to see if a file exists, we can also check to see if it has any data in it. The following code checks first if the file exists and then if it is empty.

```
inData.open("sample2.dat");

if(!inData)
   cout << "file does not exist" << endl;
else if((inData.peek()) == EOF)

   cout << "File is empty" << endl;
else
   //rest of program
```

The `peek` function actually looks ahead in the file for the next data item, in this case to determine if it is the end of file marker.

Since the `peek` function looks "ahead" for the next data item, it can be used to test for end of file in reading values from a file within a loop without priming the read.

The following program accomplishes the same thing as Sample Program 13.1 without priming the read. The portions in bold differ from Sample Program 13.1.

Sample Program 13.2

```
#include <fstream>
#include <iostream>
#include <iomanip>
using namespace std;

int main()
{
      ifstream infile;               // defining an input file
      ofstream outfile;              // defining an output file

      infile.open("payroll.dat");
      // This statement opens infile as an input file.
      // Whenever infile is used, data from the file payroll.dat
      // will be read.

      outfile.open("payment.out");
      // This statement opens outfile as an output file.
      // Whenever outfile is used, information will be sent
      // to the file payment.out

      int hours;                     // The number of hours worked
      float payRate;                 // The rate per hour paid
      float net;                     // The net pay

      if (!infile)
      {
            cout << "Error opening file.\n";
            cout << "Perhaps the file is not where indicated.\n";
            return 1;
      }
      else if ((infile.peek()) == EOF)
            cout << "File is empty" << endl;
      else
      {

            outfile << fixed << setprecision(2);
            outfile << "Hours     Pay Rate   Net Pay"  << endl;

            while ((infile.peek()) != EOF)
            {
                infile >> hours;
                infile >> payRate;
                net = hours * payRate;
```

continues

```
                outfile  << hours << setw(10) << "$ " << setw(6)
                         << payRate << setw(5) << "$ " << setw(7)
                         << net << endl;


            }  // end of while (!infile.peek())
        }         // end of default else
        infile.close();
        outfile.close();

        return 0;
}
```

Output Files

Output files are opened the same way: `outfile.open("payment.out")`. Whenever the program writes to `outfile`, the information will be placed in the physical file `payment.out`. Notice that the program generates a file stored in the same location as the source file. The user can indicate a different location for the file to be stored by indicating the full path (drive, etc.).

Files Used for Both Input and Output

A file can be used for both input and output. The `fstream` data type, which is used for files that can handle both input and output, must have a **file access flag** as an argument to the `open` function so that the mode, input or output, can be determined. There are several access flags that are used to indicate the use of the file. The following chart lists frequently used access flags.

Flag mode	**Meaning**
`ios::in`	Input mode. The file is used for "reading" information. If the file does not exist, it will not be created.
`ios::out`	Output mode. Information is written to the file. If the file already exists, its contents will be deleted.
`ios::app`	Append mode. If the file exists, its contents are preserved and all output is written to the end of the file. If it does not exist then the file will be created. Notice how this differs from `ios::out`.
`ios::binary`	Binary mode. Information is written to or read from in pure binary format (discussed later in this chapter).

Example:

```
#include <fstream>
#include <iostream>
using namespace std;

int main()
{
    fstream test ("grade.dat", ios::out)
```

continues

```
    // test is defined as an fstream file first used for output
    // ios::out is the file access flag

    int value, result;
    cout << "Please input a value" << endl;
    cin >> value;
    test << value << endl;
    // This outputs the value read in to grade.dat

    test.close();          // close the file as an output file

    test.open("grade.dat", ios::in)
    // the same file is reopened now as an input file
    // ios::in is the file access flag

    test >> result;
    // This gets a value from the file test(grade.dat) and
    // stores it in result

    cout << "result is " << result << endl;
    test.close();          // close the file

    return 0;
}
```

In the following example, we check for a file's existence before opening it. We first attempt to open the file for input. If the file does not exist, then the open operation fails and we open it as an output file.

Example:

```
fstream dataFile;

dataFile.open("grades.txt", ios::in);
if (dataFile.fail())
       // The fail directive indicates the file did not open
       // since it does not exist
{
       // The file does not exist, so create it.
dataFile.open("grades.txt", ios::out);
       // file is processed here: data sent to the file
}
else   // the file already exists.

{
    cout << "The file grades.txt already exists. \n";

            // process file here
    dataFile.close();

}
```

Just as `cin >>` is used to read from the keyboard and `cout <<` is used to write to the screen, `filename >>` is used to read from the file `filename` and `filename <<` is used to write to the file `filename`.

Closing a File

Files should be closed before the program ends to avoid corrupting the file and/ or losing valuable data.

```
infile.close();
outfile.close();
dataFile.close();
```

Passing Files as Parameters to Functions

Files can be passed as parameters just like variables. Files are always passed by reference. The `&` symbol must be included after the data type in the function heading and prototype.

Example:

```
void GetData(ifstream& infile, ofstream& outfile); // prototype of function
                                                   // with files as parameters

void GetData(ifstream& infile, ofstream& outfile)  // heading of function with
                                                   // files as parameters
```

Review of Character Input

Chapter 12 introduced the basics of characters and strings. We briefly review those concepts since they apply to files as well.

Recall that each file has an end of line marker for each line as well as the end of file marker at the end of the file. Whenever whitespace (blanks, newlines, controls, etc.) is part of a file, a problem exists with the traditional `>>` operator in inputting character data. When reading input characters into a string object, the `>>` operator skips any leading whitespace. It then reads successive characters into the character array, stopping at the first trailing whitespace character (which is NOT consumed, but rather which remains as the next character to be read in the file). The `>>` operator also takes care of adding the null character to the end of the string. Stopping at the first trailing whitespace creates a problem for names containing spaces. A program reading first names into some string variable (array of characters) has a problem reading a name like Mary Lou since it has a blank space in it. The blank space between Mary and Lou causes the input to stop when using the `>>` operator. The `get` function can be used to input such strings.

```
infile.get(firstname, 20);
```

The `get` function does NOT skip leading whitespace characters but rather continues to read characters until it either has read, in the example above, 19 characters or it reaches the newline character \n (which it does NOT consume). Recall from Lesson Set 10 that the last space is reserved for the null character.

Since the `get` function does not consume the end of line character, there must be something done to consume it so that a new line can be read.

Example: Given the following data file

```
Mary Lou <eol>
Becky    <eol>
Debbie   <eol>
<eof>
```

Note: Both the <eol> and <eof> are NOT visible to the programmer or user. There are several options for reading and printing this data.

```
char dummy;                        // created to read the end of line character
char  firstname[80];               // array of characters for the first name
outfile << "Name   " << endl;
infile.get(firstname,80);          // priming the read   reads the first name

while(infile)
{
   infile.get(dummy);              // reads the end of line character into dummy
   outfile << firstname << endl;   // outputs the name
   infile.get(firstname,80);       // reads the next name
}
```

In this example, dummy is used to consume the end of line character. input.get(firstname,80); reads the string Mary Lou and stops just before reading the <eol> end of line character. The infile.get(dummy) gets the end of line character into dummy.

Another way to do this is with the ignore function, which reads characters until it encounters the specific character it has been instructed to look for or until it has skipped the allotted number of characters, whichever comes first. The statement infile.ignore(81,'\n') skips up to 81 characters stopping if the new line '\n' character is encountered. This newline character IS consumed by the function, and thus there is no need for a dummy character variable.

Example:

```
char  firstname[80];

outfile << "Name   " << endl;
infile.get(firstname,80);

while (!infile.fail())
{
   infile.ignore(81,'\n');          // read and consume the end of line character
   outfile << firstname << endl;
   infile.get(firstname,80);
}
```

The following sample program (a modification of Program 13.2) shows how names with embedded whitespace along with numeric data can be processed. Parts in bold indicate the addition of a name to the data in Sample Program 13.2. Assume that the payroll.dat file has the following information:

John Brown	40	10.00
Kelly Barr	30	6.70
Tom Seller	50	20.00

The program will produce the following information in payment.out:

Name	**Hours**	**Pay Rate**	**Net Pay**
John Brown	40	$10.00	$400.00
Kelly Barr	30	$6.70	$201.00
Tom Seller	50	$20.00	$1000.00

Sample Program 13.3

```
#include <fstream>
#include <iostream>
#include <iomanip>
using namespace std;

const int MAX_NAME = 11;

int main()
{
      ifstream infile;            // defining an input file
      ofstream outfile;           // defining an output file

      infile.open("payroll.dat");
      // This statement opens infile as an input file.
      // Whenever infile is used, data from the file payroll.dat
      // will be read.

      outfile.open("payment.out");
      // This statement opens outfile as an output file.
      // Whenever outfile is used, information will be sent
      // to the file payment.out

      int hours;                  // The number of hours worked
      float payRate;              // The rate per hour paid
      float net;                  // The net pay
      char name[MAX_NAME];        // array of characters for the name of
                                  // a student, with at most 10 characters

      if (!infile)
      {
         cout << "Error opening file.\n";
         cout << "Perhaps the file is not where indicated.\n";
         return 1;

      }

      outfile << fixed << setprecision(2);
      outfile << "Name             Hours     Pay Rate   Net Pay" << endl;


      while ((infile.peek()) != EOF)           // no need to prime the read
      {
            infile.get(name,MAX_NAME);     // gets names with blanks
            infile >> hours;
            infile >> payRate;
            infile.ignore(81,'\n');        // ignores the rest of the line
                                           // and consumes end of line marker
            net = hours * payRate;
```

continues

```
            outfile << name << setw(10) << hours << setw(10) << "$ "
                    << setw(6) << payRate << setw(5) << "$ " << setw(7)
                    << net << endl;


      }

      infile.close();
      outfile.close();

      return 0;
}
```

Binary Files

So far all the files we have talked about have been text files, files formatted as ASCII text.[1] Even the numbers written to a file with the `<<` operator are changed to ASCII text. ASCII is a code that stores every datum (letter of the alphabet, digit, punctuation mark, etc.) as a character with a unique number. Although ASCII text is the default method for storing information in files, we can specify that we want to store data in pure binary format by "opening" a file in binary mode with the `ios::binary` flag. The `write` member function is then used to write binary data to the file. This method is particularly useful for transferring an entire array of data to a file. Binary files are efficient since they store everything as 1s or 0s rather than as text.

Example:

```
fstream test("grade.dat", ios::out | ios::binary); // This defines and opens
                                                   // the file test as an
                                                   // output binary file

int grade[arraysize] = {98, 88, 78, 77, 67, 66, 56, 78, 98, 56};   // creates and
                                                                   // initializes
                                                                   // an integer
                                                                   // array

test.write((char*)grade, sizeof(grade));  // write all values of array to file

test.close();                             // close the file
```

`test.write((char*)grade, sizeof(grade));` in this example calls the `write` function. The name of the file to be written to is `test`. The first argument is a character pointer pointing to the starting address of memory, in this case to the beginning of the `grade` array. The second argument is the size in bytes of the item written to the file. `sizeof` is a function that determines the size of its argument.

The following sample program initializes an array and then places those values into a file as binary numbers. The program then adds 10 to each element of the array and prints those values to the screen. Finally the program reads the values from the same file and prints them. These values are the original numbers. Study the program and its comments very carefully.

---

[1] Or some other alphanumberic code.

Sample Program 13.4

```
#include <fstream>
#include <iostream>
using namespace std;

const int ARRAYSIZE = 10;

int main()
{
       fstream test("grade.dat", ios::out | ios::binary);
       // note the use of | to separate file access flags
       int grade[ARRAYSIZE] = {98,88,78,77,67,66,56,78,98,56};
       int count;     // loop counter

       test.write((char*)grade, sizeof(grade));
                      // write values of array to file
       test.close();  // close file

       // now add 10 to each grade

       cout << "The values of grades with 10 points added\n";

       for (count =0; count < ARRAYSIZE; count++)
       {
           grade[count] = grade[count] + 10;
                      // this adds 10 to each elemnt of the array
           cout << grade[count] << endl;
                      // write the new values to the screen
       }

       test.open("grade.dat", ios::in);
                      // reopen the file but now as an input file

       test.read((char*) grade, sizeof(grade));

       /*  The above statement reads from the file test and places
           the values found into the grade array.  As with the write
           function, the first argument is a character pointer even
           though the array itself is an integer.  It points to the
           starting address in memory where the file information is to
           be transferred
       */

             cout << "The grades as they were read into the file"  << endl;

             for (count =0; count < ARRAYSIZE; count++)
             {
```

continues

```
            cout << grade[count] << endl;
                // write the original values to the screen
        }

        test.close();
        return 0;
}
```

The output to the screen from this program is as follows:

```
The values of grades with 10 points added
108
98
88
87
77
76
66
88
108
66
The grades as they were read into the file
98
88
78
77
67
66
56
78
98
56
```

Files and Records

Files are often used to store records. A "field" is one piece of information and a "record" is a group of fields that logically belong together in a unit.

Example:

Name	Test1	Test2	Final
Brown	89	97	88
Smith	99	89	97

Each record has four fields: `Name`, `Test1`, `Test2`, and `Final`. When records are stored in memory, rather than in files, C++ structures provide a good way to organize and store them.

```
struct Grades
{
     char name[10];
     int test1;
     int test2;
     int final;
};
```

An identifier defined to be a `Grades` structure can hold one record.

The `write` function, mentioned in the previous section, can be used to write records to a file.

```
fstream test("score.dat", ios::out|ios::binary);
Grades student;                          // defines a structure variable

// code that gets information into the student record
test.write((char *) &student, sizeof(student));
```

The `test.write` function used to write a record stored as a `struct` is similar to the `write` function used for an array with one big difference. Notice the inclusion of `(&)`. Why is this necessary here and not when writing an array? In this example we need to pass by reference which requires the `(&)` symbol. Arrays are passed by pointer. The following sample program takes records from the user and stores them into a binary file.

Sample Program 13.5

```
#include <fstream>
#include <iostream>
#include <cctype>              // for toupper function
using namespace std;

const int NAMESIZE = 31;

struct Grades                  // declaring a structure
{
            char name[NAMESIZE];
            int test1;
            int test2;
            int final;
};

int main()
{
            fstream tests("score.dat", ios::out | ios::binary);
            // defines tests as an output binary file

            Grades student; // defines student as a record (struct)
            char more;      // used to determine if there is more input

            do
            {
               cout << "Enter the following information"  << endl;
               cout << "Student's name: ";
               cin.get(student.name,NAMESIZE);

               cout << "First test score :";
               cin >> student.test1;
               cin.ignore();     // ignore rest of line

               cout << "Second test score: ";
```

continues

```
            cin >> student.test2;
            cin.ignore();

            cout << "Final test score: ";
            cin >> student.final;
            cin.ignore();

            // write this record to the file
            tests.write((char *) &student, sizeof(student));

            cout << "Enter a y if you would like to input more data\n ";
            cin >> more;
            cin.ignore();

        }   while (toupper(more) == 'Y');

        tests.close();
        return 0;
}
```

Random Access Files

All the files studied thus far have performed **sequential file access**, which means that all data is read or written in a sequential order. If the file is opened for input, data is read starting at the first byte and continues sequentially through the file's contents. If the file is opened for output, bytes of data are written sequentially. The writing usually begins at the beginning of the file unless the `ios::app` mode is used, in which case data is written to the end of the file. C++ allows a program to perform **random file access**, which means that any piece of data can be accessed at any time. A cassette tape is an example of a sequential access medium. To listen to the songs on a tape, one has to listen to them in the order they were recorded or fast forward (reverse) through the tape to get to a particular song. A CD has properties of a random access medium. One simply jumps to the track where a song is located. It is not truly random access, however, since one can not jump to the middle of a song.

There are two file stream member functions that are used to move the read/write position to any byte in the file. The `seekp` function is used for output files and `seekg` is used for input files.

Example:

```
dataOut.seekp(30L, ios::beg);
```

This instruction moves the marker position of the file called `dataOut` to 30 positions from the beginning of the file. The first argument, `30L` (`L` indicates a long integer), represents an offset (distance) from some point in the file that will be used to move the read/write position. That point in the file is indicated by the second argument (`ios::beg`). This access flag indicates that the offset is calculated from the beginning of the file. The offset can be calculated from the end (`ios::end`) or from the current (`ios::cur`) position in the file.

If the `eof` marker has been set (which means that the position has reached the end of the file), then the member function `clear` must be used before `seekp` or `seekg` is used.

Two other member functions may be used for random file access: `tellp` and `tellg`. They return a long integer that indicates the current byte of the file's read/write position. As expected, `tellp` is used to return the write position of an output file and `tellg` is used to return the read position of an input file.

Assume that a data file `letterGrades.txt` has the following single line of information:

ABCDEF

Marker positions always begin with 0. The mapping of the characters to their position is as follows:

A B C D E F
0 1 2 3 4 5

The following sample program demonstrates the use of `seekg` and `tellg`.

Sample Program 13.6

```
#include <iostream>
#include <fstream>
#include <cctype>
using namespace std;


int main()
{
            fstream inFile("letterGrades.txt", ios::in);
            long offset;       // used to hold the offset
                               // of the read position from
                               // some point
            char ch;           // holds character read at some
                               // position in the file
            char more;         // used to indicate if more information
                               // is to be given

            do
            {
               cout << "The read position is currently at byte "
                   << inFile.tellg() << endl;

               // This prints the current read position (found by the tellg
               // function)

               cout << "Enter an offset from the beginning of the file: ";
               cin >> offset;

               inFile.seekg(offset, ios::beg);

               // This moves the position from the beginning of the file.
               // offset contains the number of bytes that the read position
               // will be moved from the beginning of the file

               inFile.get(ch);
            // This gets one byte of information from the file
```

continues

```
            cout << "The character read is " << ch << endl;

            cout << "If you would like to input another offset enter a Y"
                 << endl;
            cin >> more;

            inFile.clear();
            // This clears the file in case the eof flag was set

        }   while (toupper(more) == 'Y');
        inFile.close();
        return 0;
}
```

Sample Run

The read position is currently at byte 0
Enter an offset from the beginning of the file: 2
The character read is C
If you would like to input another offset enter a Y: y
The read position is currently at byte 3
Enter an offset from the beginning of the file: 0
The character read is A
If you would like to input another offset enter a Y: y
The read position is currently at byte 1
Enter an offset from the beginning of the file: 5
The character read is F
If you would like to input another offset enter a Y: n

CAUTION: If you enter an offset that goes beyond the data stored, it prints the previous character offset.

PRE-LAB WRITING ASSIGNMENT

Fill-in-the-Blank Questions

1. The ________________ member function moves the read position of a file.
2. Files that will be used for both input and output should be defined as ______________data type.
3. The ________________member function returns the write position of a file.
4. The `ios::`____________file access flag indicates that output to the file will be written to the end of the file.
5. ________________files are files that do not store data as ASCII characters.
6. The _____________member function moves the write position of a file.
7. The _____________function can be used to send an entire record or array to a binary file with one statement.
8. The >> operator ______________any leading whitespace.
9. The _____________function "looks ahead" to determine the next data value in an input file.
10. The _____________ and _____________functions do not skip leading whitespace characters.

LESSON 13A

LAB 13.1 Introduction to Files (Optional)

(This is a good exercise for those needing a review of basic file operations) Retrieve program `files.cpp` from the Lab 13 folder. The code is as follows:

```
// This program uses hours, pay rate, state tax and fed tax to determine gross
// and net pay.

#include <fstream>
#include <iostream>
#include <iomanip>
using namespace std;

int main()
{
      // Fill in the code to define payfile as an input file
      float gross;
      float net;
      float hours;
      float payRate;
      float stateTax;
      float fedTax;

      cout << fixed << setprecision(2) << showpoint;
      // Fill in the code to open payfile and attach it to the physical file
      // named payroll.dat

      // Fill in code to write a conditional statement to check if payfile
      // does not exist.
      {
            cout << "Error opening file. \n";
            cout << "It may not exist where indicated" << endl;
            return 1;
      }

      cout << "Payrate      Hours    Gross Pay       Net Pay"
           << endl   << endl;
      // Fill in code to prime the read for the payfile file.
      // Fill in code to write a loop condition to run while payfile has more
      // data to process.
      {
          payfile >> payRate >> stateTax >> fedTax;
          gross = payRate * hours;
          net = gross - (gross * stateTax) - (gross * fedTax);
          cout << payRate << setw(15) << hours << setw(12) << gross
               << setw(12)  << net << endl;
          payfile >> // Fill in the code to finish this with the appropriate
                     // variable to be input
      }
      payfile.close();
      return 0;
}
```

Exercise 1: Assume that the data file has `hours`, `payRate`, `stateTax`, and `fedTax` on one line for each employee. `stateTax` and `fedTax` are given as decimals (5% would be .05). Complete this program by filling in the code (places in bold).

Exercise 2: Run the program. Note: the data file does not exist so you should get the error message:

```
Error opening file.
It may not exist where indicated.
```

Exercise 3: Create a data file with the following information:

```
40  15.00  .05 .12
50  10     .05 .11
60  12.50  .05 .13
```

Save it in the same folder as the `.cpp` file. What should the data file name be?

Exercise 4: Run the program. Record the output here:

____

____

____

____

____

Exercise 5: Change the program so that the output goes to an output file called `pay.out` and run the program. You can use any logical internal name you wish for the output file.

Lab 13.2 Files as Parameters and Character Data

Retrieve program `Grades.cpp` and the data file `graderoll.dat` from the Lab 13 folder. The code is as follows:

```
#include // FILL IN DIRECTIVE FOR FILES
#include <iostream>
#include <iomanip>
using namespace std;


// This program reads records from a file.  The file contains the
// following: student's name, two test grades and final exam grade.
// It then prints this information to the screen.


const int NAMESIZE = 15;
const int MAXRECORDS = 50;
struct Grades                              // declares a structure
{
      char name[NAMESIZE + 1];
      int test1;
      int test2;
      int final;

};
```

continues

```
typedef Grades gradeType[MAXRECORDS];
// This makes gradeType a data type
// that holds MAXRECORDS
// Grades structures.



// FIll IN THE CODE FOR THE PROTOTYPE OF THE FUNCTION ReadIt
// WHERE THE FIRST ARGUMENT IS AN INPUT FILE, THE SECOND IS THE
// ARRAY OF RECORDS, AND THE THIRD WILL HOLD THE NUMBER OF RECORDS
// CURRENTLY IN THE ARRAY.


int main()

{
      ifstream indata;
      indata.open("graderoll.dat");
      int numRecord;                // number of records read in
      gradeType studentRecord;

      if(!indata)
      {
           cout << "Error opening file. \n";
           cout << "It may not exist where indicated" << endl;
           return 1;
      }

           // FILL IN THE CODE TO CALL THE FUNCTION ReadIt.

           // output the information
           for (int count = 0; count < numRecord; count++)
           {
              cout << studentRecord[count].name << setw(10)
                   << studentRecord[count].test1
                   << setw(10) << studentRecord[count].test2;
              cout << setw(10) << studentRecord[count].final << endl;
           }

           return 0;
}

/*********************************************************************

*                               readIt                              *
*  This procedure reads records into an array of records from an    *
*  input file and keeps track of the total number of records. It    *
*  receives, as a parameter, a data file containing information to  *
*  be placed in the array.                                          *

*********************************************************************/
```

continues

```
void readIt(// FILL IN THE CODE FOR THE FORMAL PARAMETERS AND THEIR
            // DATA  TYPES.
            // inData, gradeRec and total are the formal parameters
            // total is passed by reference)

{
   total = 0;

   inData.get(gradeRec[total].name, NAMESIZE);
   while (inData)
   {
     // FILL IN THE CODE TO READ test1
     // FILL IN THE CODE TO READ test2
     // FILL IN THE CODE TO READ final

        total++;      // add one to total

     // FILL IN THE CODE TO CONSUME THE END OF LINE
     // FILL IN THE CODE TO READ name


   }
}
```

Exercise 1: Complete the program by filling in the code (areas in bold). This problem requires that you study very carefully the code and the data file already written to prepare you to complete the program. Notice that in the data file the names occupy no more than 15 characters. Why?

Exercise 2: Add another field called `letter` to the record which is a character that holds the letter grade of the student. This is based on the average of the grades as follows: `test1` and `test2` are each worth 30% of the grade while `final` is worth 40% of the grade. The letter grade is based on a 10 point spread. The code will have to be expanded to find the average.

90–100	A
80–89	B
70–79	C
60–69	D
0–59	F

LAB 13.3 Binary Files and the `write` Function

Retrieve program `budget.cpp` from the Lab 13 folder. The code is as follows:

```
// This program reads in from the keyboard a record of financial information
// consisting of a person's name, income, rent, food costs, utilities and
// miscellaneous expenses. It then determines the net money
// (income minus all expenses)and places that information in a record
// which is then written to an output file.
```

continues

```
#include <fstream>
#include <iostream>
#include <iomanip>
using namespace std;

const int NAMESIZE = 15;
struct  budget             // declare a structure to hold name and financial information
{
      char name[NAMESIZE+1];
      float income;        // person's monthly income
      float rent;          // person's monthly rent
      float food;          // person's monthly food bill
      float utilities;     // person's monthly utility bill
      float miscell;       // person's other bills
      float net;           // person's net money after bills are paid

};

int main()

{
   fstream indata;
   ofstream outdata;                                    // output file of
                                                        // student.
   indata.open("income.dat", ios::out | ios::binary);   // open file as binary
                                                        // output.
   outdata.open("student.out");                         // output file that we
                                                        // will write student
                                                        // information to.
   outdata << left << fixed << setprecision(2);         // left indicates left
                                                        // justified for fields

   budget person;          // defines person to be a record

   cout << "Enter the following information" << endl;
   cout << "Person's name: ";
   cin.getline(person.name, NAMESIZE);
   cout << "Income :";
   cin >> person.income;


   // FILL IN CODE TO READ IN THE REST OF THE FIELDS:
   // rent, food, utilities AND miscell TO THE person RECORD

   // find the net field
   person.net = // FILL IN CODE TO DETERMINE NET INCOME (income - expenses)

   // write this record to the file
   // Fill IN CODE TO WRITE THE RECORD TO THE FILE indata (one instruction)

   indata.close();
```

continues

```
    // FILL IN THE CODE TO REOPEN THE indata FILE, NOW AS AN INPUT FILE.
    // FILL IN THE CODE TO READ THE RECORD FROM indata AND PLACE IT IN THE
    // person RECORD (one instruction)

    // write information to output file
    outdata << setw(20) << "Name" << setw(10) << "Income" << setw(10) << "Rent"
                        << setw(10) << "Food" << setw(15) << "Utilities" << setw(15)
                        << "Miscellaneous" << setw(10) << "Net Money" << endl << endl;

    // FILL IN CODE TO WRITE INDIVIDUAL FIELD INFORMATION OF THE RECORD TO
    // THE outdata FILE.(several instructions)

    return 0;
}
```

Exercise 1: This program reads in a record with fields `name`, `income`, `rent`, `food`, `utilities`, and `miscell` from the keyboard. The program computes the net (income minus the other fields) and stores this in the `net` field. The entire record is then written to a binary file (`indata`). This file is then closed and reopened as an input file. Fill in the code as indicated by the comments in bold.

Sample Run

```
Enter the following information
Person's Name: Billy Berry
Income: 2500
Rent: 700
Food: 600
Utilities: 400
Miscellaneous: 500
```

The program should write the following text lines to the output file `student.out`.

```
Name          Income    Rent     Food     Utilities  Miscellaneous  Net Money

Billy Berry   2500.00   700.00   600.00   400.00     500.00         300.00
```

Exercise 2: Alter the program to include more than one record as input. Use an array of records.

Sample Run

```
Enter the following information
Person's Name: Billy Berry
Income: 2500
Rent: 700
Food: 600
Utilities: 400
Miscellaneous: 500

Enter a Y if you would like to input more data
Y
```

```
Enter the following information
Person's Name: Terry Bounds
Income: 3000
Rent: 750
Food: 650
Utilities: 300
Miscellaneous: 400

Enter a Y if you would like to input more data
n
That's all the information
```

The output file `student.out` should then have the following lines of text written to it.

```
Name          Income    Rent     Food     Utilities  Miscellaneous  Net Money

Billy Berry   2500.00   700.00   600.00   400.00     500.00         300.00
Terry Bounds  3000.00   750.00   650.00   300.00     400.00         900.00
```

LESSON 13B

Lab 13.4 Random Access Files

Retrieve program `randomAccess.cpp` and the data file `proverb.txt` from the Lab 13 folder. The code is as follows:

```
#include <iostream>
#include <fstream>
#include <cctype>
using namespace std;

int main()
{
      fstream inFile("proverb.txt", ios::in);
      long offset;
      char ch;
      char more;

      do
      {
            // Fill in the code to write to the screen
            // the current read position (with label)

            cout << "Enter an offset from the current read position: ";
            cin >> offset;

            // Fill in the code to move the read position "offset" bytes
            // from the CURRENT read position.

            // Fill in the code to get one byte of information from the file
            // and place it in the variable "ch".
```

continues

```
        cout << "The character read is "  << ch << endl;
        cout << "If you would like to input another offset enter a Y"
             << endl;

        cin >> more;

        // Fill in the code to clear the eof flag.

    } while (toupper(more) == 'Y');

    inFile.close();
    return 0;
}
```

Exercise 1: Fill in the code as indicated by the comments in bold.
The file `proverb.txt` contains the following information:

```
Now Is The Time fOr All GoOd Men to come to the aid of their Family
```

Sample Run:

The read position is currently at byte 0
Enter an offset from the current position: 4
The character read is I
If you would like to input another offset enter a Y y

The read position is currently at byte 5
Enter an offset from the current position: 2
The character read is T
If you would like to input another offset enter a Y y

The read position is currently at byte 8
Enter an offset from the current position: 6
The character read is e
If you would like to input another offset enter a Y y

The read position is currently at byte 15
Enter an offset from the current position: 44
The character read is r
If you would like to input another offset enter a Y y

The read position is currently at byte 60
Enter an offset from the current position: 8
The character read is r
If you would like to input another offset enter a Y n

Exercise 2: Why do you think that the character printed at the last run was another r? What would you have to do to get a different letter after the position is beyond the `eof` marker?

Exercise 3: Change the program so that the read position is calculated from the end of the file. What type of offsets would you need to enter to get characters from the proverb? Do several sample runs with different numbers to test your program.

LAB 13.5 Student Generated Code Assignments

Option 1: Write a program that will: 1) read an array of records from the keyboard, 2) store this information to a binary file, 3) read from the binary file back to the array of records, 4) store this information to a text file. Left justify the information for each field. Each record will consist of the following fields:

first name	15 characters
last name	15 characters
street address	30 characters
city	20 characters
state	5 characters
zip	long integer

You may assume a maximum of 20 records.

This assignment is very similar to the program found in Lab 13.3.

Sample Run

```
Enter the following information
Person's First Name: Billy
Person's Last Name: Berry
Street: 205 Main Street
City: Cleveland
State: TX
Zip: 45679

Enter a Y if you would like to input more data
Y

Enter the following information
Person's First Name: Sally
Person's Last Name: Connely
Street: 348 Wiley Lane
City: San Francisco
State: Md
Zip: 54789

Enter a Y if you would like to input more data
n
That's all the information
```

The output file contains the following:

```
First Name  Last Name  Street          City           State  Zip Code

Billy       Berry      205 Main Street Cleveland      Tx     45679
Sally       Connely    348 Wiley Lane  San Francisco  Md     54789
```

Option 2: Write a program that will read the radii of circles. Use an array of records where each record will have the radius of the circle read from the keyboard and the diameter and area of the circle will be calculated by the program. This information (radius, diameter and area) is stored in a binary file. The information in the binary file is then read back into the records and stored in a text output file. Left justify the information for each field. Each record will consist of the following fields:

radius	float
diameter	float
area	float

You may assume a maximum of 20 records. You may want to include the `cmath` library.

You need to know the formulas for finding the area and circumference of a circle.

This assignment is very similar to the program in Lab 13.3.

Sample Run

```
Enter the following information:
Radius of circle: 5
Enter a Y if you would like to input more data
y

Enter the following information:
Radius of circle: 4
Enter a Y if you would like to input more data
y

Enter the following information:
Radius of circle: 7
Enter a Y if you would like to input more data
n

That's all the information.
```

The output file contains the following:

```
Radius   Area    Circumference

5.00      78.54   31.42
4.00      50.27   25.13
7.00     153.94   43.98
```

Option 3: Bring in the file `employee.in` from Lab 13 folder. Write a program that will read records from this file and store them in a binary file. That file will then be used as input to create an output file of the information. The data file contains employee information consisting of name, social security, department ID, years employed, and salary. In addition to displaying the information of each record, the program will also calculate the average salary and years employed of all the records. This additional information is stored in the same output file.

Sample Data File

Bill Tarpon	182460678	789	8	30600
Fred Caldron	456905434	789	10	40700
Sally Bender	203932239	790	8	50000
David Kemp	568903493	790	9	60000

The output file should look like this:

```
Name          Social Security  Department ID  Years Employed  Salary

Bill Tarpon   182460678        789                 8               30600.00
Fred Caldron  456905434        789                10               40700.00
Sally Bender  203932239        790                 8               50000.00
David Kemp    568903493        790                 9               60000.00

The average number of years employed is 8

The average salary is $45325.00
```

APPENDIX A

Visual C++ .NET Environment

In this first lab you will become acquainted with a software environment which allows you to create, compile and run C++ programs. Visual C++ .NET is a product of Microsoft and is one component of the .NET environment. The following steps walk you through most of the commands needed for this manual.

I. Pre-lab Assignment

1. Be sure to read the Lesson Set 1 Pre-lab Reading Assignment and do the Pre-lab Writing Assignment before coming to class.
2. Make sure you have a working password or some means of logging on to your particular computer system. Check with your instructor.

II. Visual C++ .NET

In the Visual C++ .NET environment, programs are written within a project. A project allows many files to be used together to accomplish a particular goal. For that reason it is necessary to first create a project and then add existing files and/or create files that will be part of that project.

3. Make sure you are logged on the system.
4. Select **Start→Programs→Microsoft Visual Studio.NET→Microsoft Visual Studio.NET** (Your particular system may have an alternative way of accessing Visual Studio. NET. Check with your instructor).
5. You should now see the **Start Page**. Click on the **New Project** box.
6. Since the .NET environment includes many types of programming options, you must indicate which type of project you want. For this manual you will always select **Visual C++ Projects** from the **Project Types:** box.
7. There are many options for a C++ project. In the **Templates:** box select the **Win32 Project** icon (make sure it is highlighted). You may have to scroll down on the template window menu to see this icon.
8. Near the bottom you will see a **Name:** box that has the words **<Enter name>**. You need to enter a name for your project here. For this exercise enter the name `firstprog` in this box. Your instructor may have a different name for you to use.
9. The **Location:** box just below the name box is important. It indicates where the project will be stored. Your instructor will tell you what to put in this box. If in doubt just type **C:** \ in the **Location:** box. This will place the project on the root directory of the C drive.
10. Click on the **OK** button.

11. The **Win32 Application Wizard** window should start. You will need to specify some settings. Click the **Application Settings** box just under the **Overview** box.
12. This takes you to the **Application Settings** window. Click on the radio button for **Console application**.
13. Click on the check box for **Empty project**.
14. Now Click the **Finish** button.
15. This takes you to the **Start** page. You should also see a window on the right side of the larger window which says **Solution Explore – firstprog**. In this window under the `firstprog` folder you should see file icons. The only one you will need to be concerned with (for now) is the **Source Files** folder. This is where C++ programs will be stored in the project. We must either bring in existing C++ programs into the project or create new C++ programs to be placed in the project.

III. Bringing an Existing C++ program into a project

16. From the **File** menu (of an already created project, if you have not created a project go back to section II of this lesson) select **Add Existing Item**.
17. You should now see **Add Existing Item - firstprog** window. You will need to indicate where the file to be added is located. In the box called `firstprog` at the top of the window, click the down arrow. Your instructor will tell you where and how to access the programs stored for this lab course. Double click on the `firstprog.cpp` file.

    This places the `firstprog.cpp` file into the project. You should see `firstprog.cpp` under the source files folder of the **Solution Explorer - firstprog** window.
18. Double click `firstprog.cpp` under the source files folder of the **Solution Explore-firstprog** window. You should see the program displayed in the larger window.

IV. Compiling and running a program

19. Once a program is in a project it can be compiled and then run. All the compile options are found in the **Build** menu (located on a top bar of the window)
20. Click on **Build Solution** from the **Build** menu. This option compiles and links all the files in the project.
21. This program compiles without any errors. Most programs will have some compile errors that will have to be corrected and the program compiled again until there are no more compile errors.
22. We can run the program from the **Debug** menu (located to the right of the **Build** menu).
23. Select the **Start without Debugging** option from the **Debug** menu. (Look for the bright red exclamation point icon).
24. An output window pops up that has the output generated from the program.
25. What is displayed on the screen?

26. Press any key and the window disappears.
27. After each program, you should close the Visual C++ project. Select **Close Solution** from the **File** menu.
28. Do not exit Visual C++ .NET. You will need to do the other labs in Lesson Set 1.
29. You have now completed Lab 1.1 and are ready to begin Lab 1.2.

V. Write a program from scratch into a project.

1. You can write a program while in a project. In step 16, instead of selecting **Add Existing Item**, select **Add New Item** from the **file** menu. This takes you to the **Add New Item** window.
2. Enter the name that you want to call the program into the **Name:** box near the bottom of the window.
3. If you want to create a source code file, select the **C++ File (.cpp)** icon (the first one shown at the top left corner of the template window). Make sure it is highlighted.
4. Click the **Open** box. This will give you a blank window where you can code your program.
5. If you want to create a data file instead of a .cpp file, follow section V, however, in Step 3 select the **Text File (.txt)** icon. You may have to move the templates window down to see this icon. Data files will be found under the **Resource Files** folder of the **Solution Explorer** window.

APPENDIX B

Visual C++ Environment

In this first lab, you will become acquainted with a software package that will allow you to create, compile and run C++ programs. Visual C++ is a product of Microsoft and is one component of Visual Studio (a complete set of programming language environments). The following steps walk you through most of the commands needed for this course.

I. Pre-lab Assignment

1. Be sure to read Lesson Set 1 Pre-lab Reading Assignment and do the Pre-lab Writing Assignment before coming to class.
2. Make sure you have a working password or some means of logging on to your particular computer system. Check with your instructor.

II. Visual C++ Environment

1. Make sure you are logged on the system.
2. Select Start→Programs→Microsoft Visual Studio→Microsoft Visual C++6.0 (Your particular system may have an alternative way of accessing Visual C++, check with your instructor).
3. After opening any source file, you must save it to your hard or zip drive before you will be able to compile and run it.
4. Once you are in the Visual C++ package you are ready to open or create files. All files are stored in a workspace.

III. Opening an Existing File

1. Click on the **File** menu (top left corner) then select Open.

   (The above step could be done by just clicking on the open folder icon).
2. You now see a window that says Open. In the `Look in` box at the top there is a down arrow button. Selecting this helps you *browse* the drives to find where the files are.
3. Your instructor will tell you where and how to access the programs stored for this lab course, hereafter called the lesson folder.
4. We are going to open the first program. Double click on `firstprog.cpp`.
5. This brings the file into the workspace; however, we must save it to our own disk space (hard drive or zip drive). Click on File→Save As→ and now use the browse feature, explained in step 2 above, to go to your hard drive and save the file there.
6. Your window should say something like `C:\firstprog.cpp`.

7. You can now compile this program by going to the **Build** menu and selecting **Compile** (the first choice of the menu) or by clicking on the compile icon.
8. A message pops up that says the file requires an active project workspace. All Visual C++ files are stored in a workspace and must have a project created in that workspace. Just click **yes** to this message.
9. You should see some words at a bottom window that says no errors. When this occurs you are ready to run the program.
10. Click on **Build** and then **Execute** or click the execute program icon (it has a red exclamation point).
11. Another message appears that asks if you want to build a file. Again just click on **yes**.
12. The program runs and shows an output display window. What is printed on the screen?
13. Press any key and the message disappears.
14. After completing each lesson you MUST purge the Visual C++ workspace before opening a new source file. Do this by selecting File→Close Workspace. Select Yes when prompted about closing all document windows.
15. All programs brought in from the lesson folder must be saved to your hard or zip drive before compiling or running.
16. We do not explain at this point how to create a project. This is done for you when you compile a program you wrote or brought in from a lesson folder.
17. You have now completed Lab 1.1 and are ready to begin Lab 1.2.

Note: You can also create your own file from scratch by selecting File→New→Files then highlight C++ source file (if you are creating a program file) or text file (if you are creating a data file). On the right side, type in the name of the file in the box labeled file name, and determine where you want it saved by giving the drive in the box labeled Location.

APPENDIX C

UNIX

In this first lab you will learn how to create, compile, and run C++ programs using the UNIX operating system.

I. Pre-lab Assignment

1. Be sure to read the Lesson Set 1 Pre-lab Reading Assignment and then do the Pre-lab Writing Assignment before coming to class.
2. Make sure you have a login name and a working password to logon to a UNIX system. Your instructor, along with the UNIX administrator, will help you obtain an account and learn how to login.

II. The UNIX Operating System

UNIX is a very powerful operating system. However, for some users it is not quite as easy to learn as the Windows environment. UNIX requires some extra knowledge on the part of the user. This appendix should help you learn some of the basics of this operating system. Nevertheless, you will most likely need additional information from your instructor or other sources to be a successful UNIX user. This appendix is a terse, but in no way complete, introduction to UNIX.

The UNIX system organizes files in a hierarchical structure. The top of this structure is called the root directory, identified by `(/)`. Major directories are located under the root directory. For example, `/home` is the user home directory and `/bin` is the binary directory for executables. A directory called `programs` under `/home` is identified by `/home/programs`. The *path* `/home/programs/program1.cpp` shows the location of the C++ program `program1.cpp` in the `/programs` directory.

III. The UNIX Reference Manual

There is a UNIX reference manual that can be accessed during your UNIX session as long as your system has the `man` program. To get information regarding a particular command, type `man` at the shell prompt followed by the desired command. For example,

```
man mkdir
```

provides information about the `mkdir` (make directory) command. Here is a list of useful commands that you may wish to explore.

`cd`	changes the directory you are located in
`cp`	copies a file
`find`	finds a file
`grep`	locates text within a file

`ls`	displays the contents of the current directory
`man`	UNIX reference manual
`mkdir`	makes a new directory
`mv`	moves and renames a file
`pwd`	displays the name of the current directory with the full path
`rm`	removes (deletes) files
`rmdir`	removes a directory
`vi`	begins a `vi` (visual interpreter) editor session

Of course, there are many other useful UNIX commands. Your instructor will provide you with the commands you will need to use.

IV. Editing with `vi`

You can create and edit files during a UNIX session using the `vi` (visual interpreter) editor. First choose the desired subdirectory for your file. For example, if you are in the `/home` directory, enter `cd programs`. To start the editor enter `vi` at the shell prompt followed by the name of your file:

```
vi program1.cpp
```

There are two modes for `vi`: the text-entry mode and the command mode. First select the text-entry mode by typing the character `a` for append. Now you are ready to enter text.

Type the following:

```
#include<iostream>
using namespace std;

int main()
{
     cout << "Welcome to the UNIX operating system" << endl;
     return 0;
}
```

You do not need to worry about what the code means at this point. Just make sure you can enter this using the `vi` editor. To exit the text-entry mode, press the `Escape` key. This will return you to the command mode. Editing commands can be entered from this mode.

A simple example of a `vi` editing command is the command to delete a character. If you want to delete a single character, move the cursor to the desired character and type `x`. To delete multiple successive characters, move the cursor to the first character and type the desired number followed by `x`. For example, `9x` deletes the next 9 characters. Other editing commands are the following:

`dw`	deletes a word
`dW`	deletes a word that contains punctuation
`ndw`	(or `ndW`) deletes n successive words
`i`	inserts new text (changes to text-entry mode)
`O`	opens a new line above the current line (changes to text-entry mode)
`o`	opens a new line below the current line (changes to text-entry mode)

For more information on these and other editing commands use the `man` command described above or some other resource on the `vi` editor.

To save the program you just entered, make sure you are in command mode and type `:w` and then press ENTER. Your work should now be saved in `program1.cpp`.

Finally, you will need to exit the `vi` editor before you can compile and run your program. To do this, type `:q` and then press ENTER. The shell prompt should now appear on your screen.

The last two commands can be combined into one step by entering `:wq` and then pressing ENTER.

V. Compiling and Executing a C++ Program

Possible commands to compile your C++ program will depend on your particular system. Many UNIX systems have GNU C/C++ compile. In this case you may type

```
g++ -o program1 program1.cpp
```

to compile your program. Assuming you typed everything correctly, there should be no errors and an executable will be created. A shell prompt will appear without any messages. Now type `ls` and then press ENTER. You should see a new file listed named `program1`. To execute your program, type `program1` and then press ENTER. The following should appear on your screen:

```
"Welcome to the UNIX operating system"
```

This indicates that you have executed your program. If `g++` does not successfully compile your program, see your instructor to find out the command necessary for your particular system.

Often, you will want to bring in an existing C++ program from a floppy disk or some other source. Your instructor will show you how to retrieve existing files from other locations.

VI. Logging Out

To log out after completing your UNIX session, type `logout` and then press ENTER. Make sure that you do not misspell `logout`—otherwise you may be leaving your files open to the next user!

You have now completed Lab 1.1 and are ready to begin Lab 1.2.

Index